REVISIONING
THE PAST

REVISIONING THE PAST

Prospects in Historical Theology

Edited by
MARY POTTER ENGEL
and
WALTER E. WYMAN, JR.

Fortress Press   **Minneapolis**

REVISIONING THE PAST
Prospects in Historical Theology

"Theology and the Historical Consciousness" originally appeared in *McCormick Quarterly* 21 (1968).

Interior design: ediType
Cover design: McCormick Creative

Library of Congress Cataloging-in-Publication Data

Revisioning the past : prospects in historical theology / edited by
   Mary Potter Engel and Walter E. Wyman, Jr.
       p. cm.
   Includes bibliographical references and index.
   ISBN 0-8006-2614-1
   1. Theology, Doctrinal—History—Historiography 2. Theology,
Doctrinal—History—16th century. 3. Theology, Doctrinal—
History—19th century. I. Engel, Mary Potter. II. Wyman, Walter
E.
BT22.R28 1992
230'.09—dc20   92-35440
                                                        CIP

The paper used in this publication meets the minimum requirements of American National Standard for Information Sciences—Permanence of Paper for Printed Library Materials, ANSI Z329.48-1984   ∞™

Manufactured in the U.S.A.   AF 1–2614

95   94   93   92   1   2   3   4   5   6   7   8   9   10

To B. A. Gerrish
Scholar, Mentor, Colleague, Friend

Contents

Part 3
ESSAYS ON NINETEENTH-CENTURY THEMES

Acknowledgments

From Walter E. Wyman, Jr.: I would like to express gratitude to Dean David Deal and Whitman College for a reduction in teaching load during the spring semester, 1990, and to the Whitman College Aid to Scholarship and Instructional Development Committee for travel support. I am indebted for the forbearance and understanding of my family, Sara, Walter, Chris, and Rachel, who put up with my preoccupation and absence from the family circle during periods of research, writing, and editing. I would like to express my appreciation to my coeditor, Mary Potter Engel, for her invaluable contributions and consistently sound judgments.

From Mary Potter Engel: I would like to express gratitude to Walter E. Wyman for suggesting this volume and for inviting me to collaborate on it. I am indebted to United Theological Seminary of the Twin Cities for granting me a sabbatical leave in the fall of 1990. The support and flexibility of Dean Wilson Yates and President Benjamin Griffin of UTS during the academic year 1990–91 were of great help. Without that time and support this project could not have been brought to completion. My family, Win, Sam, and Miriam, brought me the joy and fortitude I needed for this work, and I am profoundly thankful to them.

From both editors: We would like to acknowledge with great appreciation the direction of our editor, J. Michael West. He encouraged us when we needed it most, asked incisive questions, and offered valuable suggestions.

We would also like to thank B. A. Gerrish for directing each of us to the vocation of historical theologian and for continuing to challenge us with his example of excellent scholarship.

Mary Potter Engel
and Walter E. Wyman, Jr.

Introduction

From its inception Christian theology has had at its core a historical task: to recover and reread the past in order to reconstruct faith for living in the present. In every age, but especially in times of great change, theologians have intentionally returned to the past as part of their strategy for reshaping and redirecting Christian communities so that they are able to respond creatively and with integrity to contemporary challenges. To this end, Matthew and Luke reread the Gospel of Mark, Augustine reread Paul, and Aquinas reread Augustine.

The dynamic force for reconstructing Christianity that is unleashed in the critical appropriation of tradition is especially evident in the various reformations of the sixteenth century. The diversity of the reform movements of that century is often understood as a consequence of a fundamental disagreement about either the strategy for reform, the doctrine of grace, or the nature, shape, and purpose of the church. One might just as easily understand this diversity in terms of a fundamental disagreement over the nature of the relationship between the past and the present, tradition and innovation. Erasmus, Luther, the Anabaptists, Müntzer, and Calvin all held different views of which past one should return to and how and why one returned to that past.

Erasmus made a critical study of the New Testament and used the practical and simple philosophy of Christ he found there to reorient Christianity away from medieval scholasticism. Luther and Calvin returned to the scriptures, Paul, and Augustine, not merely to criticize corruptions, but to reinterpret Christian faith and reconstitute and re-

1

direct the church in the world. The Anabaptists eschewed all official ecclesiastical and theological traditions in order to recover the witness of the earliest Christian community in the New Testament in its purity and replicate it in the present. Müntzer reread the prophets and apocalyptic documents of the early church as part of his strategy to bring into existence a revolutionary Christianity.

Clearly there are large differences among these reform movements. Each identifies differently the primary sources to be consulted as "tradition," the essence of Christianity, the theological view of the dynamics of history, and the vision of the reformed community. But we should not let this diversity obscure their common adoption of a historical task—the reappropriation of the past—as a fundamental element of the strategy of reform. In one way or another the historical task of all these sixteenth-century reformers was informed by the new historical-critical consciousness introduced by Renaissance scholars in the previous century. Generally speaking, the Renaissance practice of returning to the classical sources of Western tradition (ad fontes!) undoubtedly influenced the reformers' methods. More specifically, Lorenzo Valla's use of historical-critical research to expose the Donation of Constantine as a forgery, for example, could not have failed to impress religious reformers with the power of historical knowledge for the criticism of tradition in the reconstruction of the present. Without exception the leaders of the reform movements agreed that without historical knowledge, without revisioning the past, there could be no vision for the future that could move them beyond the corruptions of the present.

With the deepening of historical consciousness after the Enlightenment, the familiar practice of recovering and rereading one's forebears became even more self-conscious. One result of the modern historical consciousness was the emergence in the nineteenth century of historical theology as a distinct field within Christian theology. The classic statement of the role of historical theology is Friedrich Schleiermacher's *Brief Outline on the Study of Theology* (1811). Concerned to situate theology as a "positive science" alongside the other sciences of the university and to claim historical consciousness and the use of historical-critical methods for theology, Schleiermacher identified three major areas of theology: philosophical theology, historical theology, and practical theology. Historical theology he defined in broad terms:

Good leadership of the church also requires a knowledge of the whole community which is to be led: (a) of its situation at any given time, and (b) of its past, with the realization that this community, regarded as a whole, is a historical entity, and that its present condition can be adequately grasped only when it is viewed as the product of the past. Now these two things taken together constitute historical theology, in the broader sense of the term.[1]

Historical theology understood in this way is "the actual corpus" of Christian theology. By that expression, Schleiermacher meant that historical study constitutes the central content of theology, the actual substance of theological study, which both lays the foundation for practical theology and verifies philosophical theology. This organization of the three branches of theology is significant not merely as an architectonic solution to an organizational problem, but more importantly as the working out of the implications of the historical consciousness for religious thought. Schleiermacher's inclusive concept of historical theology signals the historicizing of theology.[2]

According to Schleiermacher, historical theology itself consists of three sections: knowledge of primitive Christianity (exegetical theology), knowledge of the total career of Christianity (church history), and historical knowledge of the present condition of Christianity (dogmatic theology and church statistics). The second, church history, he referred to as historical theology in the narrower sense, and he divided it further into history of doctrine and history of community.[3]

In the twentieth century, new developments in philosophy, the natural sciences, and the social sciences have only intensified our historical-critical and social consciousness. One of the inescapable results of this is that Christian theologians are no longer able to share with Schleiermacher and many of his contemporaries a unified vision of theology or a clear view of the differences and relationships among the subdisciplines of theology. Historical theology tends to become a specialized subdiscipline rather than being broadly understood as the actual corpus of

---

1. Friedrich Schleiermacher, *Brief Outline on the Study of Theology,* trans. Terrence Tice (Richmond, Va.: John Knox Press, 1970), 26.

2. B. A. Gerrish, *The Old Protestantism and the New* (Chicago: University of Chicago Press, 1982), 208–9.

3. Schleiermacher, *Brief Outline,* 90, 166–77.

theology. The narrower definition of historical theology as church history is now seen by many as inadequate; moreover, the sharp distinction
within church history between the history of doctrine and the history
of community has become questionable. Finally, there is no consensus
about which historical methods are legitimate and appropriate for use in
historical theology. Trite as it may sound, the state of historical theology
in the final decade of the twentieth century may be most appropriately
described as one of "creative confusion." Signs of this creative confusion about the nature, tasks, and methods of historical theology may be
found in many contemporary publications, including the essays in this
volume. What are some of those signs?

First, the distinctions and relationships Schleiermacher sketched out
among philosophical, historical, and practical theology are now being
called into question. As Schubert Ogden's essay indicates, systematic
theologians have begun to rethink these relationships; but there is by
no means a consensus among Christian theologians about how this is to
be done or what it is to look like. Ogden's essay also points to the lack
of agreement in Christian theology concerning the relationship of the
various areas Schleiermacher identified as part of historical theology in
the broader sense. There is little clarity about how exegetical or biblical
theology, historical theology in the narrower sense (as knowledge of the
doctrine and life of the Christian communities in the past), and dogmatic
or constructive theology should be related to one another. What are the
tasks and methods appropriate to each and how do they relate to one
another? Do exegetical and historical theology, adhering strictly to the
hermeneutical methods of their fields, offer critical interpretation of the
Christian witness, right understanding of it, and leave critical validation
of the Christian witness to systematic theology? Is historical theology,
practiced as criticism and clarification, the "first step," necessarily followed by constructive theology, practiced as criticism, correction, and
defense, as the "second step"?[4] In his essay, Ogden addresses some of
these questions and argues for one answer.

Second, the creative confusion that typifies historical theology in the

4. B. A. Gerrish hints at such a distinction in the conclusion of his essay "Practical Belief: Friedrich Karl Forberg (1770–1848) and the Fictionalist View of Religious Language,"
in *Probing the Reformed Tradition: Historical Studies in Honor of Edward A. Dowey, Jr.*, ed. Elsie
Anne McKee and Brian G. Armstrong (Louisville, Ky.: Westminster/John Knox Press, 1989),
382: "To criticize, or to correct, or to defend Forberg's conception of moral theology would
require another paper in the constructive, rather than the historical, mode."

present day is also evident in the blurring of the line within historical theology in the narrower sense between history of doctrine and history of the social conditions of the communities. Until recently the history of doctrine and church history (history of the life of the communities) were kept quite distinct in college, university, and seminary course offerings and in publications. Lately, these two have begun to be merged under one heading, with the inseparability of doctrine and life being stressed. This one heading is variously referred to as "historical theology," "church history," and "the history of Christianity." This raises in another way the question of the distinctive nature of historical theology, because these labels do not appear to be used with consistency and there is little methodological reflection illuminating the differences they might imply.

The question here may be put this way: Do we share an assumption that there is a difference between church history and historical theology? If so, what is that difference? What distinguishes the work of Margaret R. Miles and Jane Dempsey Douglass as historical theologians from that of Justo L. González and John Boswell as church historians?[5] All four take seriously the close mutual relationship between doctrine and the social conditions of the church. All four read history in the light of contemporary questions (sexism, Western imperialism, heterosexism, and ageism). One might argue that González and Boswell recover and reread the history of the Christian communities' ideas and lives primarily in order to understand, clarify, and expose the complexities of the past, while Miles and Douglass recover and reread it in order to offer normative judgments about that past and critical perspectives for the present.

The third and most obvious sign of the creative confusion in historical theology today is the emergence of new research paradigms alongside the still-predominant understanding of historical theology as

---

5. Margaret R. Miles, *Image as Insight: Visual Understanding in Western Christianity and Secular Culture* (Boston: Beacon Press, 1985); idem, *Practicing Christianity: Critical Perspectives for an Embodied Spirituality* (New York: Crossroad, 1988); Jane Dempsey Douglass, *Women, Freedom, and Calvin* (Philadelphia: Westminster Press, 1985); Justo L. González, *The Story of Christianity*, 2 vols. (New York: Harper & Row, 1984); John Boswell, *Christianity, Social Tolerance, and Homosexuality: Gay People in Western Europe from the Beginning of the Christian Era to the Fourteenth Century* (Chicago: University of Chicago Press, 1980); idem, *The Kindness of Strangers: The Abandonment of Children in Western Europe from Late Antiquity to the Renaissance* (New York: Pantheon, 1988).

a kind of intellectual history. Although we are still the heirs of Schleiermacher in our commitment to historical theology as part of the modern
study of history, the way we understand and practice historical theology
is quite different because the research paradigms in that broader discipline of history today have changed. In fact, they are in flux and there
is no general agreement about what the appropriate historical-critical
methods are. The diversity of historical perspectives and methods that
plagues and enriches the discipline of history is to be found in historical
theology as well.

For example, feminist scholars reread the past not only with different questions and assumptions, but with different methods and goals.
As Elisabeth Schüssler Fiorenza has argued in her essay "Remembering
the Past in Creating the Future," for women and others who have been
written out of history, part of the historical task is to remember or "un-
earth" the past that has been suppressed; for feminist theologians this
means reconstructing early Christian origins *from* a committed feminist
stance and *for* a particular community of liberation. Schüssler Fiorenza
states: " 'Entering an old text from a new critical direction' is not just a
'chapter in cultural history' but an 'act of survival.' "[6] Social and cultural
historians, to take another example, turn away from the concentration
on the documents of "high culture"—the texts produced by academics
or intellectuals—and turn instead to popular literature and evidence
of a nonliterary kind to determine what the lives of ordinary persons
might have been. The very question of what constitutes the "text" to be
interpreted is open to debate. In regard to historical theology, the list
of legitimate evidence, which expands daily, now includes ecclesiastical court records; popular religious literature such as hymns, sermons,
and liturgies; and correspondence and diaries. Nonliterary evidence includes painting before the Reformation and woodcuts during and after
the Reformation.

For example, in *Women, Freedom, and Calvin,* Jane Dempsey Douglass has investigated Calvin's view of freedom in relation to the role
of women in church order, and in the course of that investigation she

---

6. Elisabeth Schüssler Fiorenza, "Remembering the Past in Creating the Future:
Historical-Critical Scholarship and Feminist-Critical Interpretation," in *Bread Not Stone:
The Challenge of Feminist Biblical Interpretation* (Boston: Beacon Press, 1984), 113. The essay provides a critique of the "objective-realist" (value-neutral) approach to history and
an argument for the greater adequacy of a "constructionist" (committed and engaged)
approach.

uses as sources not only Calvin's *Institutes* but also popular works by Renaissance women and contemporary histories of women and the Reformation in Geneva. In *Image as Insight: Visual Understanding in Western Christianity and Secular Culture,* Margaret R. Miles investigates visual images that were "thoughtfully and purposely created by the christian community" at the sites of Christian worship; Miles does this in order to imaginatively "reconstruct the role of religious images in the life and worship of historical people" and to uncover "women's history."[7] In her *Practicing Christianity: Critical Perspectives for an Embodied Spirituality,* she turns to popular devotional manuals, "the best-seller, self-help literature of the Christian West," as sources to uncover how "historical people learned to shape their lives around Christian ideas, attitudes, and values."[8] Marilyn Massey, in *Feminine Soul: The Fate of an Ideal,* writes a "local history through the narrative and explication of three tales [widely read and used tales of moral and religious development] and their fate at the hands of contemporary thinkers."[9] In the present volume, Jill Raitt and Claude Welch offer an analysis and evaluation of the appearance of these new research paradigms in historical theology, and several of the other essays in this volume demonstrate this shift in perspectives and methods. For example, Mary Potter Engel unearths a tradition of just battery of wives parallel to the just war tradition by attending to the evidence of popular French literature. Jane Strohl seeks to illuminate and criticize sixteenth-century views of the theological meaning of suffering by juxtaposing the thought of Martin Luther and Hans Denck with contemporary African women's writings.

To add to the confusion, at the same time these changes in method and perspective are altering the shape of historical theology, the term "historical theology" is still used most frequently to refer to work that follows the more traditional understanding of this discipline as a kind of intellectual history. The fact that many of the essays in this volume are examples of historical theology done in this key illustrates this. Much creative scholarship is to be found among those who continue to understand and pursue historical theology under the paradigm of intellectual history. To mention just two examples from nineteenth-century scholarship: (1) the new critical editions of the works of Hegel and

---

7. Miles, *Image as Insight,* 5, 7.
8. Miles, *Practicing Christianity,* ix.
9. Marilyn Massey, *Feminine Soul: The Fate of an Ideal* (Boston: Beacon Press, 1985), 24.

Schleiermacher reflect painstaking textual scholarship of the highest standards, and already new interpretations of these figures are being stimulated by the availability of these new texts; and (2) Hegel, Schleiermacher, Kierkegaard, and Troeltsch all have international societies devoted to their study.

But even this intellectual history paradigm permits differing kinds of instantiation. The essays by Katy O'Brien Weintraub, Jack Forstman, Marcia Bunge, Michael Himes, and William Madges exemplify the enduring validity of the close reading of the primary texts of classic thinkers. Randall Zachman's and David Lotz's essays illustrate, in very different ways, the insights to be gleaned from connecting figures in different centuries. Walter E. Wyman's essay tracks the career of a single concept over a number of decades among several different thinkers. The coexistence of these very different and equally viable ways of doing historical theology raises in other ways the question of the nature and purpose of historical theology.

At the root of all this creative confusion are the overarching questions: What is historical theology? What are its tasks? What methods and perspectives are legitimate for carrying out those tasks? What purposes and what communities does it serve? Why do we do it? Is it, finally, worth all the effort? How would we as scholars who invest so much time probing the thoughts of dead thinkers and the lives of communities buried in the past answer the angels' question to the women in the burial ground: "Why do you look for the living among the dead?" (Luke 24:5, NRSV)?

There is no agreed-upon answer to this set of questions, as the essays in this volume, as well as those in many other contemporary publications, show. The case we would defend is that the Christian historical theologian is first of all a *theologian*. Theology is a normative discipline whose constitutive question, whose very reason for being, is the question of the *meaning* and *truth* of Christian faith.[10] Thus it is not sufficient to conceive of the historical theologian as purely an intellectual historian who seeks to understand the ideas of the past. The historical theologian is not the same as the historian of theology. The latter is essentially

---

10. This understanding of theology is shaped by and indebted to the work of Schubert Ogden and David Tracy. See Schubert Ogden, "What Is Theology?" in *On Theology* (San Francisco: Harper & Row, 1986), 1–21, and David Tracy, *Blessed Rage for Order* (New York: Seabury Press, 1975).

an intellectual historian whose subject matter happens to be religious ideas (rather than philosophical or political or economic ideas). To identify the historical theologian with the historian of theology forfeits the normative, theological character of the historical theologian's task. To be a theologian is to wrestle with problems of the meaning and truth of religious beliefs as they arise in past and contemporary forms. For the same reason, it is not sufficient to see the task of the historical theologian as coincident with that of the social historian of theology or Christianity. The work of feminists and social historians undoubtedly may have a great impact on the way the historical theologian shapes and wrestles with ultimate problems and on the way she or he struggles to interpret past ideas and movements in the light of an ultimate meaning, but it does not do away with the obligation of the historical theologian to make specific judgments about the center or ultimate context of meaning of Christian faith in and for the present.

This normative, theological character of historical theologians' task conditions all of their work, whether they are clarifying an idea, exposing a practice, reconstructing Christian origins, raising methodological questions, or reflecting on the fundamental question of the identity of Christianity. One might argue concerning the latter, for example, that one of the historical theologian's tasks is to press certain fundamental questions: Does Christianity have an essence or an identity? If so, how do we define it? Where are the major changes in its course in history and what constitutes its continuity across those changes? What are the uses of the past for the present? What criteria does one use to determine whether a given idea or practice is appropriate to the tradition? Some, perhaps all, of these questions the historical theologian may share with the historian of theology and Christianity or with the church historian. The historical theologian, however, as theologian, is *required* to raise these basic issues within and for the broader discipline of theology and to offer judgments about them.

The present volume, which is dedicated to B. A. Gerrish, reflects major themes that are the foci of his scholarly career. Each contributor—whether a former student or a contemporary of Gerrish's—seeks to embody the vocation of the historical theologian in her or his particular essay while addressing these major themes. Thus the essay in Part One offers sustained methodological reflection on the nature and task of historical theology. The essays in Parts Two and Three single out several thinkers and issues in the sixteenth and nineteenth centuries, respectively, both to illustrate and to reflect upon the variety of ways in which the craft of the historical theologian may be carried out. Parts Two and Three each contain an introductory essay that reflects critically on current scholarship regarding that century. Many of the authors of the individual studies not only *do* historical theology, but *reflect upon* their actual practice as historical theologians; thus methodological reflections are not confined to the essay in Part One, but are to be found throughout the volume.

The Afterword contains two pieces by B. A. Gerrish—an essay, written in 1968, on theology and the historical consciousness, and a postscript reflecting on the changes in historical theology that have occurred in the years since the original piece was published. In characterizing his own conception of historical theology in 1968, Gerrish wrote of "a determination to make one's theological decisions in the best company."[11] While there is something to be said for a purely antiquarian definition of the historical theologian's task—to understand the past in its own integrity, as past—Gerrish's phrase captures a far more adequate understanding. Disciplined conversation with the past—its thinkers and movements, crystallizations and dynamic tensions, beacons and shadows—in order to make one's own decisions about the meaning and truth of Christian faith in and for the present is what the historical theologian is finally about. The essays in this volume explore some of the ways in which this fundamental task may be carried out.

11. B. A. Gerrish, "Theology and the Historical Consciousness," *McCormick Quarterly* 21 (1968): 206; the essay is reprinted as part of the Afterword of the present volume.

Part 1

Methodological Reflections on Historical Theology

ONE

Schubert M. Ogden

Prolegomena to Historical Theology

I

Human beings obviously differ both in their aptitude for self-reflection and in their exercise of it. But perhaps most persons seriously engaged in doing anything find themselves reflecting sooner or later on just what it means to do it and on how it ought to be done. As and when they do so, they may naturally look for help from any who bear professional responsibility for asking and answering this kind of self-reflective questions.

In the case of those who do Christian theology, it is from the systematic theologians among them that they may especially expect to receive such help. Here, too, of course, differences in aptitude for self-reflection and in its exercise will be reflected in the help that individual theologians are in a position to provide. But to be a systematic theologian at all is to be responsible for critically reflecting on theology itself—on just what it means to do it and on how it ought to be done. This explains why among the perennial questions of systematic theology are those commonly designated "prolegomena," which is not a bad term for them, provided one construes it with Karl Barth to mean not the things that are said *before* one does theology, but rather the things that are said *first*, as soon as one begins to do it.

Like other such perennial questions, however, those included in prolegomena arise in rather different ways in different situations. They acquire their particular shape and urgency from changes in the larger context of theology in the church and in the world, changes that bear on the self-understanding of theologians both as such and as working in one or the other of its particular disciplines. Thus it is generally recognized that, throughout the modern period, systematic theologians have been forced to pay particular attention to even the most fundamental questions of prolegomena. Faced with the transition to secular culture effected by modern science and technology and a growing historical consciousness, they have had to ask with unprecedented seriousness whether there can even be such a thing as theology as a legitimate form of critical reflection. Moreover, it is widely supposed that they have become increasingly caught in an impossible situation in their attempts to answer this question: if they understand theology so that it is subject to the same standards applying to all other fields or disciplines now institutionalized in the university, they can no longer understand it in accordance with its own constitution as specifically Christian theology.

Happily, there are growing signs that this supposed dilemma is not inescapable. More and more theologians are calling for a "paradigm change in theology," which includes at its center such a change in theology's traditional self-understanding as allows it to be nothing other or less than specifically Christian theology even while rightly claiming a place in the university alongside the other fields or disciplines.[1] But there are unfortunately other signs as well that the modern struggle for a more adequate understanding and practice of theology is anything but over. This is the deeper significance of such a well-known case as that of Charles E. Curran vs. The Catholic University of America. For while important features of this case are peculiarly Roman Catholic, the basic issues it raises are thoroughly ecumenical. As theology is still widely understood and practiced in all of the churches, and even by a large number of academic theologians, it simply cannot be a field of study on a par with other fields or disciplines. Consequently, the fundamental question of prolegomena, of how theology as such is to be understood and practiced, remains even now a pressing question.[2]

Other questions pertaining to the particular disciplines of theology have also become more or less urgent as a result of ongoing changes in the larger theological context. Thus, for example, throughout the

---

1. See, e.g., Hans Küng and David Tracy, eds., *Paradigm Change in Theology: A Symposium for the Future*, trans. Margaret Kohl (New York: Crossroad, 1989); Charles M. Wood, *Vision and Discernment: An Orientation in Theological Study* (Atlanta: Scholars Press, 1985).

2. See Schubert M. Ogden, "Theology in the University: The Question of Integrity," in *Theology and the University: Essays in Honor of John B. Cobb, Jr.*, ed. David Ray Griffin and Joseph C. Hough, Jr. (Albany: State University of New York Press, 1991), 67–80.

nineteenth century right up to the present, Protestant theology has commonly been organized into the four distinct disciplines of biblical, historical, systematic, and practical theology. But among the consequences of consistently following historical-critical methods of study in theology has been the complete breakdown of the distinction between scripture and tradition that lay behind thus distinguishing between biblical and historical theology. Therefore, there is good reason to ask whether biblical theology ought not now to be regarded simply as a special case of historical theology, with the result that the field as a whole should be organized into three rather than four distinct disciplines.[3]

Yet another and more fundamental question has also continued to arise about historical theology itself as a distinct theological discipline. If its being properly historical in the now generally accepted sense of the term has required clearly distinguishing it from the other theological disciplines, its also being properly theology has appeared to blur any such clear distinction. Thus it is not surprising that historical theologians sometimes have difficulty acquiring and maintaining a clear self-understanding. Also understandable is that systematic theologians attempting to understand historical theology have at least appeared to be caught in yet another impossible situation: if they understand it so that it is subject to the same standards applying to all other studies now generally judged to be historical, they can no longer understand it in accordance with its own constitution as a discipline of Christian theology.

Here, too, however, I am convinced that the apparent dilemma is merely that and that historical theology can be so understood as to escape from it. In fact, I am convinced that there is an exact analogy between so understanding historical theology as a discipline and adequately understanding theology as a field. My purpose in what follows, then, is to develop this analogy so as to justify these convictions. If in this way I shall offer little more than a sketch of the prolegomena promised by my title, one advantage of the procedure seems clear: it should serve to situate a regional prolegomena to historical theology within its only proper context—that is, within a fundamental prolegomena to theology as such.

---

3. See Schubert M. Ogden, *On Theology* (San Francisco: Harper & Row, 1986), 8–9, 96; Wood, *Vision and Discernment*, 43–44.

II

The key to a fundamental prolegomena is rightly distinguishing theology from Christian faith and witness. This distinction, however, is a special case of a much more general one, with which it is helpful to begin in trying to understand it. I refer to the fundamental distinction between what I shall call "critical reflection," on the one hand, and "self-understanding" and "life-praxis," on the other.[4]

To be human is not only to live, but also to understand one's life and, within limits, to be free to lead it and responsible for doing so. Of course, in understanding one's life, one understands indefinitely more than oneself—not only all the others, human and nonhuman, but for relation with which one neither would nor could live at all, but also the encompassing whole of reality of which both oneself and all others are parts. But thus to live understandingly, and so also freely and responsibly, is precisely to lead one's life according to certain norms or principles of validity, whether authenticity and sincerity, or truth, goodness, and beauty. This means that one's very life as a human being involves the asking of certain questions—whether the existential question about the authentic understanding of oneself and others in relation to the whole, or other no less vital questions about the true, the good, and the beautiful. It also means, however, that the whole of one's life-praxis, and so whatever one thinks, says, or does, in effect answers these same questions, thereby making or implying certain corresponding claims to validity.

Thus, to say or imply that so-and-so is the case is to answer the question about the true and at least to imply a claim to truth in doing so. But if thus implying or making a truth claim is a typical exercise of our essentially human capacity to live understandingly, it is by no means the only such exercise. Not only do we just as typically make or imply all sorts of other claims—to authenticity and rightness as well as to goodness and beauty—but we also ask, at least under certain circumstances, about the validity of our several claims. We ask, for example, whether what is *said* to be the case really *is* the case, and, in this sense, whether the claim to truth expressed or implied by the saying is a valid claim.

---

4. Cf. Jürgen Habermas, *Erkenntnis und Interesse, Mit einem neuen Nachwort* (Frankfurt: Suhrkamp Verlag, 1973), 382–93.

This example suffices to show that our capacity to live understandingly is typically exercised not merely on one level, but on two. On the primary level of self-understanding and life-praxis, it is exercised by asking and answering the question of truth and all our other vital questions and by making or implying claims to validity in answering them. On the secondary level of critical reflection, it is exercised by critically interpreting our answers in relation to our questions and by critically validating the claims that the answers make or imply.

Distinct as they are, these two levels of living understandingly are also inseparable, each in its way necessarily involving the other. This becomes evident as soon as one reflects that so living is always done by individual women and men in community with other human beings living in the same understanding way. Thus to make or imply a claim to validity on the primary level of self-understanding and life-praxis is in effect to issue a promise to all other members of this human community—the promise, namely, to submit one's claim to critical validation as and when it becomes problematic and needs to be validated. In this way, living on the primary level of human life already anticipates living on the secondary level, which it makes both possible and, under certain circumstances, necessary. On the other hand, to validate a claim to validity on the secondary level of critical reflection is neither possible nor necessary unless some such claim has already been made or implied on the primary level. Critical reflection requires something to reflect on and a reason for doing so and, in this way, necessarily presupposes the self-understanding and life-praxis out of which it arises and which it is constituted to serve.

But if the two levels of human living cannot be rightly separated, neither can they be rightly identified. Being as different as they are united, they can only be rightly distinguished, by which I mean, so distinguished as to be seen in their unity as well as their difference. This is done, I believe, by stressing both the difference and the unity between making or implying claims to validity, on the one hand, and critically validating these claims, on the other.

The bearing of this distinction on the understanding of theology may be brought out by briefly considering the meaning of "Christian faith and witness." Construed in a purely formal sense, this phrase refers to human self-understanding and praxis insofar as they are mediated—immediately or mediately—through Jesus Christ. This assumes that the

Christian *proprium,* in the sense of what alone makes anything properly Christian, is the experience of Jesus as the Christ, or, as we might say today, the experience of Jesus as of decisive significance for human existence. One experiences Jesus to be thus significant insofar as it is decisively through him that one's own existential question about authentic self-understanding is directly and explicitly answered. But the faith that is of a piece with such experience and through which this answer is received is, in purely formal terms, an explicit self-understanding—an understanding of oneself and others in relation to the whole, decisively re-presented through Jesus as the all-encompassing love of God.

In the same way, the witness through which this faith then comes and must come to manifold expression is correctly understood purely formally as the life-praxis that necessarily follows from just such a self-understanding. Insofar as one understands oneself through Jesus, one exists in unreserved trust in God's love and in unqualified loyalty to it, which means loyalty both to God and to all—others as well as one-self—to whom God is loyal. This existence in trust and loyalty, then, naturally comes to expression either explicitly or implicitly in action— in the whole of one's life-praxis, and so in everything that one thinks, says, or does. It comes to explicit expression as praxis of the Christian religion, which, like all religion, functions as the primary form of culture that explicitly mediates authentic self-understanding and the life-praxis that follows from it. But existence in faith is also expressed implicitly through all of the other so-called secular forms of praxis and culture, both primary and secondary. Whatever one thinks, says, or does somehow expresses one's faith as a Christian, and so cannot fail to be at least implicit Christian witness.

Implicit or explicit, however, all Christian witness, like any other life-praxis, makes or implies certain claims to validity. Different as these claims clearly are materially, because of the *proprium* of Christian witness, they are nonetheless similar formally to those made or implied by other cases of life-praxis both religious and secular. Thus not only the Christian religion, but any religion, lays claim to decisive existential authority because it also claims to be the true religion—in the sense that it makes explicit the true answer to the existential question and, therefore, properly functions as the formal norm for determining all other religious truth. So, too, with implicit Christian witness, which is in no way different formally from the implicit witness of any other faith in also claiming to mediate, in its way, authentic self-understanding.

There is another important respect in which the claims to validity made or implied by Christian witness are formally the same as those of any other witness of faith. This becomes evident as soon as one reflects on the systematic ambiguity of the term "witness," which can mean both the *that* of witness, in the sense of the *act* of witnessing, and the *what* of witness, in the sense of the *content* the act conveys, either explicitly or by implication. Thus, like any other witness of faith, any instance of Christian witness, whether explicit or implicit, makes or implies a twofold claim to validity corresponding to its twofold structure as witness: insofar as it is an act of witnessing, it claims at least implicitly to be fitting to its situation; and insofar as it is an explication or implication of the content of witness, it makes or implies the claim to be adequate to this content.

What is distinctive about any instance of Christian witness, of course, is its content, which is determined by its *proprium* in the experience of Jesus as of decisive significance for human existence. But even here there is a formal similarity to other witnesses of faith, or to the other specific religions through which such witnesses become explicit. Not only the Christian religion, but any religion, is constituted as such by some explicit primal source through which its particular self-understanding is decisively re-presented. At the same time, any religion, as we have seen, lays claim to decisive existential authority because it also claims that its particular self-understanding is true and hence of universal significance. So, in claiming as it does to be adequate to its content as well as fitting to its situation, any instance of witness claims in effect to be both authorized by its explicit primal source and worthy of belief by any woman or man simply as a human being. In the case of Christian witness, this becomes the distinctive twofold claim to be both appropriate to Jesus Christ, or to Jesus as Christians experience him, and credible to human existence.

But if these are the claims to validity that are made or implied by any instance of Christian witness, then to bear this witness on the primary level of self-understanding and life-praxis is already to anticipate critically validating these claims on the secondary level of critical reflection. This is so, at any rate, on the assumption that to make or imply these claims is also in effect to issue a promise to all of the other members of the human community—the same promise, namely, to allow the claims to be critically validated whenever they become problematic and are in need of such validation. In this way, simply bearing Christian witness necessarily involves doing theology. For what is properly meant by "theology" in the specific sense of "Christian theology" is simply the form of critical reflection constituted as such by asking whether the validity claims made or implied by any instance of Christian witness are, in fact, valid claims. Is the witness in question both fitting to its situation and adequate to its content, in that it is appropriate to Jesus Christ and credible to human existence? Or, to put the same question in the more constructive form in which it may also be asked: What would be a witness that is both fitting to its situation and adequate to its content, because it is authorized by Jesus Christ and worthy of being believed by anyone encountering it?[5]

This question makes clear that the unity between Christian witness and theology runs the other way as well. The theology that the question constitutes would be neither possible nor necessary but for the prior existence of the Christian witness with its claims to be fitting and adequate, and so appropriate and credible. In fact, the theology arises out of this witness and is constituted to serve it by critically validating its claims. But if the question thus confirms the unity between theology and witness, it also reveals their difference. It makes clear that bearing Christian witness and doing theology properly take place on two distinct levels—witness being borne on the primary level of self-understanding and life-praxis, theology being done on the secondary level of critical reflection. Thus, while bearing Christian witness is a matter of answering our vital questions—specifically, our existential question about authentically understanding ourselves and others in relation to the whole—doing theology is a matter of critically interpreting this answer and of critically validating the claims that giving it at least implies.

As clear as this distinction is, however, there are reasons why it is not always easy to draw in particular cases. One such reason is that many of the concepts and terms in which theological reflection is done are naturally the same as those in which Christian witness is borne. Thus, if one considers only language, and ignores the different functions that even the identical language may perform, one may very well confuse a case of

---

5. Cf. Wood, *Vision and Discernment*, 40.

doing theology with a case of bearing Christian witness. Another closely related reason for confusion is that even the novel products of theological reflection, once they have been produced, are commonly taken up into Christian witness as its own forms of thought and speech. Here, again, the distinction may not be easy to make unless one looks beneath the obvious similarity in the formulations to the underlying difference in the purposes for using them. But perhaps the most fundamental reason why bearing Christian witness and doing theology may be hard to distinguish is that bearing witness itself can be done in two different ways, one of which is easily mistaken for doing theology.

I refer to the difference between the direct witness of Christian proclamation and the indirect witness of Christian teaching. This difference is particularly obvious in the paradigm cases, or representative forms, of both ways of bearing witness. These forms are, with respect to the first way of proclamation, preaching the word and administering the sacraments and, with respect to the second way of teaching, the instruction in Christian faith and in Christian belief and action that is generally understood to be yet a third official function of the representative minister.

In the cases of both preaching the word and administering the sacraments, witness directly offers the possibility of an explicit self-understanding and demands that it be actualized through the free personal decision of the hearer or receiver. This explains why proclamation in either case is typically cast in the form of imperatives, or of indicatives having a clear imperative meaning—as, for example, "Be reconciled to God!" (2 Cor. 5:20), or "The body (blood) of Christ, given for you." In the case of teaching, by contrast, sentences are typically cast in the indicative mood. This is true, indeed, even of the instruction in Christian action that is one important part of such teaching. This instruction does not directly call for doing things, but rather elucidates *agenda*, things to be done, given the self-understanding of Christian faith. Likewise, the instruction in Christian belief that is another important part of the same teaching does not directly call for believing things, but rather expounds *credenda*, things to be believed, insofar as one has a Christian self-understanding. The explanation of this is that Christian teaching in all of its parts is precisely not Christian proclamation. It does not directly offer the possibility of Christian faith and demand that the learner actualize it, but does this only indirectly, by clarifying the meaning of this possibility itself, both as such and in its necessary implications for belief and action.

Because of this indirectness, however, Christian teaching, in contrast to Christian proclamation, may not seem all that different from doing theology. And this is the more likely because doing theology is, in fact, necessary to Christian teaching, even as it is to the direct way of bearing Christian witness. Nevertheless, Christian teaching is not the same as doing theology, but is a way of bearing Christian witness, and therefore takes place on the primary level of self-understanding and life-praxis. This means that, for all of the indirectness with which it does so, it still intends to answer the existential question to which bearing Christian witness in either of its ways is addressed. Doing theology, by contrast, takes place on the secondary level of critical reflection. This means not only that it is related indirectly even to Christian teaching, but also that it has another and quite different intention: not to answer the existential question, but to interpret the answer given to it by bearing Christian witness and to validate the claims to validity that this witness makes or implies.

To understand this difference is to realize why any attempt to subject doing theology to the teaching office of the church must be profoundly misguided. As much as bearing Christian witness, including Christian teaching, may be quite properly subjected to such control, this is emphatically not the case with doing theology. On the contrary, doing theology cannot possibly perform the service for bearing witness that it is constituted to provide unless it is free to validate all instances of Christian witness, including not least those comprising the official teaching of the church. As a matter of fact, it is precisely the church's official teaching that is, above all, subject to, and in need of, the critical control of theology. For one of the defining characteristics of such teaching, as distinct from all unofficial teaching and proclamation, is that it does not merely imply claims to be fitting and adequate, and so appropriate and credible, but makes these claims explicitly and even formally. Consequently, the promise it in effect issues to all members of the human community is correspondingly obvious and all the more clearly in need of the redemption that doing theology alone is able to provide.

But if doing theology cannot be controlled by the church's teaching office without forfeiting its proper service to bearing Christian witness, there is no good reason why theology may not rightly claim a place in the university alongside the other fields or disciplines. On the contrary, it is only when theology is understood to be subject to the same standards applying to any legitimate field or discipline that it can be reasonably expected to validate the validity claims that are made or implied in bearing Christian witness.

This is not to ignore the specific difference between doing theology and pursuing any other form of critical reflection. Nor is it to imply that theology has to be among the fields or disciplines rightly represented in any university simply as such. The inseparable unity of theology with Christian witness uniquely distinguishes it from all other forms of critical reflection, and hence from all other fields or disciplines represented in the university. And this same unity entails that theology's right to a place in the university is not absolute but relative—deriving not from the constitution of any university simply as such, but from that of a university (for example, an explicitly Christian university) that privileges, in its way, the claims to validity that the specifically Christian witness of faith makes or implies.[6] But none of this alters the fact that theology is a form of reflection that can and must be as critical as any other and, therefore, may very well be a field of study on a par with all the other fields and disciplines. Only if it is, indeed, can it perform the service of critical validation that theology as such, as specifically Christian theology, is constituted to provide.

I conclude, therefore, that the supposed dilemma of a fundamental prolegomena is merely that. It arises not from theology itself, given the institutionalization of critical reflection in the modern university, but only from what theology is supposed to be insofar as its difference from Christian witness is missed or misunderstood. To take account of this difference and to understand it as I have done here, however, is in no way to deny the unity between Christian witness and theology. It is only rightly to distinguish them.

III

The question now is how, within this understanding of theology as a field, historical theology as a discipline is to be understood. I have

---

6. See Ogden, *On Theology*, 128–33.

already stated my conviction that there should be an exact analogy between the two understandings. But if this conviction is right, it would
seem that the key to a regional prolegomena to historical theology must
be—as in the case of distinguishing theology from Christian faith and
witness—rightly distinguishing things that cannot be rightly separated
any more than they can be rightly identified. In this case, the key would
be rightly distinguishing historical theology from theology, although
here, too, this would presumably mean so distinguishing them as to
see them in their unity as well as their difference. The fact, however,
that "theology" appears on both sides of the distinction clearly indicates
their unity, while also indicating that there can be at most an analogy between distinguishing them and distinguishing theology from Christian
faith and witness. Historical theology is itself theology, and this means
that it, too, is done on the secondary level of critical reflection, not on the
primary level of self-understanding and life-praxis on which Christian
witness is borne. But, then, how does it really differ from theology otherwise? And how can its difference be really analogous to that between
theology and Christian witness?

To answer these questions, we need to recall what has already been
said about the scope of critical reflection, both in general and in the
specific form of theology. On the foregoing analysis, critical reflection
generally is constituted by asking about the claims to validity that are
made or implied in answering our various vital questions. But if such
reflection thus necessarily includes what I have referred to as "critical
validation," this is not all that it includes. No less necessary is what I have
distinguished as "critical interpretation"; for whether the answer to a vital question is valid in whatever ways it makes or implies a claim to be
so cannot be determined until the answer itself has been rightly understood. So, too, in the case of theology, which is constituted as specifically
Christian theology by asking whether the answer to our existential question given by Christian witness is valid in the several ways in which it
at least implicitly claims to be so. Before this question can be answered,
the Christian witness first has to be understood as an answer to the existential question. Therefore, the scope of theology as constituted by its
own constitutive question is greater than this question, simply on the
face of it, might seem to indicate. Precisely as critical reflection on Christian witness, theology includes critical interpretation of this witness as
the necessary condition of critical validation of its claims to validity.

To the first question, then, of how historical theology really differs, the answer would seem to be this: historical theology differs from theology otherwise as the critical interpretation necessarily included in theology differs from the critical validation that it also includes. In other words, what is properly meant by "historical theology" is simply such critical interpretation of Christian witness as is required to answer the constitutive question of theology as such—whether the validity claims made or implied by any instance of such witness are, in fact, valid claims.

But what critical interpretation of Christian witness is thus required? From what has been said, it should be clear that at least the particular instance of Christian witness whose validity is in question has to be critically interpreted. To attempt to validate its claims without first rightly understanding it would run the risk of not validating its claims at all, but only what are misunderstood to be its claims. It is also the case, however, that this cannot be all the critical interpretation that is necessary. Part of the twofold claim made or implied by any instance of Christian witness is the claim to be adequate to its content. But, as we have seen, this claim itself is twofold, in that it is the claim both to be appropriate to Jesus Christ and to be credible to human existence. In the nature of the case, there are two, and only two, conditions under which the first part of this claim could be valid: either the particular instance of witness is itself the constitutive and, therefore, formally normative instance of Christian witness, by which the appropriateness of all other instances has to be determined; or else it is one of these other instances that so agrees with the formally normative instance that it, too, is appropriate and, therefore, substantially normative for determining the appropriateness of other such instances. Consequently, to validate the appropriateness of any instance of Christian witness is to show that one or the other of these conditions is satisfied. But to show that either of them is satisfied requires critically interpreting the constitutive and, therefore, formally normative instance of Christian witness.

That this is so if one is to show that the second condition is satisfied is obvious enough, since no instance of witness can be determined to be in substantial agreement with another unless both instances are rightly understood. But it is no less so even if one is to show that the first condition is satisfied; for whether an instance of witness is itself constitutive and, therefore, formally normative in turn depends upon its satisfying certain conditions. Specifically, it has to make or imply the claim to be appropriate to Jesus Christ by asserting or implying that Jesus is of decisive significance for human existence; and it has to be not just *an* instance of asserting or implying this, but *the* instance of doing so, in the sense of being the original and originating such instance. But, once again, whether an instance of Christian witness satisfies these conditions and thus is the constitutive instance can be determined only by first rightly understanding it.

The critical interpretation that theology requires, then, is of nothing less than all instances of Christian witness whose claims to be appropriate as well as credible and fitting need to be critically validated. Since the claims of any instance of witness may, under certain circumstances, need to be validated, any instance of witness may also need to be interpreted. This means that the scope of historical theology coincides, in principle, with the whole history of Christian witness, beginning with the earliest instances lying behind, and now accessible only through, the writings of the New Testament, and continuing right up to the latest instances comprising contemporary Christian life-praxis. If one recalls the many forms and kinds of such witness—explicit and implicit, direct and indirect, official and unofficial, and so on—the scope of historical theology will seem vast indeed.

Having recognized this, however, I want to return to what seemed to be its difference from theology otherwise and especially to the other question raised above, whether this difference can really be analogous to that between theology and Christian witness. Historical theology is different, it seemed, because the critical interpretation that theology includes is different from the critical validation that it also includes. While historical theology is concerned with rightly understanding Christian witness, theology otherwise, through its other two disciplines of systematic and practical theology, is concerned with determining whether Christian witness itself is right, in the sense of validly claiming to be both adequate to its content and fitting to its situation. Notwithstanding this difference, however, we have just seen that historical theology is also united with theology otherwise, and thus with its sister disciplines. The critical validation that they are constituted to perform requires, and hence necessarily presupposes, its critical interpretation. To this extent, we have already observed a certain analogy with the difference and unity between Christian witness and theology.

To be sure, the analogy is reversed, in that it is theology that presupposes historical theology, rather than the other way around. But given the difference that analogy implies, it is entirely consistent to allow for this reversal. And there is the more reason to do so because the unity between historical theology and theology likewise runs both ways. In other words, while doing theology presupposes doing historical theology, doing historical theology anticipates doing theology—just as bearing Christian witness anticipates doing theology, while doing theology presupposes bearing Christian witness.

This becomes evident as soon as one reflects that, in general, we seek to understand what others think, say, or do in order to answer our own vital questions. Thus the critical interpretation of the past provided by historical reflection generally is of a piece with, and is naturally oriented toward, the critical validation to be performed by systematic and practical reflection. It is no different in the specific case of theological reflection: the critical interpretation of the past provided by historical theology is never simply an end in itself, but also always the means, even if the indispensable means, to the ulterior end of critical validation, which systematic and practical theology are constituted to attain. In this sense, doing historical theology, from its end, anticipates the work of its sister disciplines, even as they, for their part, necessarily presuppose its work.

But if the analogy seems clear with respect to the unity between the disciplines, it is equally clear with respect to their difference. Corresponding to the difference between the content of Christian witness and the act of witnessing, and hence between Christian witness's claim to be adequate to its content and its claim to be fitting to its situation, is the difference between systematic and practical theology respectively. Although they are united in both having to do with critical validation, they are also different in each having to validate only one of these two claims. But just as Christian witness in both of its aspects is one thing, while theology is something else, so theology in both of these disciplines involves one type of critical reflection, while historical theology involves another. Whereas systematic and practical theology are both a matter of critically validating the claims of Christian witness to be adequate and fitting, historical theology is a matter of critically interpreting this witness so that its claims can be thus validated. This difference, admittedly, is nothing like as great as the difference in levels of living understandingly that obtains between bearing Christian witness and doing theology. And yet it is a difference in types of reflecting critically and, therefore, is certainly great enough to be analogous.

Here, too, however, there are reasons why a distinction that is clear in itself may not always seem so. One such reason is that systematic theology itself perforce has a historical aspect or phase. Because its first task, indeed, is the "dogmatic" task of critically validating the claim of Christian witness to be appropriate to Jesus Christ, its first main objective, for reasons already explained, is to identify what is to count both in principle and in fact as the formally normative instance of Christian witness. It lies in the nature of the case, however, that systematic theology can attain this objective only by pursuing properly historical methods of study and by learning from historical theology as well as historical studies generally. Thus it may not seem to be really distinct from historical theology, and the term "historical theology" may even be used to designate its own historical aspect or phase.[7] But another and perhaps more important reason why historical theology may not be clearly distinguished from the other theological disciplines is that its own proper task is described as *critical* interpretation of Christian witness.

Of course, the point in so describing it is to bring out that, while there is indeed a difference in types between the critical interpretation of historical theology and the critical validation of systematic and practical theology, the first as much as the second is precisely a type of *critical* reflection. But from what has already been said it should be clear that the critical interpretation provided by historical theology is like that of any other form of historical reflection in interpreting what has been thought, said, or done in the past in its meaning for the present. This implies that historical theology critically interprets particular instances of Christian witness in relation to the existential question to which they are properly addressed. Only by thus interpreting them as answers to one of our own vital questions can it rightly understand what they mean for us, or even what they meant for those for whom they were originally intended. But this kind of critical interpretation allows for and, under certain circumstances, requires an immanent criticism (*Sachkritik*) of what has been thought, said, or done in Christian witness by reference to its own basic intention. Thus, if an instance of witness shows

---

7. See Wood, *Vision and Discernment*, 41–45.

signs of having confused addressing its own properly existential question with speaking to some other logically different question, historical theology precisely as critical interpretation includes criticizing the witness accordingly. And the same is true insofar as the witness is otherwise self-inconsistent or the concepts and terms in which it is cast are in principle inappropriate for formulating any answer to the existential question.

Because historical theology allows for such immanent criticism, however, it may itself seem to be a matter of critically validating Christian witness rather than, or as well as, critically interpreting it. This is the more probable insofar as immanent criticism is, in fact, critical validation of certain validity claims that Christian witness, like any other life-praxis, makes or implies. Still, historical theology is not the same as systematic and practical theology, even if it, too, may include a certain kind of criticism of Christian witness. An immanent criticism is one thing, a transcendent criticism, something different; and as much as historical theology may indeed include the first, it cannot possibly include the second except by ceasing to be itself. What makes it or any other historical study properly historical is precisely its "methodical abstraction" from any kind of critical validation requiring transcendent norms, in the sense of norms that go beyond what is thought, said, or done in the objects of its study themselves.[8] Thus, while it may indeed validate the claim to be self-consistent that any instance of Christian witness necessarily implies, it may not validate any of the other claims of witness to be fitting and adequate, and so appropriate and credible. Practical and systematic theology, by contrast, are constituted for the precise purpose of critically validating these other claims, and thus of effecting the transcendent criticism that historical theology as such necessarily precludes.

Once this difference is understood, it is obvious why any attempt to subject historical theological study to systematic and practical theological control is completely out of line. However much the findings of historical theology do indeed need to be thus controlled before they are accepted as normative for Christian faith and witness, this is emphatically not the case with historical theology itself.[9] On the contrary, it

---

8. See Karl-Otto Apel, *Transformation der Philosophie* (Frankfurt: Suhrkamp Verlag, 1973), 2:112–20.

9. Cf. Willi Marxsen, *Der Exeget als Theologe, Vorträge zum Neuen Testament*, 2d ed.

cannot possibly perform the service for its sister disciplines that it is constituted to provide unless it is free to interpret all instances of Christian
witness as they need to be interpreted if they are to be rightly understood. This includes not least all instances of witness that have hitherto
been accepted as normative, both formally and substantially. That an instance of witness has been accepted as normative in no way implies that
it deserves to be so accepted. But to determine its right to be accepted
requires critically validating its claim to be appropriate; and there is no
way to validate this or any of its other claims to validity without first critically interpreting it in entire independence of systematic and practical
theological control.

But if historical theology cannot perform its proper service unless
it is done thus independently, there is no good reason for it not to be
subject to the same standards applying to all other studies now generally judged to be properly historical. On the contrary, it is only when
historical theology is understood to be subject to these very standards
that it can be reasonably expected to interpret the Christian witness so
as rightly to understand it, and thus satisfy the necessary condition of
critically validating its claims to be valid.

Of course, historical theology is specifically different from every
other historical study; and its right to be reckoned among such studies generally is exactly as relative as the right of theology as a field to
a place alongside all the other fields and disciplines institutionalized in
the university. But this in no way implies that historical theology is not
also continuous at every point with historical studies in general and,
therefore, subject to identically the same standards.

I conclude, then, that the analogy is exact between a regional prolegomena to historical theology as a discipline and a fundamental prolegomena to theology as a field. This means that the apparent dilemma of
such a regional prolegomena is exactly that. It arises not from what historical theology really is, given the now generally accepted sense of what
is properly historical, but only from what historical theology appears to
be insofar as its difference from theology otherwise is missed or mis-

(Gütersloh: Gütersloher Verlagshaus Gerd Mohn, 1969), 198–213; idem, "Historisch-
kritische Exegese?" in *Kirchlicher Dienst und theologische Ausbildung: Festschrift für Präses
Dr. Heinrich Reiss* (Bielefeld: Luther-Verlag, 1985), 53–62; idem, "Der Streit um die Berg-
predigt—ein exegetisches Problem?" in *Studien zum Text und zur Ethik des Neuen Testaments:
Festschrift zum 80. Geburtstag von Heinrich Greeven*, ed. Wolfgang Schrage (Berlin: Walter de
Gruyter, 1986), 315–24.

understood. To recognize this difference, however, and to understand it as I have argued one should is in no way to question that historical theology is constituted as a discipline of Christian theology. It is only to contend that it is also eminently historical.

Part 2

Essays on
Sixteenth-Century Themes

TWO

Jill Raitt

Why the Sixteenth Century?

The sixteenth century needs no apology for the scholarly interest it gen-
erates. Academicians from many disciplines find this vibrant century
fascinating. Renaissance scholars realize that their concerns do not end
in fifteenth-century Florence but extend northward in space and into
the sixteenth century in time. Sociologists, economists, and historians
and students of literature, art, music, and architecture find the sixteenth
century incomparably rich. None of this is news and need not be further
insisted upon.

But two important questions need to be addressed. Neither introduces a problem specific to the sixteenth century although that ebullient
age provides fine examples for the discussion of both. The two questions
arise from a change in the locus of the work of the historical theologian.
The first question is: What does historical theology imply when some
of its practitioners no longer study and teach in seminaries but in secular universities? The second question, which arises from the first, is:
How dialogical has the work of historical theologians become as they
draw upon the disciplines available in a university? Although Jaroslav
Pelikan and B. A. Gerrish have discussed the task of the historical theologian and have undertaken to answer questions that have arisen about
it,[1] neither has addressed these questions specifically. They have shed a
most helpful light on the problem of continuity and change, of dogmatic
security in the midst of theological relativity, a problem both rightly

---

1. B. A. Gerrish, *The Old Protestantism and the New: Essays on the Reformation Heritage*
(Chicago: University of Chicago Press, 1982); Jaroslav Pelikan, *Historical Theology: Conti-
nuity and Change in Christian Doctrine* (New York: Corpus Instrumentorum; Philadelphia:
Westminster Press, 1971).

identify as a primary concern for today's historical theologian. They have also discussed the relation of the Reformation to the theories of nineteenth-century historians and systematicians.

Historical Theology and the History of Religions

I wish to address here what it means that some historical theologians prefer to work in institutions with no ecclesiastical ties. How do they teach and do their research in state universities? The question is still being debated with regard to theology itself; I raise it now with regard to historical theology, an enterprise different from theology. That the work of historical theologians may influence systematic theologians' interpretations often may be the case. A historical theologian may also be a systematic theologian or become one, as has frequently happened; but I do not think that there is an indissoluble and unavoidable bond between the two disciplines so that the historian must become a systematician or have as a primary goal the service of systematic theology.[2] I would argue that systematicians had better know the history of the doctrines with which they deal; they will therefore find the work of historians indispensable. But the reverse is not necessarily the case, especially for those whose area of historical interest is other than the twentieth century. I understand historical theologians to be those who analyze the theologies of a particular period of history or trace a doctrine through history. Like historians of religion, they may be interested in the history of Christian doctrine because of the ways in which it has been influenced by other religions and cultures; in turn, they may try to grasp the influence Christian doctrine has had on European, Euro-American, and Euro-Australian religions and those indigenous cultures overwhelmed by conquest, mission, and modernity and now struggling to reassert their own voices and visions of reality. In other words, I would answer affirmatively the question asked by Harnack and cited by Gerrish: "Even if Christianity were a mistake, would it not still be fascinating . . . to trace

---

2. Pelikan says that "a dogmatic purpose still is the primary motivation for much of the research in historical theology, probably even for most of it" (*Historical Theology*, 100; see also 130).

the history of this mistake, of the earthshaking events it has brought about, of the manner it has penetrated our entire civilization?"[3]

B. A. Gerrish has also pointed to the "history of religions" side of Friedrich Schleiermacher's work insofar as he was interested in "the essence and forms of concrete religion."[4] This quotation occurs in the context of Gerrish's highlighting of Schleiermacher's fundamental concern with religious experience. Gerrish's brief for Schleiermacher, and with him for liberal Protestant theology, is that "the experiential character of Schleiermacher's entire theological enterprise . . . contains the clue to reappraising him as a church theologian in the *legitimate* succession of Luther and Calvin."[5] In other words, the great reformers of the sixteenth century, in Gerrish's view, looked to the *experience* of Christian faith as fundamental. It is not the formal, theological expression of belief that is most influential, but rather how believers experience their religion. Liturgical practice may then be a formal focal point of study; further, some historical theologians would contend that the incorporation of religious values into daily life may be a less formal but equally important area of study. The difficulty with the latter is that it is so hard to bring it into focus because it is so varied and often left unrecorded except in archives or in pamphlets, folk art, music, drama, and the like.

The experiential side of the history of doctrine has therefore widened considerably in the last half of the twentieth century. In spite of resistance, historical theologians must take into consideration the milieu in which doctrines were changed or developed. Politics, wars, the development of the printing press as a means of fostering popular communication through leaflets and books, economic changes and pressures, popular movements and urban development—all and more are part of the picture. The luxury of being a "pure" historian of ideas is no longer feasible, although I am quick to admit how much more attractive it is to me, how much more at home and competent I feel in that heady atmosphere.

Harnack came only part way, and that belatedly, toward such a view, for at first he would not admit that the liturgy itself was an object of

---

3. Gerrish, *Old Protestantism*, 238.
4. B. A. Gerrish, *Prince of the Church: Schleiermacher and the Beginnings of Modern Theology* (Philadelphia: Fortress Press, 1984), 22. By "history of religions" I mean the study of all religions, Christianity included, especially in those areas most readily shared or compared.
5. Ibid., 23; emphasis added.

study proper for the historian of theology, much less for the historian of dogma.[6] Pelikan goes a long way beyond Harnack and defines Christian doctrine as "what the Church believes, teaches, and confesses on the basis of the word of God."[7] He asserts that liturgy belongs to all three areas: believing, teaching, confessing.[8] Pelikan's emphasis, then, is not on what individual theologians taught, but on what the Christian church either gave to them or took from them. The effect of this definition and of the periodization given in Pelikan's *Historical Theology*[9] can be seen in the unusual organization of his magisterial five volumes on the history of Christian doctrine, a work that is so much more than a florilegium. Perhaps it could better be called a tapestry because the selections are firmly held within the warp and woof of what the church believes, teaches, and confesses. Pelikan understands his work to remain within that context.

While the historical theologian may find a particular doctrine or age fascinating and study it without feeling that he or she need give the story a theologically constructive conclusion, the enterprise provides a service for constructive theologians, on the one hand, and for cultural or even general historians, on the other. Antiquarianism is not the object of the field although it may legitimately be so for individual scholars within it. I would venture to say that antiquarianism is not the object of most historians and is certainly not that of theologians. The point of reviewing history is to shed light on the present, to provide tools to help answer new questions or maybe old questions that have a new twist. It was not a coincidence that B. A. Gerrish's understanding of Calvin's theology as rooted in Christian piety converged with his interest in Schleiermacher's turn to Christian experience as a necessary base for theology.[10] The study of Calvin enlightens and enlivens the study of Schleiermacher and vice versa. Gerrish tells us that his work has been dominated by three major interests: "the relation of Luther's thought to Calvin's...; the relation between classical and liberal Protestant thought; and...

---

6. Pelikan, *Historical Theology*, 88–89. Harnack limited the history of dogma to the doctrines of the Trinity and Christology. The history of theology included the other doctrines, for example, the Eucharist. This division implies acceptance of the fathers of the church and considerable reluctance to accept the theologians of the Middle Ages.

7. Ibid., 95.

8. Ibid., 97.

9. Ibid., 126.

10. Gerrish, *Old Protestantism*, 196–207.

the religious experience behind theological formulas."[11] While Gerrish may have been brought to the first two interests by his study, the third interest, I would surmise, arose also through reflection on his own experience as a theologian ordained in the Reformed tradition. This would not be idiosyncratic. Gerrish approvingly refers to Loofs: "The German historian of dogma, Friedrich Loofs, for example, held that history is simply not competent to deal exhaustively with the sources insofar as it is bound to interpret the past on the analogy of present experience."[12] For the historical theologian aware of present interests and limitations, past and present are in continual dialogue.

Questions and Discoveries

In the same way, new questions may send historians into the past to see how earlier theologians dealt with similar problems.[13] There they may find material overlooked by other researchers because former historians were not looking for, and hence did not find, the ways earlier thinkers dealt with similar questions. An example of such a provocative area is women's studies. While there was interest in the lives of sixteenth-century women in the nineteenth century,[14] digging into the works of the reformers to find their theological opinions about women has occurred primarily in the last two decades. Even more recent is scholars' interest in theologies of women that are revealed in letters and literature written by women and in rituals that include or exclude them.[15]

---

11. Ibid., 2.

12. Ibid., 234.

13. This is not to contradict Pelikan in his rejection of "the effort to elicit from the early centuries of doctrinal history a detailed answer to questions that were not raised in their present form until considerably later"; Pelikan rejects such an effort as "bad theology—and worse history" (*Historical Theology*, 84). Rather I follow Pelikan's statement that "despite the obvious dangers of overcompensating and of trimming the past to suit the present, such a reconstruction of the conventional wisdom about history can bring about a correction and an enrichment of scholarship by paying attention to the new insights coming out of current social trends" (ibid., 12–13).

14. See the bibliographies at the ends of the chapters in Roland Bainton, *Women of the Reformation*, 3 vols. (Minneapolis: Augsburg Publishing House, 1971–77).

15. A number of essays that break new ground through attention to the particularities of women's experiences and therefore of the religious insights derived from those experiences may be found in Judith Plaskow and Carol Christ, eds., *Weaving Visions* (San Francisco: Harper & Row, 1989). See also Jean R. Brink, Allison P. Coudert, and Maryanne C. Horowitz, eds., *The Politics of Gender in Early Modern Europe*, Sixteenth Cen-

An added bonus for historical theologians is that new questions illuminate further what the reformers thought not just about women, but
about human beings in general, the image of God, and even soteriology. A book like Jane Dempsey Douglass's *Women, Freedom, and Calvin*[16]
illustrates the point. Her object was not simply to find out what Calvin
wrote and thought about women; she also hoped to provide directives for Calvinists, specifically for Presbyterians still reluctant to ordain
women. Her book had to deal with subjects such as Calvin's distinction
between divine and human law (the nonordination of women is a matter of polity, not divine law), and in the process did indeed provide a
rationale for changing the tradition.

Truth Claims

These questions raise another that is becoming more and more insistent
as historical theologians move out into ecumenical and secular contexts.
It is one thing to teach students their own tradition. One can assume
that most of the students will accept the seriousness of the truth claims
of that tradition even if they question their content. But when one faces
a variety of beliefs or when the atmosphere is secular and one may assume nothing about the beliefs of the students, the problem becomes
more acute. Students take classes in Christianity in departments of religious studies in state universities for a variety of reasons: humanities
credit, curiosity, or to learn more about their own denomination, which
they often consider to be the only true form of Christianity. It may then
be difficult to persuade the students that all religions and all forms of
Christianity make truth claims. These claims must be taken seriously in
the sense that they should not be made the subject of cynicism or treated
as though they had no more importance for the claimers than one's loyalty to one's school or team. To do so would be to belittle people simply
because they base their lives on creeds other than the one we profess,
whether our creed be religious, agnostic, or atheist.

---

tury Essays and Studies, vol. 12 (Kirksville, Mo.: Sixteenth Century Journal Publishers,
1989). For studies based on women's own writing, see Sherrin Marshall, ed., *Women in Reformation and Counter-Reformation Europe: Private and Public Worlds* (Bloomington: Indiana
University Press, 1989).

16. Jane Dempsey Douglass, *Women, Freedom, and Calvin* (Philadelphia: Westminster
Press, 1985). For example, see 73–82.

Because of the probability that even in a state university many of the students in religious studies courses will be existentially engaged with one sort of truth claim or another, historical theologians teaching in state universities may lean more toward the *history* side of their profession. In such instances, Pelikan's comment is apropos:

> To a degree that is alarming for their historical expertise . . . histo-
> rians have lost the ability to resonate to the religious convictions of
> previous ages, which they therefore feel obliged to explain away
> in terms of political, economic, or psychological factors. Only if
> historical theology is prepared to deal with these factors in rela-
> tion to the beliefs and doctrines that have animated Christians
> may it claim a right to be heard in the councils of the secular
> historians.[17]

Historical theologians in state universities have a twofold obligation. They must be prepared to enter into dialogue with secular historians on their own ground and they must be willing to demonstrate the histor-ical importance of religious developments in the wider view of history. In other words, they must be mediators between two disciplines, which thereby will be mutually enriched.

In the same vein historians must be sensitive to the religious baggage students bring with them. Historians must take into account the truth claims of sources while avoiding two sets of dangers: the "dangers of a crypto-polemical method in the history of doctrine" and the dangers of trivializing the "seriousness of the documents by ignoring their claim to be speaking about an ultimate and universal truth that affects every man." Hence Pelikan states: "No theory of historiography dare be so antiseptic in its definition of scholarly objectivity that it rules out the possibility of an existential reaction to the message announced in the sources."[18]

Students often have existential reactions as they learn the origins of their own denomination or that the justification of a doctrine in their church rests on a minority opinion or that biblical scholars have under-cut an interpretation based on a faulty translation of the biblical text. A profound difficulty may emerge or, worse, may remain hidden when

---

17. Pelikan, *Historical Theology*, 80.
18. Ibid., 81; see also 158–59.

particular beliefs of students make it impossible for them to understand a historical position of another group. This has occurred too often to me. For example, an honors student who was doing C− work came in to talk about a test on the Definition of Chalcedon. Students are not asked to endorse the Definition, but they are asked to know the main theological and political issues. This particular student told me that he simply could not take seriously any proposition that affirmed the humanity of Christ. "If he is human," said the student, "then he is not divine." The student did not realize that he represented one of the poles of the controversy. He only knew that he could not understand the material he was asked to read because it contradicted his own profound conviction.

A professor can announce antiseptic goals, but that same professor cannot simply ignore the struggle of students to deal with the history presented to them and the doctrinal implications of that history.

And how antiseptic are the goals and interpretations of the professor? Most scholars understand that the claim to objectivity is weak, if not empty. The prejudices and unexamined assumptions that underlie a scholar's interest in a particular subject may also guide the study and teaching of that subject to a degree unsuspected by the scholar-professor. This need not be looked upon as a handicap. Indeed, if one had no particular interests in a particular subject, what motivation would one have to undertake the study of that subject? What questions could one generate if one had no preconceptions? Perhaps that is why Pelikan asks but does not answer the question: "Can the theological a priori be avoided in historical theology?"[19] The distance one can acquire by taking the perspective of the history of religions may help to reveal that a priori. The history of religions will undoubtedly provide a new a priori and a new set of questions. But one can never lay aside one's personal history, one's personal quest, at the levels where these are most dynamic, namely, in the depths of one's outlook on the world. The answer to Pelikan's question is, I think, that even in a secular institution, the theological a priori can neither be ignored nor avoided, at least not with pedagogical impunity.

---

19. Ibid., 103.

Changes

Equally interesting for the purposes of this essay is the fact that scholarship on the religious issues of the sixteenth century has undergone significant changes, many of which are still in progress. No longer are only denominationally interested researchers delving deeper into their founders' theologies, but scholars now follow their interests regardless of their religious preference or even religious indifference. Prior to World War II the denominational biases were frequently evident. In tandem with a denominational bias went polemical attitudes that had roots in the sixteenth century, developing rapidly even during Luther's lifetime. After the death of the major reformers—Zwingli, Luther, and Calvin—polemics among Protestants became increasingly virulent, often more bitter than the polemics between Catholics and Protestants. These divisions then became entrenched in the confessional materials that proliferated in the last quarter of the sixteenth century.

In contrast, during World War II, many European scholars saw the necessity of uniting ecumenically to support Christian principles. Ecumenicity contributed to an already increasing interest in a better understanding of the roots of the Reformation, of its relation to the Middle Ages and to modernity, and of the theology of the reformers themselves. Scholars began to study what interested them regardless of the denomination of their subject. It is common now to find Catholic scholars examining Protestant reformers and their work, producing articles and books that have become standard in the field; an example of this is the outstanding volumes on John Calvin by Alexandre Ganoczy. At the same time, Protestant scholars are able to present Catholic doctrine without bias. Jaroslav Pelikan's five-volume work on the whole of Christian doctrinal history is an outstanding example.[20]

Another change is the continuing growth of the idea that historical theology must be contextually understood. To know the theology of any theologian or church means to set that theology in its cultural, social, and political milieu. Nuances of language, terms, and phrases must be set in their own larger and often eclectic context. The development of particular theologies can be properly understood only when the theolo-

20. Jaroslav Pelikan, *The Christian Tradition: A History of the Development of Doctrine,* 5 vols. (Chicago: University of Chicago Press, 1971–89).

gians responsible for them are seen as human beings engaged in their
social, political, and cultural world. This is as true of the theologians in
the sixteenth century as of any other century. One might even argue
that it is particularly true of a time as transitional in culture and society
as was the sixteenth century, that time of discovery and renewal. The
Renaissance not only stimulated philological studies, love of the classics, and concern for the rapidly developing vernacular languages, but
also political passions. The reformers worked in the midst of social up-
heaval and pressures. The changes brought about by the use of printing
presses might be said to equal those brought about by the use of com-
puters today. The discoveries of new lands and seas might be said to
equal the space probes of today. The changes in the political map and
the restlessness of peasants and burghers resulted in social changes that
draw scholars into micro- and macro-studies of the sociopolitical worlds
of the sixteenth century. In other words, historical theology is coming to
view history as more than a temporal backdrop for the development of
particular intellectual ideas. With due respect to Gibbon, not even theologians, insofar as they are cognizant of history, may present only the
heavenly face of the church.[21]

Historical theology, taken more narrowly but retaining the need to
put such study in context, is the study of the development of a theological idea or particular aspects of theology in a given historical period.
The fundamental method is a careful scrutiny of theological texts on a
particular subject like justification or the Lord's Supper. Or the historian
of theology may concentrate on the thought of a particular theologian,
for example, Luther or Calvin, studying particular doctrines or choosing
to present a theory concerning the theologian's central dogma. Many
efforts to find Calvin's central dogma have resulted in a better understanding of his theology even though they have failed to convince other
scholars that the chosen doctrine is in fact *the* central one. Failing to locate so clear a central doctrine for Calvin as justification is for Luther,
scholars may look for the governing principles of Calvin's thought:
his christological or soteriological concern, his perspectives, his related
principles.

---

21. Edward Gibbon, *The History of the Decline and Fall of the Roman Empire*, ed. J. B. Bury, 7 vols. (London: Methuen, 1896–1900), 2/2:15 (cited in Jaroslav Pelikan, *The Excellent Empire: The Fall of Rome and the Triumph of the Church* [San Francisco: Harper & Row, 1987], vii and 36).

Challenges

All of these goals and methods, these historical-theological enterprises, remain valid, but other methods challenge their right to dominate the field of Reformation studies. The most vociferous challenger is social history; the most cunning is psycho-history. Social history itself breaks into different methods and subjects, but in each case, the argument vis-à-vis intellectual history or doctrinal history is the same: one has to take the mentality of the people into account. Who heard the preaching, read the pamphlets, and voted reforming magistrates in or out of office?

Contributing to the increasing number of areas the scholar must now study are the works on the means of publication, the printing press, the book fairs, the leaflets and fliers and their distribution. Miriam Chrisman's two volumes on printing in Strasbourg carry the reader far beyond anything that one might expect and, indeed, into the lives and minds of the bourgeoisie of a town through which churned many currents of the Renaissance and the Reformation.[22] The study of the impact of printing presses on the spread of Reformation ideas and polemics has led to the study of the popular art of the period; scholars are studying pamphlets and leaflets that were often illustrated with cartoons that leave indelible impressions even now when one sees them—cartoons like that of the seven-headed Luther and the seven-headed pope, both adapted from the beast of the book of Revelation.

It is also becoming more and more evident that no period is "pure." Every thinker is more or less eclectic. The scholar's job is to see what the eclectic mix is and what influences dominate. Thus the work of William Bouwsma reveals how much more can be understood about Calvin when someone steeped in Renaissance studies undertakes to write about a man who was himself enamored of the Renaissance's return to the classics, its emphasis on rhetoric, its praise of a moderate and moral life.[23]

New emphases have broadened the scene still more as scholars ask what women were doing besides keeping house and raising the chil-

---

22. Miriam Usher Chrisman, *Lay Culture, Learned Culture: Books and Social Change in Strasbourg, 1480–1599* (New Haven: Yale University Press, 1982), and its companion volume, *Bibliography of Strasbourg Imprints, 1480–1599* (New Haven: Yale University Press, 1982).

23. William J. Bouwsma, *John Calvin: A Sixteenth Century Portrait* (New York: Oxford University Press, 1988).

dren of the reformers. This is a subject that requires much more study, whether it be from a fascination with witch-hunts or the elegant *querelle des femmes* that overflowed from Renaissance literature into Reformation discussions of the "role of women" and into arguments about whether the Reformation was "good" for women.[24]

Another area of growth is the increasing interest in the development of confessionalism and the neo-scholasticism that marked the seventeenth century. This subject raises theological questions such as the relation of scripture to tradition within Protestantism. During that period those engaged in polemical debates increasingly shored up arguments with appeals to the later councils and even to the scholastics themselves. In this connection, the theological battlefield moved from engagements over the nature of the Eucharist to wars over the natures and person of Christ. In addition, at every point, scholars must now be aware of the way in which polemics affected the people whose lives and property were jeopardized by a change in the theological wind.

A phenomenal increase in interest in spirituality has resulted in several fine new series that have included Protestants.[25] No longer is mysticism the province of Catholics only and as such an area highly suspected by Protestants. The relation of spirituality to theology in general is now taken for granted and so must be included in studies by historians of theology.

Old problems have not been solved even though excellent studies argue persuasively on one side or the other. At what point does the modern period begin? To what degree are Protestants Catholic and how Protestant were many Catholics prior to the Reformation? Such questions may never be resolved and that may be all to the good. Arguing about them can result in fresh research and insights into the periods under debate.

Historical methods have also undergone fundamental challenges,

---

24. For example, see Allison P. Coudert, "The Myth of the Improved Status of Protestant Women: The Case of the Witchcraze," in Brink, Coudert, and Horowitz, *Politics of Gender.*

25. For example, see the Paulist Press series *Spiritual Classics of the Western World.* The first volumes appeared in 1978; more than sixty volumes later, the series continues to grow. Each volume provides a scholarly introduction plus complete works by the author. Included are not only those expected—for example, Julian of Norwich, Augustine, and Teresa of Avila—but also the spiritualities of Native Americans and Protestants like William Law, the Shakers, and so on. Another example is the series published by Crossroad Press, *World Spirituality,* destined to be twenty-five volumes. The Christian volumes (1985–89) include essays on the reformers and later Protestants.

such as those posed by the *annalistes*. Other disciplines ask new questions of the historian of theology. Passions flare in attack and defense when psychologists attempt to analyze Luther and Calvin. With regard to the question of the use of psychology in understanding historical personages and events and in teaching about them, I find a solution proposed by Peter Iver Kaufman to be convincing.[26]

New Boundaries

Gradually, in fact too slowly, interest in the religious aspects of the sixteenth century is expanding beyond a too great fascination with the countries bordering on the Rhine, especially Germany. England's reformation is no longer being regarded as so *sui generis* that it can be considered apart from the continental reformation. It is no longer considered to be simply a series of parliamentary acts under the bullying insistence of a king determined to have male issue. Rather the underlying religious concerns that stirred beneath the actions of court and parliament are also being recognized as *sine quibus non* in England's series of compromises, changes, quarrels, settlements, and incivilities. In short, England is being studied as a country over which blew the same winds stirring the continent. France, torn by the wars of religion, is also being increasingly studied in terms of the international involvements in its wars including both aid and interference dictated by religious motives. Indeed, sociological studies of small areas of France, whether rural or urban, are more advanced than similar studies of many other nations. Italy and Spain remain largely peripheral although there is a need to better understand how the Italian Renaissance and some of its converts to forms of Protestantism influenced the religious revolution in the rest of Europe. But what of the lands of central Europe, especially Poland, that sanctuary for the persecuted Anabaptists and Unitarians? And what about the neglected Scandinavian reformations that seem to become interesting only when scholars turn to the signing of the Formula of Concord or to Scandinavian intervention in continental wars?

Another fascinating line of study that promises to develop rapidly

---

26. See Peter Iver Kaufman, "Social History, Psychohistory, and the Prehistory of Swiss Anabaptism," *The Journal of Religion* 68 (1988): 527–44; idem, "Historians and Human Behavior: Biography as Therapy," *Clio* 18, no. 2 (1989): 179–87.

among historical theologians is the relation of Europe to the non-European world. Heretofore, these areas have largely been the province of Roman Catholic historians, especially Jesuits and Franciscans whose orders established missions in the American and Asian continents during the sixteenth century. Protestant interest in these distant lands did not develop until after the defeat of the Spanish Armada when British and Dutch traders saw the advantages of colonizing the Pacific and Atlantic rims and when dissident religious groups dared to cross the Atlantic because the marauding Spanish and English galleons no longer posed such a threat.

Nevertheless, it was during the heyday of Portuguese and Spanish naval power that exploration was quickly followed by trading ships, colonies, and missions. Queen Isabella inquired of her theologians whether the "Indians" brought to Spain by Columbus were human—that is, had souls and therefore could not be enslaved and should rather be sent missionaries. Although debate continued, the official responses were that Indians were indeed human. That position was adopted also by Emperor Charles V and Pope Paul III.[27] In Roman Catholic lands laws were thus established that were different from those that guided the Jamestown settlers,[28] who decided that the blacks brought to their shore in 1619 were not entirely human and therefore could not be saved and, as non-Christians, could thus be enslaved. European exploration and settlement in the Americas therefore have to be understood in the larger European context, not just as a part of the history of the colonies and of Spain, Portugal, and Roman Catholic missionaries. The same must be said about the settlements in India, the work of Francis Xavier in Japan, and that of Matteo Ricci in China.

In addition, one must ask: What impact had these prolonged contacts and resultant reports and imports on Europeans? The expansion of the known world and the importation of exotic foods and materials had to bring about a gradual shift in Europeans' perceptions of their world

27. For a good discussion of the issues (however controversial Todorov's historical accuracy), see Tsvetan Todorov, *The Conquest of America: The Question of the Other*, trans. Richard Howard (New York: Harper & Row, 1984), esp. 161. I owe this reference to Philip Arnold.

28. Ibid., 161–62. Similarly, in the papal bull of 1537, Paul III declares: "Acknowledging that the Indians as true men not only are capable of receiving the Christian faith but, as we have been informed, eagerly hurry to it, . . . we command that the aforesaid Indians and all other nations which come to the knowledge of Christians in the future must not be deprived of their freedom and the ownership of their property."

and of themselves. Attentiveness to these geographical and economic shifts could result in a rich new area of sixteenth-century studies.[29]

Christians who have learned to engage in ecumenical dialogue may find dialogue with historians of religions more threatening as Christianity is treated as one religion among others. Hackles rise when historians dare to suggest that many strands in Christianity, in fact many denominational allegiances, are owed to distant or not-so-distant "pagan" elements. Nevertheless, these currents and challenges turn the mill wheel of the dedicated historian. As we approach the twenty-first century, the health of historical theology seems assured. New challenges and problems keep youthful the discipline and the minds of its best practitioners.

---

29. See Geoffrey Atkinson, *Les nouveaux horizons de la renaissance française* (Paris: E. Droz, 1935). I owe this reference to Charles Nauert.

THREE

Mary Potter Engel

Historical Theology and Violence against Women: Unearthing a Popular Tradition of Just Battery

Authentic liberation of women from the oppressive attitudes, struc- tures, and practices of a patriarchal society entails the transformation of women from the "appropriate victims" of sexual terrorism to free and responsible persons who cooperate with equals to build a just and car- ing society for all.[1] Historical theologians can contribute to this radical transformation by exposing and analyzing the ways in which women have been oppressed in the past; recovering the challenges and alterna- tives to women's oppression buried in the past; and using both of these to reconstruct the view of history that informs our lives today.

Historical theologians are beginning to respond to this feminist chal- lenge. In-depth examinations of the theory and practice of the subor- dination of women and recoveries of long-buried spiritual traditions of women are appearing more frequently. None of this work, however, has

---

1. Rebecca E. Dobash and Russell P. Dobash have popularized the phrase "appro- priate victim" in their *Violence against Wives* (New York: Free Press, 1979), 32. Carole J. Sheffield defines "sexual terrorism" as the use of ideology, propaganda, and indiscrim- inateness to perpetrate violence and the threat of violence against women in order to control through fear and maintain the patriarchal definition of women's place ("Sexual Terrorism," in *Women: A Feminist Perspective,* ed. Jo Freeman [Palo Alto, Calif.: Mayfield Publishing Co., 1979], 3–19).

been incorporated in general church history or history of theology text-books. Jaroslav Pelikan's five-volume history of doctrine, *The Christian Tradition*, though critical of histories of theology that ignore the eccle-sial context of doctrinal development, does not include women as part of the church.[2] Williston Walker et al.'s *A History of the Christian Church*, one of the classic church histories still widely used today, contains only a few mentions of women.[3] At least three factors contribute to this silence. The first and most obvious is the androcentrism of those who recorded the histories and those who interpret them today. The world of the con-quered is not known or recorded by the conquerors and therefore is not heard by later interpreters. The second factor is the focus in history of theology on intellectual history. If one considers only the development of ideas important, the reality of most women's lives will not come to light. The third factor is the focus in church history on the organization and development of the church as institution. If one considers only the public life of the community significant and not the private lives of ordi-nary Christians, the reality of most women's lives will not come to light; for they were often restricted to the domestic realm.

In the last few decades social historians have criticized histories of theology and church histories as histories of the elite who influenced public life. These social historians have argued that for a more represen-tative or comprehensive history, sources other than published treatises or official church documents must be consulted. In order to gain access to the lives of ordinary men and women, they have turned to court, convent, and consistory records, household inventories, private letters, pamphlets, woodcuts, and other visual art.

The turn to social history is necessary but not sufficient for exposing violence against women, as the few general histories that adopt a more social-historical approach and take gender distinction seriously show. Justo L. González's excellent two-volume work, *The Story of Christianity*, which begins to move beyond "the history of the conquerors" model in so many ways, ignores violence against women.[4] Barbara J. MacHaffie's

---

2. Jaroslav Pelikan, *The Christian Tradition*, 5 vols. (Chicago: University of Chicago Press, 1971–89).

3. Williston Walker et al., *A History of the Christian Church*, 4th ed. (New York: Charles Scribner's Sons, 1985).

4. Justo L. González, *The Story of Christianity*, 2 vols. (San Francisco: Harper & Row, 1984).

Her Story: Women in Christian Tradition, though it focuses on women's lives as they intersect and parallel official church history, is also silent on this issue.[5] And Margaret R. Miles's *Image as Insight* and *Practicing Christianity,* both attempts to tell the history of Christianity from a feminist social-historical point of view, do not contain any references to violence against women.[6]

This silence about violence against women is notable not only in general histories of Christianity but in studies of marriage in Christianity and histories of the family as well. Martin Ingram's *Church Courts, Sex and Marriage in England, 1570–1640,* while concerned with divorce practices, does not mention violence.[7] James Casey's *The History of the Family*—which analyzes the politics of the family, considers marriage contracts, and situates the family in society—does not mention domestic violence.[8] Clearly the turns to a feminist perspective and social history are not enough to bring to light the violence women have suffered.

We are left with the conclusion that violence against women, a key factor in society's oppression of women, has received "selective inattention" in historical theology.[9] At best this neglect suggests to students of historical theology that the violent reality of women's lives is of no significance for our understanding of the history of theology and spirituality. At worst it is a sign of the tradition's continuing complicity in the practice of violence against women.

Breaking the Silence

This silence about Christianity's role in the cultural practice of violence against women is beginning to be broken. More often than not, however, those breaking it come out of the broader feminist movement or the movement to end violence against women. Two early historical over-

5. Barbara J. MacHaffie, *Her Story: Women in Christian Tradition* (Philadelphia: Fortress Press, 1986).

6. Margaret R. Miles, *Image as Insight: Visual Understanding in Western Christianity and Secular Culture* (Boston: Beacon Press, 1985); idem, *Practicing Christianity: Critical Perspectives for an Embodied Spirituality* (New York: Crossroad, 1988).

7. Martin Ingram, *Church Courts, Sex and Marriage in England, 1570–1640* (New York: Cambridge University Press, 1987).

8. James Casey, *The History of the Family* (Oxford: Basil Blackwell, 1989).

9. Richard J. Gelles, *The Violent Home: A Study of Physical Aggression between Husbands and Wives* (Beverly Hills, Calif.: Sage Publications, 1974), 13.

views of sexism have been instrumental in focusing attention on the
link between the Christian tradition and the violence of wifebeating.
Not in God's Image, a collection of legal, philosophical, theological, and
popular sayings against women from antiquity to the present in European culture, contains a wide variety of statements of the inequality of
women and several quotations that explicitly recommend wifebeating.[10]
Elizabeth Gould Davis's *The First Sex* also contains references to physical cruelty against wives.[11] Both these works are frequently quoted and
cited by researchers in domestic violence who want to set a historical
context for this issue. For example, many of the primary source quotations in Del Martin's *Battered Wives,*[12] Dobash and Dobash's *Violence
against Wives,* and Nancy Hutchings's *The Violent Family* come from these
two sources.[13] *Not in God's Image* and *The First Sex* have played an important role in uncovering the history of violence against women by
breaking open the question of the relation of Christianity to this violence. They will not prove of much help in the future, however, for they
(1) do not provide an analysis of the individual quotations in their contexts; (2) suggest rather than demonstrate that a connection between an
ideology of inequality and recommendations to batter exists; and (3) do
not focus on wifebeating.

Two pieces by Terry Davidson, the essay "Wifebeating: A Recurring
Phenomenon throughout History" and the historical chapter of her
book *Conjugal Crime,* do focus on wifebeating and the Christian tradition.[14] Pulling together legal, religious, and historical data drawn from
Not in God's Image, Davidson sketches in large and bold strokes the complicity of Christianity—from its earliest days to the present—in the crime
of wifebeating. Both pieces are notable because they are the first to focus
on the relation between Christianity and wifebeating and the first to acknowledge a connection between the church's teachings on inequality

---

10. Julia O'Faolain and Lauro Martines, eds., *Not in God's Image: A History of Women in
Europe from the Greeks to the Nineteenth Century* (New York: Harper & Row, 1973), 145, 152,
168–69, 175, 202.
11. Elizabeth Gould Davis, *The First Sex* (New York: Putnam, 1971), 254–55.
12. Del Martin, *Battered Wives,* rev. ed. (San Francisco: Volcano Press, 1981).
13. Nancy Hutchings, *The Violent Family: Victimization of Women, Children, and Elders*
(New York: Human Sciences Press, 1988).
14. Terry Davidson, "Wifebeating: A Recurring Phenomenon throughout History," in
Battered Women: A Psychosociological Study of Domestic Violence, ed. Maria Roy (New York:
Van Nostrand Reinhold, 1977), 2–23; idem, *Conjugal Crime: Understanding and Changing the
Wifebeating Pattern* (New York: Hawthorne Books, 1978), chap. 5.

and its practice of contempt for women, its legitimation of women as objects of antagonism and its explicit violence against women.

Although Davidson's works have played a critical role in furthering the discussion, they will not be of much help in future investigations because they: (1) assume rather than explore or argue for the connection between inequality and violence; (2) do not use primary sources; and (3) do not provide an analysis of the quotations used. They end up telescoping a wide variety of materials culled from the works of others into an overly generalized condemnation of the church that allows little room for distinctions in the kind or degree of sexism from person to person, culture to culture, or period to period. "The Christian church," Davidson concludes, "from Constantine on, has had a record of practicing and recommending physical abuse to women."[15]

Two other works connecting Christianity and wifebeating, Rosemary Radford Ruether's "The Western Religious Tradition and Violence against Women in the Home" and Joy Bussert's brief historical discussion in her book *Battered Women,* are welcome continuations of Davidson's research. Both are built on the recognition that wifebeating is rooted in the "basic patriarchal assumptions about women's subordinate status."[16] Both claim that there is a connection between the inferiority of women in a dualistic system and the justification of violence against them. Both call for radical reform. But these works, too, are of limited value. Neither analyzes the connection between the ideology of gender inequality and the practice of violence against women. Both single out dramatic quotations for effect, raising the question of whether such statements are exceptional or normative. And both run far too quickly over twenty centuries.

The fact that Davidson, Ruether, and Bussert have kept this issue before us and the directness and clarity of their claims are to be commended. But if the investigation of Christianity's roles in tightening the knot of gender inequality and the practice of violence against women is to proceed, their work must be complemented by more circumspect (though not necessarily less radical) conclusions supported by detailed

---

15. Davidson, "Wifebeating," 7.
16. Rosemary Radford Ruether, "The Western Religious Tradition and Violence against Women in the Home," in *Christianity, Patriarchy, and Abuse: A Feminist Critique,* ed. Joanne Carlson Brown and Carole R. Bohn (New York: Pilgrim Press, 1989), 31; Joy Bussert, *Battered Women: From a Theology of Suffering to an Ethic of Empowerment* (New York: Lutheran Church in America, 1986).

historical analyses of primary sources. As scholars begin to research specific aspects of this issue, they will pay attention to distinctions between periods, geographical areas, cultures, and personalities. They will base their generalized conclusions on analyses of sources that utilize the categories of gender, the intersection of gender, class, and race, and the intersection of gender and local culture. For example, it has been argued that sexism increased in the late Middle Ages and Reformation periods with the arrival of a preindustrial capitalist economy.[17] It has also been argued that local contexts need to be considered more carefully when one generalizes, because life in medieval Paris was not equivalent to life in Basel, Heidelberg, or Canterbury.[18] These survey essays, then, serve best as invitations to further studies that will supplement and critique them.

Detailed analyses of primary sources mentioning violence against wives have begun to appear. Much has been done by social historians, for example, to further our understanding of wifebeating in France and England from the fifteenth to the nineteenth centuries.[19] Much of this work, however, has not paid attention to the way in which the Christian tradition has informed or contributed to this practice. Two books do contribute detailed historical research into the issue of violence against women specifically within the context of Christianity—Edward J. Bayer's *Rape within Marriage* and Steven Ozment's *When Fathers Ruled.*[20] Bayer's study is an exercise in constructive church history, concentrating on canon law discussions of marital rape from 1600

---

17. Roberta Hamilton, *The Liberation of Women: A Study of Patriarchy and Capitalism* (London: George Allen and Unwin, 1978).

18. H. C. Erik Midelfort, "Toward a Social History of Ideas in the Reformation," in *Pietas et Societas: New Trends in Reformation Social History,* ed. Kyle C. Sessions and Phillip N. Bebb (Ann Arbor, Mich.: Edwards Brothers, 1986), 11–22.

19. Carol Bauer and Lawrence Ritt, "A Husband Is a Beating Animal: Francis Power Cobbe Confronts the Wife-Abuse Problem in Victorian England," *International Journal of Women's Studies* 6 (1983): 99–118; Leonore Davidoff, "Mastered for Life: Servant and Wife in Victorian and Edwardian England," *Journal of Social History* 7 (1969): 406–28; R. Emerson Dobash and Russell Dobash, "Community Response to Violence against Wives: Charivari, Abstract Justice and Patriarchy," *Social Problems* 28 (1981): 563–81; Margaret May, "Violence in the Family: An Historical Perspective," in *Violence and the Family,* ed. J. P. Martin (Chichester: John Wiley and Sons, 1978), 135–67; Roderick Phillips, "Women and Family Breakdown in Eighteenth-Century France: Rouen 1780–1800," *Social History* 1 (1976): 202–18.

20. Edward J. Bayer, *Rape within Marriage: A Moral Analysis Delayed* (Lanham, Md.: University Press of America, 1985); Steven Ozment, *When Fathers Ruled: Family Life in Reformation Europe* (Cambridge: Harvard University Press, 1983).

to 1749 and their implications for current Roman Catholic ecclesiastical decisions. Ozment's book is an exercise in the social history of the Protestant ideas of marriage and the family. Drawing on an impressively wide variety of popular materials, including "housefather" books, woodcuts, and vernacular pamphlets, Ozment focuses on Swiss and German family life during the Reformation. Both authors make significant contributions to the study of Christianity's role in the history of violence against women. Neither, however, focuses on wifebeating. And neither stresses the connection between gender inequality and the practice of violence against women. In fact, Ozment's argument seems to obscure this relation. His choice to highlight exceptions to the rule of male dominance rather than the rule itself, his stress on occasional references to restraint of wifebeating, and his recurrent qualifications of the patriarchal structure of the Reformation family appear to be evidence of his reluctance to consider violence against women as an established pattern in the Christian tradition.[21]

Recently, occasional references to wifebeating have appeared in social-historical articles on marriage and divorce in the Reformation. For example, William Monter's study of Geneva based on the consistory records of 1559–64 notes that several men were excommunicated for beating their wives.[22] While it is encouraging to see scholars paying attention to these kinds of details, there is still insufficient information available to draw significant conclusions from such data. Thomas Safley's caution about the difficulty of drawing conclusions from studies of litigation that are hampered by narrow chronological limits is pertinent here.[23]

Furthermore, even when we do have sufficient data, we will still need to analyze the meaning of these statistics in their social and historical contexts. Safley's work on the actions of the Basel marital court between 1529 and 1554 points to the need for this. He reports that out

---

21. For example, he comments that there was not a "total subjection of the wife" because "authority was shared by husband and wife" (*When Fathers Ruled,* 11); and "despite male rule an ordered equality existed between husbands and wives" (ibid., 99). He also consistently places the terms *sexist* and *patriarchal* in quotation marks (ibid., 12, 99).

22. William Monter, "The Consistory of Geneva, 1559–64," in *Renaissance, Reformation, Resurgence,* ed. Peter De Klerk (Grand Rapids, Mich.: Calvin Theological Seminary, 1976), 81 n. 34, 82 n. 36.

23. Thomas Safley, "Protestantism, Divorce, and the Breaking of the Modern Family," in *Pietas et Societas,* 44.

of 148 divorces granted in Basel in this period, nineteen were granted on grounds of "deadly abuse."[24] Three things are important to note here as we consider how to interpret such information. First, although deadly abuse is the third leading cause for divorces granted, it is not a well-recognized cause. Second, these statistics do not by themselves enable us to conclude how common wifebeating was, for as Safley himself notes, often divorces were granted on other grounds, such as adultery or impoverishment, even when abuse was part of the claim. Third, the court was reluctant to grant divorces on the grounds of abuse alone except in cases of the most extreme abuse. In other words, it was not physical abuse but "deadly abuse"—that which caused premature births, insanity of the wife, or the maiming or death of the wife—that could be claimed as a grounds for divorce in the Basel court.[25] Such a qualification is critical for understanding the excommunications and other disciplinary actions recorded in legal and ecclesiastical records. Rather than assuming that the excommunication of several men for beating their wives indicates the Basel court's rejection of all battery as anti-Christian, we need to ask if it is not rather the case that it indicates the acceptance of wifebeating, as long as it took place within prescribed limits of moderation. In other words, these men may have been punished not for beating their wives, but for beating them without just cause or immoderately.[26]

Grethe Jacobsen's article "Women, Marriage, and Magisterial Reformation" raises similar cautions about interpreting court statistics. Jacobsen notes that the marital court records of Malmø, Denmark, contain explicit directives to the wife to be "humble and obedient" and to the husband to discipline her physically, "within reason," if she is not.[27] Thus, while women were able to make use of the courts, and the courts *sometimes* ruled in their favor on the grounds of deadly abuse, one cannot conclude that the courts were in women's

24. Ibid., 45–46.
25. Ibid., 46–47.
26. Safley's claim that "abuse" served as a grounds for divorce in Basel, therefore, must be qualified ("Protestantism," 49), as must Ozment's report of a colleague's conclusion: "Wife-beaters in Protestant towns and territories were haled before the marriage court or consistory, and nowhere more speedily than in Geneva, which by century's end had gained the reputation of 'the woman's Paradise'" (*When Fathers Ruled,* 208 n. 79).
27. Grethe Jacobsen, "Women, Marriage, and Magisterial Reformation: The Case of Malmø, Denmark," in *Pietas et Societas,* 71.

favor, supported egalitarian marriages, or condemned all physical abuse.

What can be learned from these recent social-historical studies that include some mention of wifebeating is that we need to move beyond extrapolations from limited data to more detailed analyses of gender relations if we are to understand the complex ideology controlling the oppression of women in any given period or local culture. While it is encouraging to see wifebeating recognized, the conclusions of many of these studies remind us of the importance of a feminist perspective for interpreting the findings. In particular, if one does not see a connection between ideologies of inequality and the practice of violence, one may too quickly interpret a move toward companionate marriage as a critique of wifebeating. And if one does not allow for the possibility that the rule may be one of justified violence against wives, one may too quickly interpret the existence of calls for moderation or greater restraint of wifebeating as indications of a shift to greater justice for women.

These studies also point to the fact that sources have been and will continue to be a problem for historical theologians investigating violence against women. Today we know that a very small percentage of marital violence is reported and the official records of intimate relationships are not always easy to interpret. These problems are compounded for the historical theologian. What we can do is continue to investigate records of divorce proceedings and other legal documents to determine the incidence and meaning of wifebeating. And we can turn our attention to more popular sources—such as accounts of public shamings, sermons, and so on—that will help us uncover community attitudes toward and practices of violence against women.

Finally, these studies raise the question of the periodization of history. Once we include gender relations and violence against women in the mix of factors that determine how we identify significant shifts in history and divide it into periods, we may end up with a different picture of the past. Ozment's argument for an advance for women in the Reformation over the Middle Ages, for example, is based on the assumption that the medieval church's exaltation of celibacy and virginity led to a gross denigration of marriage and women, which the Protestant Reformation successfully countered with its notion of companionate marriage. Thus, for Ozment, the Protestant Reformation represents a significant advance for women and retains its status as a major period.[28] But if, as I will soon argue, the Reformation did not challenge the ideology of inequality and continued to accept wifebeating, within limits, as the rule, it can by no means be said to represent an unqualified advance for women. If we count Christianity's teaching and practice of violence against women in our assessment, we cannot say a reformation has occurred for women.

In order to complete a comprehensive history of Christianity's relation to women that includes attention to violence against women and in order to reconstruct a genuinely common and liberating history of Christianity that includes both women's and men's experiences, we need more studies in historical theology that

1. recognize that violence against women has occurred and does occur and that it is an urgent problem;

2. focus on different kinds of violence against women, including rape and wifebeating, instead of lumping these with other instances of sexism;

3. operate from a feminist perspective—that is, analyze rather than ignore, simply acknowledge, or explain away the connection between ideologies of inequality and the practice of violence;

4. are interdisciplinary, paying attention to a wide variety of texts and especially to the interplay of the Christian religion with other dimensions of culture;

5. take a social-historical approach, paying attention to (*a*) the private lives of ordinary women as they are recorded in private letters and in court, consistory, convent, and church records; and (*b*) the cultural attitudes toward violence against women that are suggested in visual images, pamphlets, sermons, and so on;

6. engage in detailed analyses of limited time periods and locales rather than remain at the survey level;

7. move beyond argument by means of exceptional statements (either positive ones as in Ozment's argument or negative ones as

28. Ozment, *When Fathers Ruled*, 9.

in Ruether's and Bussert's arguments) and probe for complex patterns that normalize violence against women and that can be used to interpret individual statements of or decisions about violence against women;

8. recognize that new discoveries will have implications for our understanding of the "development" and periodization of the Christian tradition.

Wifebeating in Popular French Literature from 1150 to 1565

As a way of pointing in this direction of future research in historical theology and violence against women, I will summarize here my recent study of wifebeating in popular French tales and sermons from 1150 to 1565. The *fabliaux*—ribald, rhymed tales of the follies of family life recounted for public entertainment—were widespread from the early thirteenth through fourteenth centuries. A variation on the ancient genre of fables, they use men and women rather than animals to teach moral lessons. These tales, recited in public by traveling storytellers (*jongleurs*), passed into written culture when anonymous editors collected them for publication. They finally gave way to prose versions treating the same subject matter with an equally irreverent and bawdy approach. These *nouvelles* or *contes* were extremely popular until the sixteenth century.

Collections of *exempla,* brief concrete illustrations of vice and virtue used by uneducated priests to teach their illiterate congregations religious or moral doctrines, began to appear in the eleventh and twelfth centuries. Maurice de Sully (d. 1196), Alain de Lille (d. 1202), and Jacques de Vitry (d. 1240) were early apologists for the use of *exempla* in preaching, arguing that sermons should not only edify but entertain, the better to hold the interest of mass audiences. Their use of *exempla* in their folk sermons in the vernacular and their compilation of sets of popular *exempla* as sermon starters for local priests to use reflect the renaissance in preaching that occurred during this period. Early collections, such as Eudes de Cheriton's *Parables,* contained mainly ancient fables, illustrations from nature, or lives of saints. Later collections expanded to include descriptions of actual situations, and eventually *fabliaux* and *nouvelles,* and gained great popularity in the fourteenth and fifteenth centuries. This practical, eclectic style of preaching that drew on secular as well as religious stories became so abused that the use of stories or fables was prohibited at the Council of Milan in 1565.

I chose these genres for several reasons. First, each was a well-used form of mass oral communication that depended on the common human desire to be entertained rather than on the education of speaker or audience. Second, each was an effective medium for training the majority for social life. In illustrating the working of vices, the *fabliaux* and *nouvelles* handed down social expectations to and circumscribed the behavior of the non-nobility—peasants, farmers, and the growing bourgeoisie. Likewise, sermons in the vernacular taught lay people the Rule of the Order of Marriage. Third, in keeping with their pedagogical intent, each of these genres was constructed with actors who were stereotypes rather than characters. Fourth, each focused on the everyday lives of men and women, highlighting sex, sexuality, and gender.

Fifth, although two genres (the *fabliaux* and the *nouvelles*) are secular and the other (the *exempla*) is religious, each form of popular communication conveys a remarkably similar message concerning wifebeating. In fact, each genre influenced the other. The *fabliaux* writers were well-acquainted with the *exempla* of the church. In turn, the secular stories influenced by the early sermon manuals found their way into later preaching manuals. The dynamic interplay of the secular and religious worlds evident in these literary forms suggests that mono-dimensional or mono-causal theories of women's oppression are inadequate.

Finally, together the collections of *fabliaux* and *nouvelles* and the sermon manuals provide a rich resource for understanding gender relations in this period that can supplement the information provided by canon law, secular law, and statistics. As Michel Foucault states, "Methods that are employed at all levels and go beyond the state and its apparatus" contribute a great deal to ensuring certain power relations.[29] The normalization and control of gender relations one finds in this popular literature make these genres perhaps more potent supports for and indicators of the complex relationship between the ideology of subordi-

---

29. Michel Foucault, *The History of Sexuality,* trans. Robert Hurley (New York: Random House, 1980), 1:89.

nation and the practice of violence than ecclesiastical and secular laws. At the very least, they provide us with new ways to interpret marital statistics.

I approached these sources with the feminist conviction that ideologies of inequality and the practice of violence are inextricably linked. I also approached them with the suspicion that those studies pointing to the abatement of wifebeating in the Protestant Reformation had highlighted evidence of limitations to wifebeating and minimized the larger social patterns that insured women's subordination and accepted violence against them. These assumptions did not prepare me for the shock of discovering in this literature a popular tradition of justifying violence against wives. As I read the sermons and tales, I slowly began to see the outlines of a pattern of gender relations in which the practice of violence against wives was justified by means of an ideology of gender inequality and served to maintain such an ideology. I describe the pattern I found as follows: All women are created to be subordinate to men. All wives, therefore, are subordinate to their husbands. Because the health of society depends on this ordered relationship, if a wife is insubordinate in any way, not only domestic peace but the entire social fabric is threatened. The husband, then, has not only a right but a duty to discipline her. This social responsibility may be called the "office of chastisement."[30]

The right to exercise this legitimate office of chastisement is not absolute. As with all divinely ordained offices, the duties of the office of chastisement must be executed within limits set by society. I discovered the limits to this office specified in six conditions. First, the wife must be the aggressor, that is, initiate the conflict by stepping outside the boundaries of behavior set for Good Wives. This is the *condition of just cause*, based on the assumption of female subordination. Second and third, the discipline must be administered after other corrections have failed and in moderation, that is, so as to correct effectively (i.e., not maim or kill). These are the *conditions of last resort and just means*. Fourth and fifth, the wife must be disciplined not out of rage or revenge but out of love, with an aim to preserve the peace of the household and the right order of society. These are the *conditions of right intention and just end*, which are based on the distinction between punishment and correction. Sixth, it must be the husband as head of the family who administers the blows. This is

---

30. Phrase taken from A. Salmon, ed., *Coutumes de Beauvaisis* (Paris, 1899), par. 335.

the *condition of right authority,* based on the assumption of male dominance. Violence against wives is acceptable moral and social behavior
when some or all of these conditions are met.

Given that these conditions had not been uncovered before, my first
task was to name them, as the above paragraph shows. To the entire
interlocking set of conditions for justifying violence against wives, I gave
the name "just battery of wives."

All six conditions for justifying wifebeating are implicit in the tales
and sermons. The condition of just cause is associated with the use of
female stereotypes. Five stereotypes, Gateway to Ruin, Temptress, Adulteress, Deceiver, and Shrew, together form the antitype to the Good Wife
(*preude fame et sage*), who is wise in conserving and administering her
husband's goods, solicitous of his welfare, understanding of his failings,
submissive to his sexual desires alone, honest, and willingly deferential
and obedient at all times. The type of the Good Wife and the antitype of
the Bad Wife contribute to a theory of just battery by providing specific
material for the just cause rule. If a wife does not adequately fill the role
expected of her, to be a good wife wisely administering the household
and her body (the two commodities entrusted to her care though owned
by her husband), she *deserves* to be disciplined.

The *fabliaux* and *exempla* clearly connect the use of these stereotypes
with the condition of just cause. They often portray wives being beaten
because they have caused economic ruin by squandering money to satisfy their covetousness, wasted their husband's reputation by satisfying
their lust in adultery, or broken the peace of the household by giving
in to their proud and defiant natures in acts of subordination. Thus, the
use of stereotypes undergirds the condition of just cause by specifying
just causes for violence against women in particular circumstances. The
use of these stereotypes also undergirds the condition of just cause in
another, equally powerful and more insidious way: by implying that all
women eventually behave in these ways. Therefore, even when one's
wife is not acting wrongly, she is perceived as being on the verge of
revealing her true nature as Gateway to Ruin, Temptress, Adulteress,
Deceiver, or Shrew. In other words, the use of these stereotypes implies
that all women inevitably act out of their evil nature and therefore are
always deserving of whatever chastisement they receive. The *fabliaux*
contain several examples of husbands beating their wives because they
feared their wives would commit adultery or squander their resources in

other ways. Although some of the tales warn against acting on suspicion alone, the pervasive use of these stereotypes engenders a fear and hatred not easily controlled by instructions to beat wives only when they have *actually* committed a fault or exhortations to treat wives with mercy and understanding.

The conditions of last resort and just means are evident in one of the most arresting *fabliaux*, "Sir Hate and Lady Hateful." The tale begins with the claim to have

> Proved by logic
> That whoever has a cantankerous wife
> Is furnished with a wicked beast.[31]

The story opens with examples of Lady Hateful's constant quarrelsomeness and creative unwillingness to "serve him the way he wanted." Sir Hate tries to coddle and soothe her, but to no avail. When she throws the fish he has brought for dinner in the dirt and he is shamed before his neighbors by her lack of respect for him, he finally becomes angry and challenges her to a contest for the right to rule the household. She agrees and he takes off his pants and puts them in the yard, telling her that whoever can get to them first wins. Before witnesses they battle it out, each one promising to inflict the worst possible. Before they begin a character named Simon warns Sir Hate to use restraint and

> Be careful not to strike
> With anything which will do
> Harm to your wife, except your hands.

Sir Hate gives her a "Persian blue" eye. She almost knocks him over. He knocks her in the teeth, causing her blood to flow freely and him to exclaim triumphantly, "I've painted you two colors!" She recovers enough to hit him on the ear, and he responds by threatening to kill her. When he almost breaks one of her ribs, she draws back and calls for peace from the witnesses. Simon's wife, Peacewell, comes to her aid, but Simon threatens to beat her if she interferes again, and she "keeps quiet because she feared him." The fight continues.

---

31. James Wilhelm and Lowry Nelson, Jr., eds., *The French "Fabliaux,"* 2 vols. (New York: Garland, 1984–85), 1:45.

When Lady Hateful is upended in a basket and Sir Hate, having put on the pants, returns to finish by giving her "penance," Simon intervenes. He sends Sir Hate away with the warning, "Don't do any killing!" and asks Lady Hateful if her pride has finally been beaten down. She equivocates and Simon refuses to help her until he extracts this promise from her:

> That you will be under the control
> Of Sir Hate forevermore,
> And that you will never do
> Anything that he forbids....
> For you will serve your lord
> Just as a decent wife ought to do.[32]

Freed from her prison, she proves very willing to serve her husband, "since she feared his blows," and Sir Hate lived happily thereafter.

The moral of this story is clear: wives are to be subordinate to their husbands; insubordination *should* be corrected by the husband; this correction is to be peaceful and verbal first; if and when this does not work, threats of violence may be used (as when Simon corrects Peacewell); when this, too, does not work, correction may take the form of blows; and these blows, given with the hand, should harm the wife enough to correct her but not maim or kill her. It is clear here that insubordination provides just cause for battery, and that battery should be done in moderation. It is not as clear that battery is always the last resort, as the *fabliau*'s concluding moral shows:

> If your wives lord it proudly
> Over you at any time in any evil way,
> You should not be so lazy
> As to endure it long,
> But do exactly as
> Hate did with his wife,
> Who would not respect him before,
> Except in the smallest way she could,

---

32. Ibid., 1:57–59.

> Until the time that he
> Had beaten her on her bones and back.[33]

A particularly violent *conte*, "The Woman Whose Balls Were Cut Off," ends with a similar message: "Blessed be those who chastise their bad wives and shamed be those who submit to their wives; a curse on wives who defy their husbands."[34]

There are similar tales in the *exempla*. One man, for instance, tricks his disobedient wife into violently piercing her finger with a nail, whereupon she learns to obey him.[35] Alan of Lille, in his instructions on how to preach to the estate of married persons, refers to the knot of inequality, insubordination, and the office of chastisement by noting that "the flesh, like a woman, may obey the spirit, and the spirit, like a man, may rule his flesh as if it were a woman."[36] The implication is clear: if the woman offends you, it is your Christian duty to subdue her.

The *exempla* do not teach as clearly the conditions of last resort and just means. They do not warn against "deadly abuse" as many *fabliaux* do, and, in fact, suggest that it may be acceptable. Jacques de Vitry tells of a man whose wife was so contrary that he tricked her into drowning herself and then turned it into a community joke.[37] He also includes a tale of a contrary woman who continued in her defiance even after her husband had cut out her tongue.[38] Further, the *exempla* go beyond promoting the husband's office of chastisement and add to it the wife's office of suffering. Etienne de Bourbon has an entire section entitled "The Gift of Force," and Bozon expounds at great length on Proverbs 27:6: "To be hit by one's friend is better than to be kissed by one's enemy."[39] This justification is not as apparent in the secular tales, though one can find occasional references there to women's "crown of thorns."

33. Ibid., 1:61.

34. Nora Scott, ed., *Fabliaux des XIIIe et XIVe siècles: Contes pour rire?* (Paris: Union Générale, 1977), 204.

35. Thomas Frederick Crane, ed., *The "Exempla" or Illustrative Stories for the "Sermones Vulgares" of Jacques de Vitry* (London: Folklore Society, 1890), 226.

36. Alan de Lille, *The Art of Preaching*, trans. Gillian R. Evans (Kalamazoo, Mich.: Cistercian Publications, 1981), 164.

37. Crane, *Exempla*, 225.

38. Ibid., 223.

39. Etienne de Bourbon, *Anecdotes historiques, légendes et apologues*, ed. A. Le Coy de la March (Paris: Renouard, 1877), 202–335; Nicholas Bozon, *Les contes moralisés de Nicole Bozon, Frère Mineur*, ed. Lucy Toulmin Smith and Paul Meyer (Paris: Firmin Didot, 1889), 49–55, 61.

The conditions of right intention and just end are not as clearly present as the other four conditions in any of the genres, but there is enough evidence to suggest that they do operate as part of a pattern of gender relations for justifying violence against wives. Some of the tales and sermons move toward a distinction between punishment (harm done out of anger or meanness) and correction (harm done with the loving intention of persuading the woman to assume her rightful place in the household). Almost all assume the condition of just end—that is, that the harm is to be administered toward the end of reestablishing peace in the household and right order in society. The right order, as the following shows, is a patriarchal one.

Finally, the condition of right authority—that is, the assumption that the husband is the rightful "master" of the house whose duty is to maintain order by controlling those "under" him—pervades the tales. It lies behind the construction of the stereotypes. It serves as the foundation for the condition of just cause, as is especially evident in the tales concerning the specific just cause of insubordination. It provides the basis for the conditions of right intention and moderation with its use of hierarchical monism to set the spirit/male as director over the flesh/female. The development of the notion of the office of chastisement exercised under the other conditions makes it clear that it is the husband's duty to beat his wife when necessary and his shame when he fails to do this. In addition to promoting these themes, many of the tales depend for their humor on the technique of reversal of expectations. Scenes of wives beating their husbands are funny precisely because it is assumed that right authority for this behavior can belong only to the male.[40] A condition of right authority, therefore, is also embedded in the tales.

Exceptions and the Rule

This set of conditions for justifying wifebeating found throughout the *fabliaux, nouvelles,* and *exempla* suggests that a continuing, popular tradition of just battery existed during this time in French history. On the

40. This is supported by Dobash and Dobash's study of *charivari* (ritualized ridicule for unacceptable domestic behavior). Men thought to be dominated by their wives were shamed in public because such behavior was "an extraordinary threat to the patriarchal order" ("Community Response," 566).

basis of my research I was not able to conclude that this tradition took exactly the same form in each of the five centuries and in each of the three genres. I was able to conclude, on the basis of the remarkable similarity among conditions or rules for husbands' treatment of wives in these different genres across these centuries, that it is likely that an ongoing popular tradition justifying wifebeating existed.

This provisional conclusion calls into question those social-historical interpretations of the Reformation that stress the improvement of domestic conditions for women in comparison to conditions in the Middle Ages. Specifically, it challenges those studies that support this interpretation by arguing that (1) the instances of violence against wives in the popular literature of this period are exceptions to a new rule of restraint of wifebeating, and (2) the instances of exhortation to moderation in this literature constitute a prohibition against all battery. In light of the existence of an ongoing popular tradition of just battery, these interpretations appear to be overly optimistic assessments of gender relations; for they obscure the rule of the subordination of women, justified violence against them, and the connection between these two.

One can find instances of both extreme violence against wives and explicit rejections of wifebeating during the medieval, Renaissance, and Reformation periods. The question is: How does one interpret this contradictory evidence? What is the rule, the normative pattern for gender relations, against which other evidence is to be interpreted as "exceptions"? Is the rule that of increasing justice toward wives, and the exceptions those instances of physical cruelty that remain? Or is the rule that of an ongoing tradition of just battery, and the exceptions those instances in which wifebeating is rejected? My investigation of popular sources leads me to adopt provisionally the latter as a more accurate interpretation of these centuries.

The stories I highlighted are not exceptions to a rule of equality, mutuality, and conciliation, but rather extraordinary cases that illuminate ordinary circumstances. There are *fabliaux* and at least one *exemplum* that warn husbands of the dangers of irrational jealousy, false accusations of adultery, unreasonable expectations for the completion of wifely chores, and immoderate hitting. The point of these stories, however, is that *unjust* punishment leads to no good and is therefore unacceptable, not that any or all correction or chastisement is unacceptable. None of the stories I read challenges the just battery theory I have described: that correction of wives by violent means is justifiable on the conditions of just cause, last resort, moderation, right intention, just end, and right authority.

Take, for example, two tales that appear to condemn wifebeating. "The Doctor in Spite of Himself" is the story of the cure of an alternately rageful and repentant husband. Three of the king's men hear the wife's graphic tale of unmerciful beatings *for nothing* and decide to bring the husband to the court as a doctor. When he is unable to cure the king's daughter, he is beaten. So he learns the injustice of his behavior toward his wife and returns home never to beat her again but to love and cherish her.[41] In the *fabliau* "The Braids," a man who is outrageously jealous of his wife violently beats her on account of his suspicions. Finally she can stand it no longer and commits adultery. The *jongleur* concludes:

> He does not do well
> Who harms his wife *too much;*
> If she commits folly with her body
> When away from home,
> She has good reason
> To bring shame upon her husband.[42]

Both tales criticize wifebeating only because it is done *for no reason.* Because both assume that there can be just cause for wifebeating, they do not call into question the theory of just battery but confirm it.

Likewise, stories that teach moderation, such as "Sir Hate and Lady Hateful," do not reject but confirm the theory of just battery. One of the woodcuts Ozment uses to support his theory of greater justice for wives in the Reformation, *The Nine Lives of a Bad Wife,* has an accompanying text that ends thus:

> So punish your wife modestly,
> And if there is any honor in her,
> She will become an obedient wife. . . .
> But if she remains self-willed,
> And refuses what is fair and reasonable,

---

41. Phillipe Menard, ed., *Fabliaux français au moyen âge* (Geneva: Droz, 1979), 1:83–94. See Bozon's version of this story, which begins, "A man was contrary to his wife and often beat her *without reason*" (*Les contes moralisés*, 62; emphasis added).

42. T. B. W. Reid, ed., *Twelve "Fabliaux"* (Manchester: University of Manchester Press, 1977), 33; translation mine; emphasis added.

> And opposes you in all you request,
> Ever disobedient and rebellious,
> On those occasions when she spurns your cooperation,
> You may punish her with blows—
> Yet do still with reason and modestly,
> So that no harm is done to either of you.
> Use both a carrot and a stick
> To bring about companionship.[43]

The call for moderation one reads in this moral is not indicative of a self-critical moment within a society moving toward greater justice for women in the domestic sphere, but confirmation of the existence of an ongoing tradition of just battery.

The Ideology of Gender Inequality and Just Battery

In addition to questioning the exception/rule argument as support for interpreting the Renaissance/Reformation period as one of greater justice toward women, this argument for the existence of an ongoing popular tradition of just battery of wives raises the question of how to assess the work of advocates of women during this period. For example, Christine de Pisan (d. 1429) and Margaret of Navarre (d. 1549) are two women often studied and cited by scholars as examples of women who, if not feminist, did indeed make significant contributions to understanding and improving women's lives by crying out against injustices done to them. By raising objections to insults and slurs against women, both women challenged the popular misogynism conveyed through stereotypes. Both condemned physical violence against women. In *The Heptameron,* her own set of *nouvelles* creatively combining the traditions of the *fabliaux* and *exempla,* Margaret of Navarre criticizes battery, saying, "For with beating there is an end to love."[44]

Their criticisms of female stereotypes and the use of violence against wives are important steps toward rejecting the popular just battery tradition and are historically significant as such. I do not believe, however,

---

43. Ozment, *When Fathers Ruled,* 77.

44. Margaret of Navarre, *The Heptameron of the Tales of Margaret, the Queen of Navarre* (1558; reprint, Paris: D. Trenor, 1902), 403. See also "Tale 46," 397–405, which focuses on preaching and wifebeating.

that these criticisms constitute a clear countertradition defending wives' unqualified right to freedom from being beaten by their husbands. Both Christine de Pisan and Margaret of Navarre continue to accept the subordination of women to men and the principle that insubordination is just cause for battery. In her popular manual of advice for women of all classes, *The Treasure of the City of Ladies,* Christine de Pisan counsels wifely submission and lauds the virtue of obedience.[45] In her *Book of the City of Ladies,* after crying out, "How many harsh beatings—without cause and without reason—how many injuries . . . have so many upright women suffered?" she immediately goes on to teach that "men are masters over their wives" and not the reverse.[46] Even though she makes it clear that the husband's authority is not to be misused, her assumption of the conditions of right authority and just cause suggests that she continues the tradition of just battery. Margaret of Navarre appears to reject battery outright. But she accepts the subordination of women, saying, "It is reasonable that the man should rule us, but it is not reasonable that he should forsake and ill use us."[47] The question here is how she would differentiate proper from ill use. Is all physical violence against wives ill use? Or only that which does not fulfill the condition of just cause? On the basis of my reading of the popular tradition of just battery, I would guess that the second is more likely.

Much more work needs to be done on the criticisms of and challenges to wifebeating in this period. By raising questions about the work of two of the most outspoken advocates of women during this time, I want to suggest that it is likely that in spite of calls for moderation and criticisms of wifebeating during this period, the popular tradition of just battery of wives was not interrupted. Such an interruption cannot occur until the linchpin of the tradition, the subordination of women to men, is removed. In assuming the subordination of women to men and accepting the conditions of right authority and just cause, Christine de Pisan and Margaret of Navarre may have unwittingly perpetuated the tradition of just battery even as they argued against wifebeating. The ideology of gender inequality, which serves as the basis for the condi-

---

45. Christine de Pisan, *The Treasure of the City of Ladies or the Book of the Three Virtues,* trans. Sarah Lawson (New York: Penguin, 1985), 62–65, 138–41.

46. Christine de Pisan, *The Book of the City of Ladies,* trans. Earl Jeffrey Richards (New York: Persea Books, 1982), 119–20.

47. Margaret of Navarre, *Heptameron,* 355.

tions justifying violence against wives, is inseparable from the practice of violence against them. As long as female subordination is accepted, therefore, the tradition of just battery will continue.[48]

A Popular Tradition of Just Battery and the Just War Tradition

Secular and religious popular French literature from 1150 to 1565 provides evidence for the existence of a continuing, identifiable tradition of just battery of wives. The six conditions for justifying violence against wives found in these tales and sermons constitute a pattern for connecting an ideology of inequality with the practice of violence against women in such a way that wifebeating is justified. This popular tradition of just battery provided a powerful, informal determinant of the rule for the normal and acceptable treatment of wives and reveals the pattern of gender relations operative in France during this time. Evidence for criticism or moderation of this rule may be read as confirmation of it rather than as an indication of a trend toward greater justice toward wives. Evidence of women's domestic lives from legal and ecclesiastical records, in order to be adequately interpreted, should be set against the background of this evidence for a dominant social rule of just battery of wives.

How far such a tradition of just battery of wives extends culturally and historically has yet to be determined. I deliberately chose the terminology of just battery not only because it accurately reflects the pattern of gender relations I discovered, but also to call attention to the analogy between this tradition and the just war tradition. While the just war tradition varies over the centuries (as the popular tradition of just battery may), it exists as a clearly identifiable tradition with a set of criteria that forms its nucleus: right authority, right intention, just cause, right means, last resort, and just end.

---

48. Murray A. Straus has said, "Full sexual equality is essential for the prevention of wifebeating" ("A Sociological Perspective on the Prevention and Treatment of Wifebeating," in Roy, *Battered Women*, 233). Other scholars, not necessarily agreeing with Straus's implied theory of social causation, have also connected sexual inequality and male violence against women. See Peggy Reeves Sanday, *Female Power and Male Dominance: On the Origins of Sexual Inequality* (Cambridge: Cambridge University Press, 1984); Dobash and Dobash, *Violence against Wives*, 33–34; Frances Power Cobbe, *Wife Torture in England* (London: Contemporary Review, 1878).

By referring to the popular tradition I unearthed as one of just battery, I do not intend to suggest that the criteria developed for justifying
violence in the public realm can be imposed upon the domestic sphere.
Although the conditions I have identified as constituting the just battery
tradition resemble the just war criteria, they emerged from the stories
and sermons themselves. I also do not intend to suggest that the two traditions functioned in exactly the same way. In fact, there are important
differences. One is that the moral tradition of the just war acknowledged
the tragedy in the use of all violence, while this does not seem to be the
case in the just battery tradition. Another is that the just war criteria were
announced, defended, and debated in public, whereas those of the just
battery tradition were tacit assumptions. A third is that the just war tradition is still accepted as a moral guideline by the majority in Western
culture. By contrast, the just battery tradition, though not without pro-
ponents, has been challenged to such an extent that most persons now
believe that violence against wives can never be morally justified.

By referring to this popular tradition connecting gender inequality
and violence against wives as just battery, I do intend to suggest the
possibility that a moral tradition of justifying violence may exist in the
domestic sphere in Western Christian culture that is comparable in extent, longevity, influence on behavior and attitudes, and significance for
the study of morality and history to the moral tradition of justifying violence in the public sphere. This possibility must be investigated. And,
if it turns out that such a domestic counterpart to the just war tradition
does indeed exist, we must be prepared to alter dramatically the way we
tell the story of our past, the way we identify its high and low points,
the way we label its significant advances and "dark ages."

Conclusion

If historical theologians do not probe new sources with questions about
power relations between men and women and do not investigate the
connections between an ideology of gender inequality and the practice
of violence against women, we will unwittingly perpetuate a tradition of
silence that is complicity. Whatever historical and theological judgments
we make on the basis of our research, we must continue to investigate
these issues.

As historical theologians committed to ending violence against women, we must be willing to allow our present commitments to influence what we look for and what we see in the past. And we must be ready to alter dramatically our constructions of the past on the basis of what we find. The possible existence of an ongoing popular tradition of just battery of wives certainly challenges us in these ways.

As persons who are committed to ending violence against women and who are also historical theologians, we must be willing to admit that our study of the past can transform our lives and our time as well. For example, we need to open ourselves to the possibility that discoveries of the interconnection of the ideology of gender inequality and the practice of violence against women in the Middle Ages, Renaissance, and Reformation may inform our understanding of patriarchy and our practice toward women in the present. Specifically, such an analysis of a popular tradition of just battery of wives may teach us today that if contemporary Christianity and society are to counter the practice of justifying violence against wives, they must move beyond teaching the complementary offices of chastisement and suffering to a mutual covenant of love between equals built on integrity, trust, and responsibility.

For this to happen, three steps are essential: condemnation of any and all violence against women; eradication of stereotypes of women; and rejection of all theories of inequality. As long as we do not root out the contemporary versions of the stereotypes of woman as Gateway to Ruin, Temptress, Adulteress, Deceiver, and Shrew, we will not break with the just battery tradition. And as long as we do not unequivocally reject all ideologies of gender inequality, we will perpetuate that tradition, for there will always be at least one just cause for battery of wives: insubordination. Only when we have accomplished all three steps will we have completely interrupted the popular tradition of just battery and moved to a gender "arrangement based not on force and deception but on consensual reciprocal dependence."[49] Only when women are free and responsible selves rather than appropriate victims will we be able to speak of justice for women. Only when all women are able to live at home and abroad free of the fear of violence by men will we be able to speak of a Renaissance or Reformation *for women.*

---

49. Albert Memmi, *Dependence: A Sketch of the Portrait of the Dependent* (Boston: Beacon Press, 1985), 155.

FOUR

Katy O'Brien Weintraub

Why We Must Think in the Best Company: Erasmus's Ratio Verae Theologiae *and the Limits of the Human Mind*

> *But when mind is poured into mind, and one intelligence formed by another, it is not possible for the pupil not to resemble his teacher, who is like the parent of his mind.*[1]

The advice to think with the best minds has had a long career in the history of scholarship, but this advice seldom was offered with more urgency or more reasoned judgment than it was by Erasmus of Rotterdam (1467?–1536). Erasmus, living in a very excited intellectual world, understood the need for making genuine choices among the best minds. For him, the choices were clear: Should one follow the lead of the great scholastic minds who formed impressive systems of interpretation or should one return to the source of theology and try to recapture the still fresh methods of the first great interpreters of scripture, the early fathers of the church, and in doing so, absorb the classical culture of which they were a part? The dangers of his choice were perhaps less clear to him: Would the deeper understanding of Christianity that both sides sought be perverted, on the one hand, by resort to ancient logic

---

1. Erasmus, *Collected Works of Erasmus* (hereafter CWE), 86 vols. (projected) (Toronto: University of Toronto Press, 1974–), 23:31.

created by natural reason or, on the other, by reliance on the morally ambiguous tool of rhetoric? Erasmus's questions thus became: Should one become a scholastic and play the role of a conserver of a great theological tradition? Or should one join the Christian humanists in their enthusiasm for the uncorrupted sources of Christianity, and use truth regardless of its apparent source, thereby emphasizing a belief in the unity of creation and a faith that God would never, under any circumstances, abandon creation? In Erasmus's day the desire to think with the best minds became a very complicated matter. Both of these approaches to scripture were pursued by great minds; in order to make the choice, Erasmus obviously had to decide which approach to theology was best and then find the best minds within that tradition.

The options for theology at a given moment in the history of Christianity are often provided by the available questions and answers within the wider culture. The sixteenth century was by any reckoning a tremendous stage for the conflict between conservers of varying traditions: those who wished to conserve the tradition of scholasticism and those who wished to conserve or resuscitate the tradition of the fathers of the church, of ancient Christianity. As compelling as this choice could be for individual theologians, it was made possible not so much by new theological insights as by developments in the wider intellectual culture in northern Europe.

In the early years of the sixteenth century, the rediscovery of lost works of the ancients reminded Europeans that classical Latin had a beauty and grace long forsaken in their culture. Medieval grammarians had been more preoccupied with the metaphysical relation between the words and the things they signified, and thus did not concern themselves with teaching the rules of using the language. The task at hand was obvious: restore the study of grammar to the old path of describing the best usage and teach students to express themselves in a pure, preferably Ciceronian, style. Indeed, those who chose to reject scholastic questions as irrelevant and injurious to the theological enterprise relied first on this new view of the Latin language. Erasmus was a beneficiary of the earlier language studies of Rudolph Agricola, the great humanist who had proposed a reformation in the understanding of dialectic and who taught the teacher of Erasmus, Alexander Hegius. Alexander Hegius's own contribution to the reformation of language studies was a scathing attack on the metaphysical approach to grammar, *Invectiva in modos significandi.*[2] Erasmus lived the whole of his scholarly life with the way cleared toward the beautiful style of classical Latin. In fact Erasmus was fully persuaded that a concern with language was essential, and agreed with Galen that it was not reason that separates human beings from the animals, but language.[3]

The reformation of language studies would have far-reaching consequences for the study of theology as well. Was it perhaps impossible to expound medieval Christianity in this new idiom? Was it perhaps the humanists' emphasis on texts of classical literature and moral philosophy and their devaluing of the medieval interest in classical logic and metaphysics that led them to be dissatisfied with the prevailing scholastic theology? Did the very language that they used lead the Christian humanists to ask different questions and arrive at different answers than their scholastic colleagues? Did the excitement of the revival of the tools of classical culture lead humanists to suspect that a return to the sources of Christianity and their most ancient interpreters might lead to possibilities that would be even more exciting? These questions are, of course, too complicated to answer in an essay, but they should not be forgotten in an attempt to understand the tasks and preoccupations of the Christian humanists of this period. Trained to understand the literary exertions of antiquity and made sensitive to the moral philosophy of antiquity, young humanists were educated to expect that the Bible would also respond to these literary and moral questions. Given the choice between the admirable scholastic schools of interpretation and the approach of the fathers of the church, humanistically trained students would naturally lean toward the fathers as the more genuine interpreters of scripture.

Predictably, Erasmus chose the way of the fathers as the best approach to scripture. While he professed respect for the best minds among the scholastics, he maintained that their methods were foreign to the text and, especially in the hands of their lesser-minded followers, led the student away from the actual meaning that scripture was intended to communicate. Erasmus understood scripture as essentially

2. James H. Overfield, *Humanism and Scholasticism in Late Medieval Germany* (Princeton, N.J.: Princeton University Press, 1984), 76. For the text see Josef IJsewijn, ed., "*Invectiva in modos significandi,* Text, Introduction, and Notes," *Forum for Modern Language Studies* 7 (1971): 299–319.

3. Erasmus, *Desiderii Erasmi Opere Omnia* (hereafter *LB*), ed. Jean LeClerc, 10 vols. (1703–6; reprint, Hildesheim: Georg Olms, 1962), 1:913D.

a literary text and maintained that the student should use literary methods to understand it. It is the story of God's relation to human beings and should be treated as a story and not as a philosophical treatise. He argued that the scholastics, believing that scripture was an allegorical presentation of metaphysical reality, had brought the powerful tool of logic to the analysis of scripture and had lost control of this tool. In the hands of the lesser-minded scholastics, logic had driven theological inquiry away from the true meaning of scripture. Because scripture was presented to human beings as a literary text and its message accommodated[4] to the limitations of human understanding, the theologian's only source of aid would be the tools of language and literature and a clear vision of the nature of the human mind. In a real way, Erasmus saw scripture as a work of divine rhetoric: a work of persuasion that was miraculously addressed to all audiences, that would address each reader on his or her own terms, and that would provide exactly the understanding that was suitable for each reader.[5] Distrustful of approaches to scripture that espoused either pure reason or mystical union, Erasmus advised a more balanced method that relied on the accumulated labor of the best minds in the continuing effort to understand its message. Language, more than reason, is the tool that allows human beings to cooperate with each other, that makes education possible, and that can be used to form a community of thought across the ages.

Erasmus recognized one unfortunate fact that spans the ages and that we recognize too: most of us, even most scholars, do not deserve to be counted among the best minds. Even the best minds remain limited vessels, and for Erasmus, that is precisely why we need the company

---

4. Erasmus uses the concept of accommodation to explain not only how scripture speaks differently to different readers, but also how divine wisdom is communicated to human understanding through scripture. This concept is clearly dependent upon the rhetorical injunctions to fit the speech to the audience, to meet the audience where it lives, and to proceed to raise its members above or beyond themselves.

5. Erasmus, *Ausgewählte Werke* (hereafter *RH,* followed by a page number), ed. Hajo Holborn and Annemaria Holborn (Munich: C. H. Beck, 1933), 141–42: "Haec omnibus ex aequo sese accommodat, submittit se parvulis, ad illorum modulum sese attemperat, lacte illos alens, ferens, confovens, sustinens, omnia faciens, donec grandescamus in Christo. At rursum ita non deest infimis, ut summis etiam sit admirabilis." (This doctrine in an equal degree accommodates itself to all, lowers itself to the little ones, adjusts itself to their measure, nourishing them with milk, bearing, fostering, sustaining them, doing everything until we grow in Christ. Again, not only does it serve the lowliest, but it is also an object of wonder to those at the top.) Translation available in John C. Olin, ed., *Christian Humanism and the Reformation* (New York: Fordham University Press, 1975), 96.

of the best minds so desperately. While Erasmus addressed many of the questions suggested by this dictum in a number of his works, it is fitting that the most concise statement of his views occurs in his handbook for the training of professional theologians, *Ratio Verae Theologiae* (1518).[6] His formulation of the issue in the *Ratio* is pedagogical: What can our understanding of the functioning of the human mind teach us about how best to teach aspiring theologians? Erasmus addresses this handbook to prospective teachers and claims that the method he has outlined is not meant for the best minds, but above all for beginners.

> Though the divine Augustine has discussed, both carefully and co-piously, almost the same subject matter in four books put under the title *De Doctrina Christiana*, ... we will do the same, not only more briefly, but also rudely and without art. As one might expect, this work is by no means intended for excellent men, but we expend this modest energy in order to aid the rude, the common, and those of naturally inferior capacities.[7]

In part reflecting a typical humanistic expression of humility, this statement also indicates the degree to which pedagogical motives guide this work. Augustine may have pioneered research into theological rhetoric; Erasmus is more interested here in making this tool available to "those of naturally inferior capacities."[8] While recognizing that few individuals of Augustine's abilities will ever exist, Erasmus appears to hope that lesser minds can still profit from Augustine's insights, and here attempts to bring these lessons to the general class of theological students. At the same time, Erasmus aims at more than a simple restatement of Augustine's treatment of signs; there are new battles to be fought concerning theological method. He addresses the teachers of beginning students for a very good reason.

Believing that most minds function within the constraints of habits and expectations, Erasmus counseled teachers to instill the very best

---

6. The standard edition remains that in *RH*.
7. *RH* 178. Cf. Erasmus, *Adagia*, 1.1.35.
8. The relation between Erasmus's *Ratio* and Augustine's *De Doctrina Christiana* has been closely investigated by Charles Béné, *Érasme et Saint Augustin* (Geneva: Droz, 1969), esp. 215–80. It is always difficult to prove influence; however, on the basis of the evidence Béné has gathered, I am comfortable in saying that Erasmus was influenced by Augustine. It has been a popular sport among students of Erasmus to argue whether he was more attracted to Jerome or to Augustine, but that issue seems beside the point here.

habits in their students from the very beginning of their studies. For Erasmus, the problem is a matter of sensitivity. When reading scripture, the source of theology, will students be sensitive to the proper issues presented or will they attempt to import their own concerns into the world they meet there? The question concerning sensitivity asks whether students will recognize the true voice of scripture, which, according to Erasmus, is always directed toward the human experience of the divine. As a literary and rhetorical work, scripture is addressed to the intended audience of human beings; thus, according to the rules even of human rhetoric, the message must be addressed in human terms. The formation of this sensitivity in a student requires training in both the human experience of life and in the divine intention for human life. Training in the human experience of life should occur in a program of studies dedicated to the *bonae litterae*—good letters—prior to theological studies.[9] The student must be introduced to the full range of human thoughts and emotions and to the ideal model of human life. Otherwise, the messages of the lessons provided in the stories in scripture will remain unrecognized by those who have not been trained to expect them.

Patterns of expectations wield a pervasive and perilous influence even over the best minds, as Erasmus reminds us in the preface to one of his editions of Jerome.

> One of the leading scholars in Italy was handed by someone a page torn from a manuscript in such a way that there was no heading to reveal the author. The man who gave it him observed that it looked like the work of some quite recent writer. Now the learned man was one of those whose passion for antiquity makes them despise anything modern. Immediately he protested against the filthy style, as he then thought it, heaping abuse upon the barbarian author who had spoilt good parchment with such uneducated rubbish. His scorn was unlimited and unceasing, until the other man showed him that what he had condemned so heartily was a bit of Cicero. The learned man accepted the correction and laughed to see how badly his fancy had misled him. So great is the force, even in good scholars, of a pre-existing convic-

---

9. *RH* 189.

tion, and nothing is so likely when one forms a judgment to distort or cloud one's vision.[10]

Erasmus does not tell this story to ridicule the scholar from Italy, but rather to warn all scholars of the extent to which they are slaves to their expectations. In the story, the preexisting conviction that the manuscript was the product of a recent writer immediately invoked a set of expectations in the scholar. The scholar expected to find a squalid style in the writing and that is what he found. As is clear from the course of the story, these expectations do not function on an altogether conscious level. If they did represent a standard according to which a conscious judgment was made, then the scholar would have quickly noticed that this writing did not fit into his view of modern writing and would have questioned the dating of the document.[11] Interestingly, the quality of this scholar's mind is aptly demonstrated by his willingness to be instructed; once the error produced by his reliance on his expectations was revealed to him, he was able to see how his expectations had misled him. In short, he was able to examine the functioning of this tool of his mind and find it unreliable; he was able to judge his tools and understand their shortcomings. One might go further to suggest that it is the graciousness bestowed by a liberal education that allows this scholar to admit his mistake freely and with good humor. Erasmus's care to assure the reader that this was a "leading" and "good" scholar indicates that the moral of this story is not to be taken lightly. This story cannot be dismissed simply as a clever practical joke played on a foolish man. In fact, even "good" minds function, at least in the first instance, according to habits and expectations. This is a trap into which many could fall if they were not aware of their expectations or if they had formed inappropriate expectations.

Expectations are formed in many ways; perhaps the most seductive expectations are formed by experience, and in the realm of the mind, experience is formed most permanently by training. Education thus becomes the most important concern of the liberally educated scholar. Habits and expectations limit the horizon of the scholar, prescribe the

---

10. Erasmus, *Opus Epistolarum Des. Erasmi Roterodami* (hereafter *EE*, followed by letter number), ed. P. S. Allen, H. M. Allen, and H. W. Garrod, 12 vols. (Oxford: Clarendon Press, 1906–58), EE326. See *CWE* 3.

11. One is, after all, always more likely to question new information than to question one's accepted theories.

limits within which the mind functions, and even determine what issues
will be recognized by the scholar. In the realm of theology, Erasmus is
most worried by the expectations formed by a scholastic training. In the
Ratio, he relies on a physiological analogy to expand on this concern.

> For as it happens that whoever has had his tongue and palate
> tainted with wormwood, from then on everything he eats or
> drinks tastes of wormwood,... so it happens with those who
> spend a good part of their life in sophistical hairsplitting:... for
> these divine literature does not taste like that which it is, but like
> that which they bring with them.[12]

This analogy and its message provides another hint as to just how
seriously Erasmus had been thinking about education and how central
to his thought the injunction "return to the sources" was. It is no acci-
dent that this analogy depends on taste and judgment, for the ability to
judge words and things is the hallmark of the educated mind.[13] Early
training is especially important to the student, and training has important implications for later scholarship. This training circumscribes the
vision of the theologian; one senses only what one has been trained to
sense. If the student has been habituated to look for certain types of issues in a source, he or she will find just those issues whether they are
there or not and will not be open to others. In fact, the whole experience
of the source is determined by this training. With this warning, Erasmus
again suggests the difficulty of rising above one's training. It is possible,
though extraordinary, to find one who can function with a mind truly
open to the source and open to unexpected evidence. The pedagogical answer, of course, lies in training beginning theologians in the true
method of theology, and in trying to educate them beyond themselves,
to help them learn to examine the very tools of their enterprise.

The true method of theology must be discovered by a studied judgment of the nature of the source of theology. At every turn in his

---

12. *RH* 192: "Fit enim, ut qui palatum ac linguam multo absinthio habent infec-
tam, iis quicquid deinde biberint aut ederint absinthium sapiat....Ita qui bonam vitae
partem...in sophisticis cavillationibus...iis divinae litterae non sapiunt id quod sunt, sed
quod illi secum afferunt."

13. *LB* 1:521A: "A person who is not skilled in the force of language is, of necessity, short-
sighted, deluded, and unbalanced in his judgment of things as well" (translation from
CWE 24:666).

argument, Erasmus continues his confrontation with the scholastics. If one believes that the subject matter of theology is the whole of reality and God's hand in creating and maintaining it, and if one believes that God's activities are rational, then the scholastic method based on logic may be valuable in discovering theological truth. In some ways, the scholastics took the heroic stance that nature, the second book of revealed truth, could teach theologians almost as much about divine truth as scripture itself could. If, in contrast, one believes with the Christian humanists that one can see the truth one is meant to know primarily through the window of scripture, that scripture is God's chosen means of revealing the divine to humans, then one must turn to more literary methods in order to discover theological truth. For the Christian humanists, the fact that God chose to communicate with us through scripture and thus through language has a special significance. The theologian must take care to learn the divine language and its rules, but above all, the sources themselves must be treated with the greatest of respect. The purity of the sources should remain inviolate, unassailed by the syllogisms of the dialecticians, aided only by the careful hand of the textual critic. More importantly, exegetes must recognize the effects of their own tools on the exegesis, and responsible parties must recognize the effects of early training upon the whole life of the individual.

The insight that trained minds tend to function in certain customary ways—that is, that habits of mind are built through years of training that affect even the perception of the individual—is a very sophisticated notion for a thinker of the sixteenth century. There are earlier views of the operation of the mind that might feed such an insight. Plato's concept of learning as recollection and Augustine's story of the woman who had lost a coin and could find it only because she knew what she was looking for represent two notions of memory that could, in some way, contribute to Erasmus's insight.[14] These two views of memory rely on the existence of templates within the mind by which the individual judges the truth of a fact or experience. Without this preexisting standard, the individual has no way of recognizing the truth. Plato and Augustine presented their statements as metaphysical observations on the functioning of the human mind. Erasmus, whether or not he shared a full appreciation

---

14. Plato, *Meno*, 81d (Stephanus number): "For seeking and learning are in fact nothing but recollection"; Augustine, *Confessions*, 10.18.

of this metaphysical aspect, was more occupied with educational problems and thus was more concerned with the implications for training.
In fact, these ideas of Plato and Augustine present a philosophical approach to epistemology, but Erasmus's epistemology appears to be more
self-reflective.[15]

Erasmus's approach to epistemology may be formed by rhetoric just
as his theology is. The art of rhetoric provides its own method of discovery in the use of topics or commonplaces. A rhetorician is trained
to think in terms of the common ground upon which arguments may
be built and without which no communication can occur.[16] Topical analysis is the first task of the rhetorician in the formation of arguments.[17]
The rhetorician then proceeds through a series of judgments to arrive
at the most persuasive argument. Thus judgment of new instances in
comparison to existing topics is the most habitual mode of thought for
the rhetorician.

Erasmus's version of the way the mind apprehends truth is at once
less mystical and less interested in memory than either Plato's or Augustine's and more interested in the way a mind addresses new material.
In Erasmus's view, the preexisting standard of judgment is provided by
training and this standard functions as a sensitizing agent building the
pattern of expectations in the mind. It trains the individual to ask certain types of questions and makes the mind sensitive to certain types of
evidence and answers. The best kind of training makes one sensitive to
the tools themselves as well, but this level of consciousness is not always
possible. If the student can be made sensitive to the tools and their effects
on the investigation, then a truly liberal education has been achieved.
Erasmus himself was able to achieve such a level of consciousness and

---

15. Erasmus's well-known reticence toward philosophical solutions extends to grand
formulations of epistemology. At the same time, he does have an operative understanding
of how the human mind works and how it apprehends reality, and this understanding
does appear both consistent and productive with regard to his theology.

16. As Aristotle points out, everyone uses rhetoric although most do so without understanding the art (*The Art of Rhetoric* 1.1.).

17. For a simple instance, if one were to try to prove the case that Protestantism makes
Christians fat, the topics available are Protestant/Catholic and thin/fat. Because everyone
has a general or common understanding of what fat is, this provides the starting point
of discussion. The case may proceed through argument, example, or other proof. In this
case, example would probably serve best, and the best example is the first Protestant—up
until 1520, Martin Luther was very thin and after that significant date he began to gain
significant amounts of weight.

could see the importance of developing the right kinds of habits of mind in beginning theologians.

At the very least, the student should be trained to do something very well; in order to achieve this, the student should be given the training that is specifically designed for that individual's ultimate scholarly activity. If all students are not capable of examining their preexisting standards of judgment and if some can only function habitually with them, the best course for theological studies is to provide students with those habits of mind that best fit the source of theology. Training in dialectic will habituate the student to search the sources for occasions of debate; training in poetics and rhetoric will accustom the student to interpreting allegories,[18] to recognizing human drama, and to explaining those lessons in a moving and persuasive way.

Of course one of the greatest challenges to the student of scripture is to reconcile what Erasmus calls the "variety"[19] of Christ's teachings. The interpretation of scripture is not a simple task. Even apart from the frankly obscure passages in scripture, there are passages in which Christ speaks differently to different people, in which he acts in apparently unexpected ways, and in which he seems to contradict himself. These apparent anomalies can be very upsetting to the untrained mind; even the trained mind requires a finely honed ability to judge these passages for what they are: rhetorically determined expressions of a unified message. Christ, the perfect rhetorician, tailors his speech to his audience, to the times, and to the circumstance, but it is only through training that students learn to judge these passages properly.

According to Erasmus, the substantive training of theological candidates must include the construction of the standards of judgment that will enable them to handle literary sources. Theological standards of judgment are required as well; one of these standards may even be seen as dogmatic: it is the *scopus*, Christ and his teachings, through which all

---

18. An interesting point here is that Erasmus's own pattern of expectations lead him to believe that much of classical literature was composed allegorically, a position that is clearly untenable. This was a humanistic commonplace, notably shared by Petrarch. It may be that this was the only comfortable approach for Christians toward the ancients, or it may be that their training taught them to see allegories, and these they saw.

19. Manfred Hoffmann has wisely drawn attention to the importance of the term *varietas* in connection with Erasmus's treatment of accommodation. See Hoffmann's *Erkenntnis und Verwirklichung der wahren Theologie nach Erasmus von Rotterdam* (Tübingen: J. C. B. Mohr [Paul Siebeck], 1972), 93–95.

other theological statements are viewed, and through which the whole
life of the believer is transformed. Other standards serve the method
of determining the meaning of scriptural passages. These various standards of judgment and habits of mind are the tools of the theological
enterprise and are especially necessary for the beginner.

To answer these requirements, Erasmus suggests the use of individual dogmas as the standards of judgment to provide a frame of reference
for the beginning theologian for the early confrontations with scripture.

> In my judgment, it would be more pertinent to the matter if the
> beginning theologian learned our dogmas reduced to a survey
> or compendium drawn as much as possible from the evangelical
> sources, or secondarily from the apostolic letters, so that he always
> has fixed standards [scopos] to which he can refer everything he
> reads.[20]

These standards or dogmas—or most simply, the teachings of Christ—
function as theological topics for the rhetorically trained theologian.[21]
The application of rhetorical tools to the theological task functions
heuristically in research as well as persuasively in composition. The
rhetorical device of topics, or commonplaces, aids the theologian in
gathering the elements of an argument, and Erasmus proposes these
dogmas as theological topics. These standards function as signposts or
categories to which any newly encountered scriptural passage may be
related. Here dogma is not the enforced answer to a question so much as
the terms of the question. These dogmas have been derived from scripture by the teacher as topics for the student; in one sense, they are topics
to be understood through a studied engagement with the source.

A simple instance might be a topic such as charity. The theological
student would cull scripture for direct statements concerning charity
and parables in which charity is portrayed. The elements of the argument having been collected, the student would then, through the
practice of the rhetorical art, arrange these elements persuasively to produce a sermon or treatise on the value of charity and support them

---

20. *RH* 193: "Illud mea sententia magis ad rem pertinuerit, ut tirunculo nostro dogmata
tradantur in summam ac compendium redacta, idque potissimum ex evangelicis fontibus,
mox apostolorum litteris, ut ubique certos habeat scopos, ad quos ea quae legit conferat."
21. For a fuller discussion than I can afford here, see my dissertation, "The Shape and
Function of Dogma in the Theology of Erasmus" (Ph.D. diss., University of Chicago, 1987).

with an argument designed to move the audience to acts of charity in their own lives and finally to persuade the audience that genuine acts of charity are important expressions of one's Christianity. This, in short, is Erasmus's idea of the true task of the theologian.[22]

Of course, a topic such as charity is a simple instance, and scripture hardly ever presents its voice simply. The real problems for theologians come not when searching for proof texts that will support an argument for one of these fixed standards but when, in reading scripture, they find a passage that not only does not fit into one of the theological categories, but even contradicts it. Erasmus suggests several strategies for overcoming these apparent inconsistencies. One of these is the method of *collatio*,[23] collation or comparison of texts. It may happen that the same message is presented more clearly in another passage concerning the same issue, or it may be that through a comparison of a number of passages the true interpretation slowly emerges.

As much as the theologian is meant to struggle with the text, in the end, human beings simply need help in understanding the divine both from the divine and from fellow humans. Erasmus believes that the divine Spirit has accommodated its speech to our speech, in short reached out to its creatures and fitted its message to the capacity of the human mind. Erasmus turns to a metaphor of light in casting one of the most intriguing statements of the action of accommodation: "But the brightness of eternal truth reflects one way in a smooth and polished mirror, another way in iron, another way in a crystal-clear fountain, and yet another in a polluted swamp."[24] The essential character of this light does not change depending on where it shines; it is the appearance of the light that changes. Erasmus uses the ingenious metaphor of light to stand for eternal truth. The appearance of light does change as its surroundings change and yet the light itself retains its nature. Divine truth, then, remains true even if it is expressed by an idiot or a heathen.

---

22. *RH* 193: "Yet the principal goal [*scopus*] of theologians is to explain divine letters wisely; to render an account of the faith, not of frivolous questions; to discourse gravely as well as efficaciously about piety; to provoke tears and inflame spirits to heavenly things."

23. Ibid., 291: "Sive quid erit disserendum, aderit ad manum parata supellex, sive quid explicandum, facilis erit locorum collatio." (If you need to discuss something, you will have your tools ready to hand; or if you need to explain something, a comparison of passages will be easy.)

24. Ibid., 204: "Sed aliter relucet aeternae veritatis fulgor in levi terosque speculo, aliter in ferro, aliter in limpidissimo fonte, aliter in lacuna turpida."

Such a vision of theological truth applied to scripture may give the superficial appearance of a relativistic theology, but ultimately this relativism resolves itself into the essential character of Christian theology. The relativism that momentarily exists is aimed at the needs of the times and persons involved. Persons capable of accepting more of the truth may be trained to see it more clearly within the accommodated form even though the complete truth is reserved. The accommodation is provided for the protection of those who are not strong enough to live with the whole truth, to fit the requirements of the times, and to translate divine wisdom into human terms. Erasmus's analogy suggests that it is not the light that changes, but people's perception of the light.

Epistemologically this implies that theological knowledge is always in some sense subjective, that the mind that interprets the divine light reflects it in a specific way, and that the way it appears depends on the quality of the mind that represents it. The expression of theological knowledge is the expression of a personal understanding. Here Erasmus adds a further complication to the human quest for knowledge of the divine. Theological truth is mediated not only by the miraculous language of scripture, but also by the mind of the theologian who presents it. The mind through which this light is focused or reflected does modify its appearance, and by implication, the clearer the lens through which this light shines, the clearer will be the image of the original light.

The best minds, then, present the theologian with the clearest vision of the divine light he or she seeks to understand. Relying on the guidance of the best minds, theologians can move beyond the understanding that they could achieve on their own. We need the guidance of only the best minds because, "in fact, the quality of food does not affect the habits of the body as much as reading does the soul and morals of the reader."[25] At the same time, the question of how one is to identify the best minds remains. The beginning students of theology will be introduced to the best minds by their teachers. Only fully trained theologians have the standard of judgment that enables them to identify the best minds.

For Erasmus, this ultimate standard of judgment is provided by the life and teachings of Christ, by what he calls "the marvelous circle and consensus of the whole story of Christ."[26] Christ embodies a remarkable

---

25. Ibid., 296: "Neque enim perinde ciborum qualitas transit in corporis habitum ut lectio in animum ac mores legentis."

26. Ibid., 209: "Mirabilem illum orbem et consensum totius Christi fabulae."

and unique consistency of thought and action,[27] and the closer a given theologian comes to portraying this unity the more truly Christian is that theologian's interpretation. Erasmus advises beginning students to learn from the ancient interpreters.[28] They employed the correct method of interpretation, were closer to the source, and thus could see it more clearly. Fully trained theologians will have a firm grasp on this unified message, an understanding forged through their studied engagement with the source of Christian doctrine, and will be able to judge the fidelity of the interpreters they encounter. The best minds will reflect the light of divine truth best.

The "marvelous circle and consensus of the whole story of Christ" widens over time to include the interpretations offered by the apostles and the ancient interpreters and ultimately comes to form a circle and consensus of Christian doctrine.[29] This body of belief and practice is based on the consensus of the best theologians over the long time span of Christian history. Finally, all depends on the faith that there is a single unified message expressed by the Christian religion and primarily presented in scripture. Erasmus does not demand a theology based on *sola scriptura*. Perhaps because of his rhetorical stance, he believes that as times and circumstances change, certain aspects of Christian teaching change as well.

For Erasmus, there is a core of Christian teaching, which he calls dogma, which remains true for all time; other aspects, especially ceremonial custom, can and should change over time. Erasmus firmly believes that even concerning disputed questions of theology a study of the best theologians' pronouncements over the centuries will reveal a consensus of opinion within the Christian church. Erasmus believes that the human mind functions best in concert with other human minds; that this common effort, in which the moderns learn from the ancients, both preserves and furthers the understanding of the church. This tradition, which had been built up over the centuries and which Erasmus often

---

27. Ibid., 211: "At circulum hunc et omnium rerum inter se congruentium harmoniam in solo Christo reperies." (But you will find in Christ alone this circle and consistent harmony of all things among themselves.)

28. Ibid., 284: "Prima sit cura librorum omnium veteris novique testamenti sententiam *ex priscis illis interpretibus* perdiscere" (my emphasis). (His first concern should be to learn the meaning of the Old and New Testaments from those ancient interpreters.)

29. Ibid., 286: " ... ad orbem illum doctrinae Christianae" (... to that circle of Christian doctrine).

refers to as the *consensus totius Ecclesiae*, is a common effort and cannot be denied by private authority. Erasmus does accept the corporate character of theology just as he accepts the consensus of the church as authoritative though not unchanging. Finally, Erasmus believes that language was given to humans in order that they work together in order to understand the divine more fully as times and circumstances change.

Erasmus's presentation of the true method of theology can also provide a pattern for the practice of historical theology. He recommends that pretheological training include geography and biology and that part of the theologian's task is to understand the occasion, audience, and context of scriptural statements; those recommendations clearly suggest that any attempt to discover the pure theology of a scriptural passage is at best misguided and always doomed to produce a faulty understanding. All theology is filtered through the human mind, which is dependent upon the medium of language, and language is flavored by times and circumstances. This does not imply that the source for theology is not divine, but rather that the unavoidable medium for theology is human. Erasmus believed that scriptural messages were miraculously presented to fit biblical times and circumstances and that these must be in some sense translated to the theologian's own time. The theologian then is, above all, interpreter and judge of theological statements and sentiments. The ultimate criterion of truth for Erasmus is whether such statements fit; they must fit both the consensus of the whole church and the present times and circumstances.

Erasmus defines essential Christian teachings as those that fit any time and circumstance—these teachings are dogma, are unchanging, and ought to be so simple that they need no interpretation and can be understood even by the simplest believer. This is the limit Erasmus draws to the influence of individual mind and culture on theology. For the rest, the nonessential Christian teachings and the body of ceremonial practice, Erasmus seems to have attempted to form or to discover a theological culture embodied in the consensus of the whole church and of the best theologians. Theology thus becomes a shared and corporate human enterprise that remains an ongoing attempt to refine our understanding of the divine; this enterprise proceeds not at all in distinction from the divine but with necessary divine help.

Erasmus's dual insight that the human mind needs the company and assistance of other minds and that our knowledge of the divine is restricted to reflections through human minds and human language may also prove helpful to the historical theologian of today. Erasmus did not view either of these insights as occasions for sad plaints of alienation. For him, the implications were joyful and marvelous. His recognition of a human measure for theology led him to a theology based on rhetoric, cooperation, toleration, and education. His understanding of the task of theology led him to appreciate the complex richness of human interaction with the divine. His epistemological stance led him to worry about the training beginning theologians would receive. The wisdom provided by his own training in classical culture taught him that as times and circumstances change, language changes. He believed that the expression of certain aspects of theology should change to fit the demands of the times and circumstances.

Erasmus's human measure of theology implies that we must think of theologians not as mere material vessels of pure rationality, but as human beings who live and struggle in the world. Because no theologian lives within the limits of theology alone, historical theologians studying particular theologians in the past cannot ignore the cultural conditions and tensions in which those persons lived. All live within a culture and must be studied in this context even if they themselves are interested only in combating its influence on the prevailing theology of their times. As much as theology claims to describe an ultimate reality, it nonetheless describes this reality in the terms of the prevailing cultural conditions. There is no escape from the culture that forms an individual; the repertoire of questions and available answers provided by a culture helps to form the individuals born into that culture and describes the horizon beyond which they cannot see. The investigation of the pertinent elements of the cultures in which theologians live will therefore provide an enrichment to our understanding of their theologies and may help us understand the theological moves that they make. Historical theology will prove its worth only when it moves beyond merely describing connections between theologies previous and subsequent to the theologian we seek to study and becomes a genuine attempt to understand how our understanding and perhaps even our experience of the divine change as the times and circumstances change. Erasmus's approach to the study of scriptural passages through their contexts may have a good deal to teach us about the best approach to the study of the history of Christian theology.

FIVE

Jane Strohl

Suffering as Redemptive: A Comparison of Christian Experience in the Sixteenth and Twentieth Centuries

Central to any telling of the story of Jesus Christ is his passion. His suffering and dishonorable death, denoted by the sign of the cross, are both the source of Christianity's power and the cause of its offense. St. Paul insisted that Christ's passion manifests God's intent to overcome human wisdom and strength with divine foolishness and weakness. Christ crucified, "a stumbling block to Jews and foolishness to Gentiles," proves to be he "who became for us wisdom from God, and righteousness and sanctification and redemption" (1 Cor. 1:23, 30), much to the world's surprise. The suffering of Christ, although vindicated by the resurrection, is not effaced by it. The resurrected one remains the crucified one, and this continuity of identity in the chief character of the Christian story has important implications for the lives of all persons who interpret their histories through the narrative framework of the gospel.

There is no greater test for a religious tradition than its ability meaningfully to incorporate into its mythos the overwhelming reality of suffering. The Christian tradition has attempted to explain suffering under two broad rubrics: suffering as *imitatio* and suffering as discipline. In the first case believers bear willingly the afflictions and deprivations that befall them in the course of making their confession of faith.

This does not mean that believers must court trouble or inflict hardship upon themselves, although many Christians have done precisely that as a testimony of their love for Christ and their contempt for the world and the flesh. Moreover, it would seem that distinctions among kinds of sufferings are specious here. To bear punishments inflicted directly for confession of the Christian faith—for example, a resulting loss of political rights or social status, imprisonment, or even martyrdom—is certainly an unambiguous example of taking up one's cross and following. Yet the more common ills besetting humanity are equally susceptible to the power of confession. Illness, poverty, societal indifference or discrimination, familial discord, vocational disappointment—in the midst of any of these to confess God as sovereign and merciful is an act of courage and grace. Further, the sufferings of the faithful become part of the redemptive work of Christ and thus contribute not only to the salvation of the individual but to the transformation of all whom Christ claims for his own. What is true for St. Paul is true for everyone who confesses Christ before the world and thus, consciously or not, serves to call it to account: "I am now rejoicing in my sufferings for your sake, and in my flesh I am completing what is lacking in Christ's afflictions for the sake of his body, that is, the church" (Col. 1:24).

Suffering is also understood as God's instrument of discipline and punishment. If the conception of suffering as imitation reflects a confidence in people's ability to respond to Christ and to embody the exemplary humanity set before them in the incarnation, this perception of suffering focuses on the countervailing force of human sinfulness and on its persistence and virulence. It suggests that the human being as sinner must be coerced into an encounter with God and that continuing forceful measures must be taken to maintain the relationship on proper terms.

In both cases suffering, whether perceived as embraced or inflicted, is understood to offer an extraordinary opportunity. Here one is likely to encounter Christ most intimately and to penetrate the mystery of salvation with a clarity unattainable under other circumstances. Suffering itself, then, is transformed by the encounter, as is the sufferer, for to be brought into communion with Christ is to be enriched rather than diminished. However, the relationship to God and the knowledge of the self that result are experienced differently, depending on how one appropriates the suffering that serves as their instrument.

The purposes of this essay are to explore several primary texts relevant to the issue of the Christian understanding of suffering as *imitatio* and as discipline and to bring their viewpoints into conversation with one another. Martin Luther, representative of sixteenth-century thought on this issue, presents suffering as necessary to make room for faith. His view of suffering as a divine antidote to human resistance will be explored and then considered in the light of several contemporary essays written by African women who are Christians. They too recognize the redemptive power of suffering in their lives, but they find in suffering preeminently a revelation of God standing with them rather than against them. This essay will conclude with some discussion of the purposes and principles of historical theology as I conceive them and have sought to employ them in the present study.

A Sixteenth-Century View: Martin Luther

The theology of Martin Luther portrays God as jealously demanding sole possession of the believer's heart. One is to be justified by the grace of Christ through faith alone, and that means relinquishing one's grip on all other supports and clinging only to the God made known in the gospel. In a memorable sermon preached on the text of Matthew 15:21-28, Luther presents the conduct of the Canaanite woman seeking healing for her daughter as normative for all Christians. She exemplifies the faith that justifies, which is not a question of assent to doctrine or of the observance of certain ethical and moral principles. Rather, it is a matter of persistence in one's relationship to God, of crying out and expecting to be heard, and of holding God to be truthful in the Word proclaimed in God's name. The Canaanite woman turns to Jesus, trusting in his mercy, and finds him cold and unkind. At first he ignores her. Upon her repeated entreaties he rejects her because she is not of the house of Israel, stating that it is not fair to take the children's bread and give it to dogs. The woman, however, does not let these adverse circumstances deter her. She continues to act on the conviction that he has both the power to help her and the compassion to do so. "She said, 'Yes, Lord, yet even the dogs eat the crumbs that fall from their master's table.' Then Jesus answered her, 'Woman, great is your faith! Let it be done for you as you wish.' And her daughter was healed instantly" (Matt. 15:27-28).

Luther comments on the text as follows:

Now he [Jesus] is silent as a stick. Look, this is truly a hard blow, when God shows himself stern and wrathful, and hides his grace so high and deep, as those well know who have felt and experienced it in their hearts, so that they think he will not hold to what he has said and will let his word become false.[1]

Luther distinguishes between the hidden and the revealed God (the *deus absconditus* and the *deus revelatus*), the former remaining an enigma that neither human reason nor human faith can ever fathom. This is the God behind or beyond the cross, the one who predestines, the one who does will the death of sinners and is not clothed in the Word. The revealed God, in contrast, is defined by the Word and bound to it. The person of Jesus and his history, the proclamation of forgiveness and new life made by his authority and in his name—these establish the character of God among God's people and for God's self. Thus, insists Luther, if God were to appear in majesty and say, "You are not worthy of My grace; I will change My plan and not keep My promise to you,"[2] he would hold God to the promise made publicly and remind God that God cannot go back on that Word.

The Canaanite woman finds herself in precisely such a dilemma, only it is not God in untempered majesty, the *deus absconditus,* who confronts her with inscrutability. Rather, it is the *deus revelatus,* the Word made flesh, who now presents himself hidden behind an air of indifference, even hostility. Yet she perseveres, and as she believes God to be, so is the God she finds. For Luther this is what is required of every Christian whose circumstances in life cast doubt on God's loving-kindness. They must let nothing, not even God's seeming rejection, keep them from crying out and praying, holding on to God as God's self is made known in the gospel.

This was written to comfort and teach us all so that we might know how deeply God hides his grace for us and how we should think of

---

1. Martin Luther, *Werke,* ed. J. F. K. Knaake et al. (Weimar: H. Boehlau, 1883–1986), 17/2:201.
2. Martin Luther, *Works,* ed. Jaroslav Pelikan (St. Louis: Concordia Publishing House, 1955–86), 6:131.

God not according to our own ideas and feelings but in strict accordance with his Word. For here you see that although Christ takes a harsh stance, still he does not give a final negative judgment. Indeed, all his answers sound like "no," but they are not "no." Rather, they are left hanging in suspense. For he does not say, "I will not listen to her," but rather keeps silent, saying neither yes nor no. . . .

This shows the situation of our heart when it is tried and tempted. . . . It concludes that there is only "no" there, but that is untrue. For this reason the heart must turn from such feelings, seize and cling to the "yes" deep and hidden beneath and beyond the "no," just as this woman does. We must acknowledge God to be in the right when he judges us. Then we have won him and caught him in his own word.[3]

Faith is the refusal to let go. It is the Christian's willingness to let God be divine, indeed one's insistence that God do so, and thus, according to Luther, faith succeeds in fulfilling the first commandment, "You shall have no other gods before me" (Exod. 20:3). In his 1531 lectures on Paul's epistle to the Galatians, Luther counsels his readers to run to Christ the physician, who heals those who are broken in heart and saves sinners. The judgment of reason will tell them that Christ is angry with sinners, but they are to kill reason and believe in Christ: "If you believe, you are righteous, because you give glory to God, that he is almighty, merciful, true, etc. You justify and praise God; to be brief, you yield to him his divinity, and whatsoever else belongs to him."[4] As a result, the sin that remains in believers is not held against them but is forgiven for Christ's sake.

To yield to God divinity and all else that is rightfully God's does not come easily to people. Broken human nature struggles against such surrender even after tasting grace. God requires total dependence, intimacy with no reservation on the believer's part. The response is ambiguous. For if, on the one hand, people long to let God shoulder the burden of their fear and failure, they dread, on the other hand, being so vulnerable. Human beings feel safe only in a relationship with some degree of reciprocity; that, at least, was Luther's criticism of a doctrine of sal-

---

3. Luther, *Werke,* 17/2:203.

4. Martin Luther, *Martin Luther: Selections from His Writings,* ed. John Dillenberger (Garden City, N.Y.: Anchor Books, 1961), 131; translation emended.

vation that allowed a role for human works in the justification of the
sinner. In Luther's view, works so understood inevitably become obstacles between believers and God. Dependence upon such achievements
to secure their claims before the Lord turns their very right doing into
violation of the First Commandment. Luther warns that to seek by one's
own efforts to insure or advance one's salvation is to have another god
in addition to the one who alone should command believers' trust.

For Luther it is only through the experience of anguish and temptation that one can receive true knowledge of the God who justifies the
ungodly.[5] Suffering thus serves to create and sustain the proper relationship between redeemer and sinner. Every loss, every doubt, every
experience of weakness and human limitation reminds believers that
they are utterly dependent on a divine action over which they have no
control at any point. Thus, while Luther does at times interpret tribu-
lations and temptations as punishments inflicted by God upon sinful
peoples and individuals for their condemnation, more characteristic of
his thought is the perception of such crosses as inflicted out of love,
not simply wrath, so as to prepare God's children for the reception
of faith. Suffering erodes whatever defenses humans seek to place between themselves and God's absolute demands. It serves to empty one

---

5. "For the only understanding anyone can have of what it means that God is wise,
good, mighty, and merciful is speculative and metaphysical, just as one can conceive some
idea of the goodness or wisdom of a prince that is pure speculation. But when it comes to
practice, when God snatches Joseph from the embrace of his parents, his grandfather, father, and the whole household, and he is hurled into prison in a foreign land on the charge
of adultery and remains there in constant expectation of death—will anyone interpret this
as the good will of God?

"Therefore, we should know that God hides himself under the form of the worst devil.
This teaches us that the goodness, mercy, and power of God cannot be grasped by speculation but must be understood on the basis of experience. Just endure and wait for the Lord.
Hold fast. Be content with his Word, just as Joseph has the Word of faith. He knows that
he is the son of Jacob, who received from God the promise concerning the future Seed and
blessing. Yet when all things appeared to be the contrary of the promise that was given,
he undoubtedly sobbed and complained about his wretched condition. But the Lord said
to him: 'Wait. Act manfully. Let your heart take courage (Ps. 27:14). Hold fast.' Again he
was minded to sigh and to wish: 'O how I would like to return to my father! Hold fast.'
Or 'If only a way out of prison would present itself! Hold fast. What if I shall have to perish in prison with the greatest disgrace? Hold fast.' These alternate changes from comfort
to distress were observed in Joseph's heart until at length he looked about and said with
wonder: 'Ah, I could never have hoped for this liberation or understood this power and
goodness of God which he has shown in my case!' Then his heart leaps for sheer joy. Then
he exults with his whole heart. He congratulates himself on his disgrace, death, and imprisonment. Thus Joseph is an illustrious example when he sobs and when he exults after
the trial has come to an end" (Luther, *Works*, 7:175–76).

of all self-righteousness so that one may be filled with the righteousness of Christ; Luther insists that the creature must come to God with an empty heart. Moreover, this process of humiliation and conflict is required throughout believers' lives.

> If there were no temptation to exercise the faith of believers, you know what would be the fate of such untroubled, idle, self-indulgent Christians. They would end up in the same state as has the pope. Since temptations are the rue, myrrh, aloes, and antidote against all worms, pus, rottenness, and excrement of this body of sin, it follows that they are not to be despised nor are they to be sought or chosen according to our own will. On the contrary, we are to bear temptations cf whatever sort God determines to inflict upon us, since he knows which temptations of what nature and in what amount will be best suited and most beneficial to us.[6]

The pain of recurring doubt and deprivation reminds forgiven sinners that they have nothing and no one to fall back on but the God revealed in the gospel of Jesus Christ. It is such training that enables them to stand firm in the Word as did the Canaanite woman.

Luther's view of suffering was no minority view in the sixteenth century. The position that suffering is a necessary and divinely inflicted discipline was already well established in medieval Catholic theology and pastoral care. Such chastisement was viewed as edifying and conducive to spiritual health. Many saints suffered disease or mental affliction. God thereby taught such chosen ones patience and crowned their faith with meritorious virtue. For Luther, of course, the humble acceptance of one's fate could not offer the advantage of accruing merit; it could not be transmuted into a work worthy of heavenly reward. Nonetheless, such submission was the proper response of justifying faith and hence pleasing to God. For if suffering is construed as a reminder to believers of their total dependence upon God, to acquiesce in this discipline is a potent confession of belief in God's trustworthiness, benevolence, and power ultimately to bring imperishable good out of earthly anguish.

---

6. Martin Luther, *Werke,* Kritische Gesamtausgabe *Briefwechsel* (Weimar: H. Boehlau, 1930–83), 10/3720: lines 1–11.

The view of suffering espoused by Luther appears among other sixteenth-century reformers. The radical Hans Denck, for example, also presents God as *ayn eyferer,*[7] unwilling to share honor with any other beloved in the heart of the believer. In contrast to Luther, Denck insists that the seed of salvation is implanted in the soul of every person and must be tended. His exhortations to take advantage of the grace of God available to his hearers sound much like Luther's insistence that, with respect to the evangelical gospel, Germany should buy while the market is good. Yet Denck, unlike Luther, regards the human will as able to respond to such exhortations. Free will after the Fall is very likely to be self-will but is not inexorably subject to such bondage.

Denck does not, however, minimize the power of sin. The seed of salvation present in the soul requires further cultivation by God before the human will is able to use it rightly. If the heart given to Christ must be empty, it depends upon God to begin stripping it of its pretensions.[8] Luther disagreed vehemently with Denck's teaching on the indwelling Word and the will's ability to assert itself in obedience to God's address. Yet the two reformers are in agreement as to the virulence of human resistance to the Word and the necessity of divinely inflicted suffering to bring people to knowledge of their sin, not just once but repeatedly throughout their lives. Only when one is able to stand empty before God and confess one's need of a savior does one receive what is required. Suffering, when it creates such a condition, proves to be a sign of God's favor and a prelude to the experience of justifying grace.

The ultimate effect of this commonly held position, however, is quite different in the respective theologies of Luther and Denck because of the

---

7. Hans Denck, *Schriften,* ed. Walter Fellman (Gütersloh: C. Bertelsmann Verlag, 1956), 2:35.

8. "When we are deepest in damnation we allow ourselves and everything that relates to us to be torn asunder with unspeakable pain (Job 7:20). This is like a pregnant woman who at the time of her birth has to accept her suffering. Indeed, she does so willingly even though she cannot yet rejoice in her offspring until she sees it alive (Jn. 16:21). This is the eye of the needle through which the uncouth camels have to pass, yet cannot (Mt. 19:24). Indeed, we cannot do it ourselves but must suffer God to do it for us (Phil. 4:13). To him nothing is impossible (Lk. 1:37). As long as any of the elect vaunt themselves to be something without the knowledge and love of God (Gal. 6:3, 1 Cor. 13:1), he drives and tests them until they submit to being nothing and the false nothing is consumed (1 Cor. 3:7). At that point the eye of the needle, the narrow gate to life, becomes wide enough; the yoke of Christ (which to the world appears bitter and unbearable), becomes to them wonderfully useful and easy (Mt. 11:30)" (Hans Denck, *Selected Writings,* ed. and trans. Edward J. Furcha with Ford Lewis Battles [Pittsburgh: The Pickwick Press, 1975], 86–87).

latter's rejection of the doctrine of a hidden God. There is for Denck no gulf between what humanity knows of God through the revelation of the Word and what God knows of God's self. The divine will proclaimed publicly is not undermined at any time by some secret decree.

> O, if only the whole world would come, the Lord is wonderfully prepared to embrace it. He calls all people and offers his mercy to everyone. His earnestness and desire to do all that he has promised are sincere. Is it not, therefore, malicious when our scribes say that he invites some to the table and yet it is not his will that they come? The good spirit of God has not commanded them to say such things, for all that God does, he does simply. It is not the case that he says, "Come here," and secretly thinks and wills that the person remain where he is. Nor does he give grace to someone and then secretly will to take it away again or effect in us repentance for our sins and then secretly prepare a place in hell for us. In all his gifts God is steady and true.[9]

This differs sharply from a passage such as the following in which Luther discusses the potential conflict between the will of the *deus revelatus* and that of the *deus absconditus:*

> God incarnate . . . has been sent into the world for the very purpose of willing, speaking, doing, suffering, and offering to all everything necessary for salvation. Yet he offends very many, who being either abandoned or hardened by that secret will of the Divine Majesty do not receive him as he wills, speaks, does, suffers, and offers, as John says: "The light shines in the darkness, and the darkness does not comprehend it" (John 1:5); and again: "He came to his own home, and his own people received him not" (John 1:11). It is likewise the part of this incarnate God to weep, wail, and groan over the perdition of the ungodly, when the will of the Divine Majesty purposely abandons and reprobates some to perish. And it is not for us to ask why he does so, but to stand in awe of God who both can do and wills to do such things.[10]

---

9. Denck, *Schriften*, 2:46.
10. Luther, *Works*, 33:146.

Denck's position makes the necessity of self-emptying easier to accept, for at the end, or at the root, of the suffering that Christian faith entails, the sufferer encounters one who is straightforwardly trustworthy. For all Luther's emphasis on the cross as the only lens through which one can even begin to view the *deus absconditus,* he does not succeed in neutralizing the fear that, as he and Denck both recognize, drives the sinner to flee the hand of God.[11]

A Twentieth-Century View: African Women

The next set of texts to be examined comes from essays by contemporary African women who are Christians. One is struck immediately by the particularity of their viewpoint. The authors do not claim to speak for *the* human experience but rather identify themselves as a distinct subgroup within the church and humanity, whose witness is ignored by the whole at its peril.

This is in marked contrast to Luther, who presents his view as normative for Christian faith in general and at all times. Indeed, since the rise of historical consciousness in the nineteenth century, such universalizing of any particular theological viewpoint is, at the least, problematical. Within Christianity a pluralism exists that one can no longer confidently explain, as Luther did, in terms of some communities remaining faithful to the gospel and others falling into error. What Ernst Troeltsch says about the absoluteness of Christianity in relation to other religions is true of any particular expression of Christian faith in relation to its siblings. We cannot accord it absolute validity. Our own experience bears witness to its spiritual power, but that certifies its truth only for us. Other communities rightly regard their experience of Christ as equally valid.[12]

---

11. "However, you show by your restlessness that you seek yourself and not God for his own sake, for you are always trying to find a hiding place where you may escape the hand of God. Because you are a wretched bit of grass, you fear that he will crush you if you hold still for him. So it always seems to flesh and blood before one sacrifices oneself. Where one seeks blessedness, there seems to be only damnation, and that is not to the liking of our perverted nature. If one held still, then there would be time and place for the spirit of the lamb to bear witness and say, 'This is the only way to blessedness,' that is, to lose oneself. For since God and all God's doing is the very best, then God's acting to break down, which is so repellent to our nature, must be infinitely better than all the making and creating in heaven, on earth, and under the earth" (Denck, *Schriften,* 2:33).

12. Claude Welch, *Protestant Thought in the Nineteenth Century* (New Haven and London: Yale University Press, 1985), 2:288–89.

While Christianity is inextricably bound up with European and American cultures, it has also been a vital force in various societies outside those limits. It is now a vital force in a number of markedly different societies. To speak of Christianity in the contemporary world, one must attend to the experience and witness of these communities. The truths of one group cannot simply be substituted for those of another, but they can be mutually influential, serving each other as part of the experience by which persons come to discern afresh the present power and meaning of Christian faith. I have chosen to use the work of African Christian women because by virtue of their race, gender, and ethnicity, they have generally been excluded from theological discussion. Yet their witness is certainly as deserving of consideration as that of those whose own construction of the Christian ethos permits such neglect.

Thérèse Souga, a Roman Catholic from Cameroun, states that being a woman in African society means keeping silent and being discounted. She reflects on the weakness evident in the life of Jesus and concludes that having borne in his person the condition of the weak, he has experienced an essential aspect of womanhood.

> In the light of Christ, if Jesus is the God who has become weakness in our context, in his identity as God-man, Jesus takes on the condition of the African woman. The African woman can tell herself: Christ has been concerned with, and has been touched by, the situation that I am living.[13]

Indeed, womanhood is presented in these essays as a socially constructed reality, defined by its assigned tasks and the human characteristics that are strengthened as a consequence. Thus, Jesus as compassionate nurturer of humankind reveals "all that we know of perfect womanhood."[14] He takes upon himself what is traditionally regarded as women's work, tending the sick (the healings) and providing sustenance for others (the teachings; the feeding miracles).[15] The authors see in Jesus one who was not constricted by the taboos around gender that

---

13. Thérèse Souga, "The Christ-Event from the Viewpoint of African Women: A Catholic Perspective," in *With Passion and Compassion: Third World Women Doing Theology,* ed. Virginia Fabella and Mercy Amba Oduyoye (Maryknoll, N.Y.: Orbis Books, 1988), 28.

14. Elizabeth Amoah and Mercy Amba Oduyoye, "The Christ for African Women," in *With Passion and Compassion,* 44.

15. Ibid., 39, 44.

permeate their own societies. Christ received women into his company; he ate with them; he acted on their behalf, even healing what was clearly a gynecological complaint (Matt. 9:20–22). In all this Christ recognized and promoted the integrity of women as persons, and this honoring of their condition speaks against those who would hold them to be inferior on account of their sex and the role they assume within the culture. Thus, for the authors of these essays the actual biological maleness of Christ is not a stumbling block. The humanity taken up by him in the incarnation includes activities, experiences, and values that women recognize as distinctively their own. These women, who bear a threefold burden of suffering because of their poverty, their race, and their gender, encounter Christ in the midst of their despised condition.

These essays do not convey a dominant awareness of the sinner as strong in her or his hostility to God. If for Luther the central problem was the willful perversity of humankind that requires God to crush it repeatedly, what is at issue for these women is the weakness that threatens to undo them. This is the result of external factors, the positions they are obliged to occupy in cultures that deny them autonomy in the political and social arena and then demean them for their inferiority. Even within the church their vulnerability is used as an occasion for discrimination and domination, yet their condition is not necessarily one of self-effacement. There is a difference between self-sacrifice and being sacrificed, although their societies do not generally honor that distinction.[16]

Mercy Oduyoye, in an essay reflecting on the roles of African women in the church's mission, writes the following about the vocation of women in her society:

> Women confined to home and hearth during traditional festivals spend the time happily preparing the delicacies which the ordinary routine of life prevents them from making. In the event a joyful feast is laid for all, but more important, feeding the hungry is transformed from a chore to a work of art.
>
> Women deprived of male support in time of war, by immigration or death, have proved that history-making does not belong

16. Mercy Oduyoye, "Churchwomen and the Church's Mission," in *New Eyes for Reading: Biblical and Theological Reflections by Women from the Third World,* ed. John S. Pobee and Bärbel von Wartenberg-Potter (Oak Park, Ill.: Meyer-Stone Books, 1987), 77.

to men alone and hence blazed new avenues—later to be labelled "women's role"—until men find it convenient to join in.[17]

Women do this, she states, because they have in themselves the ability to adapt for the purpose of survival and more importantly the ability to be creative as beings linked with the Creator-God. Many women have concluded that the survival of a healthy society depends upon their sacrificial lives. Indeed, faced with the obligation to serve others, they have constantly created new ways to meet the demands, coming to the conviction that self-emptying does not deprive their lives of substance and content. For them suffering becomes generative rather than destructive. It gives definition to the self; it marks out the contours of a particular biography as one is laid open to the demands of others, limited by the constraints of these relationships, and yet challenged by them to go beyond one's present boundaries. In turn their endurance affects the world that demands it of them, and as with Christ, their very weakness becomes a force for change. Their discovery of his presence in the defining conditions of their lives transforms their self-understanding. The encounter with Christ calls the powerless to be bold in their witness and confident of their honored state as especially vivid images of him.

> Through the initiatives that she [the Christian woman] will be emboldened to undertake, she is responsible for inviting the man to have a different vision of reality, to wake him up to the situation of the little ones and of the weak who are likely to be crushed. In an aggressive situation, where one might think she would be annihilated, as she takes on this situation with faith in Christ, she grows. Like the church, which sings about the happy fault that brought us such a Savior, the woman can see her situation of weakness as a treasure that opens her up and sensitizes her to situations of injustice and oppression. Her belonging to Jesus Christ increases within her this thirst to know him, to live from him, to work to make the gospel take root in this society of hers.[18]

The suffering and subsequent empowerment of African women serve, on the one hand, as an indictment of their culture's sinfulness and, on

---

17. Ibid.
18. Souga, "Christ-Event," 29.

the other, as a sign of hope for its redemption. Their experience becomes an instrument of God's judgment and of God's grace for the world.

These African women understand themselves to be uniquely qualified to speak for all those who suffer.

> She [the African woman] is oppressed by her African brother; she is oppressed by other women who are not African; she is oppressed by non-African men. Especially when the hierarchical scale on the international level is taken into account, the African woman is at the very bottom of that scale. She incarnates the mass of the poor and the oppressed.[19]

They call attention to the terrible vulnerability of women and children and of the poor to domination. Too often such persons suffer violence as they are "disciplined" by those in authority over them. The stories are legion of their being subjected to physical and psychological abuse, of being reduced to utter dependence and stripped of any rights of their own. To such ears, the God described by Luther, the God who uses suffering to produce faith and whose grace is often hidden under harsh externals, only offers more of the same.

Is one justified then in dismissing this view as no longer applicable, indeed even as false in the light of the situation experienced by these twentieth-century African women? What is the test of the truth of a theological conception? To be sure, both interpretations of suffering, as discipline and as imitation, find support in scripture as well as in various parts of the Christian tradition preceding the particular articulations under examination here. Yet inherited constructions of meaning are tested by contemporary perspectives and problems, and in the end the determination of how one's suffering relates to divine reality is a creative act, a formulation of truth in and for a specific life or group of lives. The decision is made on the basis of the adequacy of a particular view for discerning meaning in one's circumstances and for producing certain desired consequences. Such pluralism holds the danger of the loss of a constant identity in Christianity, but the faith is not without norms (though these too remain within the process of historical development and change rather than loom over it as some kind of absolute).

---

19. Louise Tappa, "The Christ-Event from the Viewpoint of African Women: A Protestant Perspective," in *With Passion and Compassion,* 33.

The two views examined here do share some common objectives—they both seek to understand suffering as the means of coming into relationship with Jesus Christ and this fellowship as effecting liberation from what undermines life—but they achieve these ends differently.

For Luther the gravest danger lies in human nature itself. According to him, people indeed may experience themselves as powerless, frustrated repeatedly by circumstances beyond their control, yet in their relationship to God they are anything but weak and ineffectual. The problem, then, is that humans are virulent in their rebellion, aggressive in their efforts to set terms with their Creator and to domesticate God. That is why God has to break the will rather than simply persuade it. By taking sin so seriously, Luther actually exalts the saving work of Christ. To free us from our enemies, the Lord must free us from ourselves, shattering the pot in order to form it anew. God in Christ is willing to do even that in order to deliver those whom God loves.

The African women do not deny the presence of sin in individuals that must be purged. However, such an interpretation of suffering does not suffice to give meaning to what they endure. The greatest obstacle for them in answering God's call to life is the evil inflicted by the sins of others, the restrictions and abuses imposed by societal structures and personal relationships that demean African women. The power of Christian faith as they experience it is that it allows them to overcome these limitations, to use them as Christ did his weakness to challenge and change their world.

Neither conception can be dismissed as untrue. The sixteenth-century formulation may be judged unacceptable by many who identify themselves as Christian, but it remains a valid expression of the faith for many others, who find in it a convincing construction of reality as they experience it. Indeed, it would be hard to recognize as a form of Christianity any theology that lost sight of sin as a defining characteristic of human existence. For Luther this is expressed primarily in terms of humanity's age-old rebellion against God; the African women call attention to the human victims of human sinfulness. While Luther's view is not untenable, it requires supplementation to be adequate to the world we know. If all must be taught the vanity of being in competition with God, there are many who need to experience the honor of being able to stand in their own right before God and other people. The enforced denial of self can no longer be offered to them as a means of grace, most certainly not by those who contribute to and benefit from their affliction. This is the distinction between being sacrificed and voluntary *kenosis,* to which the African women are so acutely sensitive.

Methodological Reflections

Having identified an issue of central importance to Christian theology, suffering, I have chosen several theological texts from the sixteenth and the twentieth centuries and put them in conversation with one another. Because of my Lutheran commitments, I have taken Luther for my point of orientation and the object of critical scrutiny as to the adequacy of his view for contemporary Christian self-understanding. Granted that historical theology is not the exclusive preserve of self-conscious adherents to some present form of the Christian faith, yet for those working within the Christian tradition, the discipline is pursued with certain objectives that presuppose a commitment to care for the faith. Its practitioners are those described by Ernst Troeltsch as believing that Christianity does have a future.

> He who affirms Christianity and who strives to work out the ideas in it which have a living power for the future, in his own work and in the work of his colleagues, will at the same time see the essence in the light of these ideas and emphasize that in the past which is amenable to the possibilities of the future.[20]

To reach maturity, to understand why certain constructions of reality have become part of one's person, each of us must explore our family history and the domestic dynamics and external forces that have shaped it. It is no different with a religious community whose values and behaviors make claims upon us. One must know the history and come to terms with it, not just of one's immediate household of faith but of the extended kin as well. Historical theology seeks to preserve the tradition both by correction and development. The discipline requires cultivation of a critical stance both over against falsifications of the nor-

---

20. Ernst Troeltsch, "What Does 'Essence of Christianity' Mean?" in *Ernst Troeltsch: Writings on Theology and Religion,* trans. and ed. Robert Morgan and Michael Pye (Atlanta: John Knox Press, 1977), 158.

mative expression of a community's faith and against these normative expressions themselves.

Historical theology at its best hovers on the border between a descriptive and a prescriptive discipline. It examines how certain persons and communities conceive the faith under particular circumstances. The discipline appreciates the historicity of these documents and examines them as cultural data. Yet within the Christian church historical theology must go a step further. It must allow for the living claim such documents make upon those who now inhabit the tradition these authors helped form. Within the church all the theological disciplines are directed toward proclamation. Historical theology explores various expressions of the gospel as instructive for contemporary witness. It serves to call the church and its members regularly to account by helping and obliging them to reflect on their present possession of the tradition in light of its past.

SIX

Jack Forstman

Coherence and Incoherence in the Theology of John Calvin

The Sources for the Knowledge of God in Calvin's Theology

Calvin's most exhaustive biographer, Emil Doumergue, judges that Calvin was a man "tormented by an incomparable need for certitude."[1] The judgment is understandable. Calvin intended in the *Institutes* to give an ordered presentation of what human beings can know about God, and a casual reading draws the eyes to focus repeatedly on the phrase, "It is certain...." One observes a pervasive assurance and the never-failing claim that apparent difficulties can be readily resolved.

Doumergue's judgment, however, obscures three considerations that are important in reading Calvin. First, to speak of Calvin's obsession with certainty inevitably causes one to focus on his conviction that the Bible as a whole is true. But in this certainty he does not differ from most in his own time and before in Christianized Europe. Second, to put such an emphasis on Calvin's "need for certainty" is likely to cause the reader to picture him as one who wanted to know everything. But in his historical context the insistence on the sole and final authority of the Bible functioned for Calvin as a limit to the knowledge of God. We are certain, he held, of this much and no more, and we should not try to extend this knowledge by the use of "spiritual" exegesis. Calvin, then,

---

1. Emil Doumergue, *Jean Calvin: Les hommes et les choses de son temps* (Lausanne: Georges Bridel et Cie Editeurs, 1910), 4:60.

was a theologian whose range of knowledge was not nearly as broad as that assumed by his counterparts who employed several kinds of exegesis and acknowledged supplementary sources of knowledge. Third, and most important, Doumergue's judgment, by causing us to focus on the objective knowledge Calvin thought he found in the Bible, leads us also to neglect the relational knowledge of God (faith), in which the knowledge of God can never be divorced from the knowledge of self.

The bondedness of the knowledge of God and the knowledge of self is the theme with which Calvin begins the *Institutes,* and it is a theme to which he repeatedly alludes. He brings it to a focus in describing the knowledge of faith at the beginning of book 3. He admits that because the knowledge of faith cannot be divorced from our fickle and fallible selves, it is "not unattended by doubt" (*tangatur dubitatione;* 3.2.17, OS 4:27.27)[2] and even unbelief (3.2.15, 17, 18, 21, 24, 37). To see that Doumergue's judgment only obscures this third consideration yields a problem for reflection that can have remarkable issue. Strictly speaking, Doumergue is still right. Calvin's admission of a measure of doubt and unbelief comes in the context of his explanation of what he means by stating that faith is a "firm and certain knowledge" (*firmam certamque cognitionem;* 3.2.7 passim, OS 4:16.33).

In Calvin's work there are two separate and distinct sources for the knowledge of God. One source—the Bible—is objective. It represents God as an object and yields information and knowledge about God and God's plan. The Bible informs us about God. It tells us what we otherwise could not know with certainty.[3]

---

2. English quotations from the *Institutes* are from the Battles translation (*Institutes of the Christian Religion,* trans. Ford Lewis Battles [Philadelphia: Westminster Press, 1960]). References are first to book, chapter, and paragraph (e.g., 1.1.1) and second to the critical Latin text, *Calvini opera selecta* (*OS*), noting volume, page, and line or lines (e.g., 4:27.8–12).

3. To be sure, the knowledge given in the Bible is not entirely straightforward. It was necessary, Calvin thought, for God to "accommodate" the language of the Bible to our dull capacity to understand.

Excursus: The controversy about whether or not Calvin thinks we can have a knowledge of God from nature is illuminative for our topic at one point. It is clear from book 1, chapters 3 and 5 of the *Institutes* that Calvin approved both ontology and cosmology as modes for knowing God. That the human mind is endowed by "natural instinct" (*naturali instinctu*) with "an awareness of divinity" (*divinitatis sensum*) is "beyond controversy" (*extra controversiam;* 1.3.1, OS 3:37.16–17). Moreover, the universe is so skillfully ordered that human beings are "compelled" (*cogantur;* 1.5.2, OS 3:45.4; cf. OS 3:46.11) to see God reflected in it as in a mirror (1.5.1). Actually it is astonishing how much Calvin thought one could know about God by these natural means. But, however much we are able to know about God from nature, this human capacity serves finally only to justify the condemna-

The other source for the knowledge of God in Calvin's thought is relational. It is relational in the sense that what one claims to know about the object (God) is bound to the subject (the self) such that the appropriate form of sentences includes reference both to the object and the subject. Its classic statement is Calvin's definition of faith: "Now we shall possess a right definition of faith if we call it a firm and certain knowledge of God's benevolence towards us, founded upon the truth of the freely given promise in Christ, both revealed in our minds and sealed upon our hearts through the Holy Spirit" (3.2.7, *OS* 4:16.31–35). The coupling of object and subject in this definition is consistent with the mode of speech Calvin began to use intensively at the beginning of book 3. It recalls, however, the language of the first two chapters of the *Institutes* where he mulls over the interconnection of the knowledge of God and knowledge of self in trying to determine a place to begin.

Almost every sentence in the first chapter of book 1 alludes both to ourselves and to God, moving first from the former to the latter (1.1.1) and then vice versa (1.1.2), declaring at the end that "the order of right teaching" requires that we begin with the knowledge of God (1.1.3). In the first paragraph: "No one can look upon himself without immediately turning his thought to the contemplation of God." And: "Our very poverty discloses the infinitude of benefits reposing in God." In the second paragraph: "It is certain that man never achieves a clear knowledge of himself unless he has first looked upon God's face." It appears that theology is at the same time anthropology and vice versa.

---

tion of humankind. Because we are corrupted we will always distort the truth with the result that this knowledge can never be "certain or solid or clear-cut" (*certum, vel solidum, vel distinctum;* 1.5.12, *OS* 3:57.24). It is this insistence that leads him to assert the need for God's own voice in scripture if we are to know anything about God with certitude.

What is most striking about these chapters on the knowledge of God from nature is the argumentation or lack of it. It should come as no surprise even to the most devoted disciple of Calvin that the positive material in book 1, chapters 3 and 5 is not included in books that collect the important texts in natural theology. Calvin either substitutes assertions for arguments, or his arguments are poorly developed and weak. The reason is not difficult to find, and it is instructive. Already in these early chapters he is assuming the truth of the Bible, and what he writes in book 1, chapters 3 and 5 is above all an exposition of Romans 1. That is, the quality of argument is less important to Calvin than its concurrence with scripture. The cogency of thought is assessed not by canons for cogency but by its end point. This procedure is far removed from Anselm's *credo ut intelligam. Intelligere,* if we mean by that term "to understand, to make sense of something in some way similar to the way people make sense of other things," plays no role in this exposition, as we shall see that it plays no role in Calvin's belief that the Bible is true in all its parts or in the doctrine of geminal predestination based on that belief.

This coupling of the knowledge of God and self pervades the rhetoric of the second chapter as well. "Now the knowledge of God, as I understand it, is that by which we not only conceive that there is a God but also grasp what befits us and is proper to his glory, in fine, what is to our advantage to know of him" (1.2.1, *OS* 3:34.6–9). It appears that all Christology is at the same time soteriology and vice versa. Indeed, a bare knowledge of God—we may say, a purely informational knowledge of God—is of no avail: "It will not suffice simply to hold that there is One whom all ought to honor and adore, unless we are also persuaded that he is the fountain of every good, and that we must seek nothing elsewhere than in Him" (1.2.1, *OS* 3:34.27–30). "What help is it in short to know a God with whom we have nothing to do?" (1.2.2, *OS* 3:35.16–17). This question explains the difference between the useless question, "What is God?" (*Quod sit Deus?*), and the theologically appropriate question, "Of what sort is God?" (*Qualis sit Deus?*) (1.2.2, *OS* 3:35.12, 13). That is: How is God to us? Thus the proper knowledge of God couples with piety, which Calvin understands as "that reverence joined with love of God which the knowledge of his benefits induces" (1.2.1, *OS* 3:35.4–5).

One would think that this kind of language should lead Calvin directly to his discussion of faith where the distance between God or Christ and human beings collapses by action of the Holy Spirit and where he deals with the salvific appropriation of God's act in Christ. However, he does not move immediately to the subject matter of book 3 because of what he considers the requirement of piety. The pious mind, we are told, not only "acknowledges" God as "Lord" and "Father" but also "deems it meet and right to observe his authority [*imperium*] in all things" (1.2.2, *OS* 3:36.18–19), and he asserts "that no drop will be found either of wisdom and light, or of righteousness or power or rectitude or of genuine truth, which does not flow from him, and of which he is not the cause" (1.2.1, *OS* 3:34.34–37). The principle of biblical authority intervenes, but we must observe that all religious parties in sixteenth-century Europe assumed that the Bible is a true account of God and of God's acts in the world. Like the others, Calvin never questioned this assumption though he tried to use the Bible more strictly and in a more limiting way than most in his day and before.

The Bible as the repository of truth about God introduces a different mode of the knowledge of God and a different kind of rhetoric. Now we are dealing with what is true without respect to its appropriation. It is what even the demons know (James 2:19). To be sure, this knowledge limits us to God's deeds and plan, not granting humankind a knowledge of the essence of God, but it is nonetheless a knowledge that one can, so to speak, look at (that is, observe outside of its relation to oneself), and any connection with "us," as Calvin most often uses that personal pronoun, is only by inference or by application.

Coherence and Incoherence in the Sources for the Knowledge of God

In trying to establish the biblical source for the knowledge of God, Calvin raises severe problems for the modern reader that in almost all cases would not have bothered the sixteenth-century reader.

The less severe problem is, one might say, aesthetic, though it is not without substance. As an explanation of the certainty of the knowledge of God in the Bible, Calvin refers to the internal testimony of the Holy Spirit. In the sixth chapter of the first book, after the opening discussion of where to begin and after asserting the availability but, finally, the unreliability of the natural knowledge of God, he claims that a certain knowledge of God requires that it come directly from God and that it be free of any human element. We have this source in scripture. "Then we may perceive how necessary was such written proof of the heavenly doctrine, that it should neither perish through forgetfulness nor vanish through error nor be corrupted through the audacity of men" (1.6.3, *OS* 3:63.18–20). As a confirmation of this divine source Calvin points in chapter 7 to the Holy Spirit as the author and confirmer of scripture.

Here is the aesthetic problem. Given the careful ordering of material in the *Institutes,* one must observe that the introduction of the Holy Spirit at this place is a disturbance of good order. The structure of the *Institutes* is clear. By one way of viewing it, it sets forth the twofold knowledge of God (*duplex cognitio Dei*), first God the Creator (book 1) and then God the Redeemer (books 2–4). From this view of the structure the doctrine of the Holy Spirit belongs under the overarching doctrine of God the Redeemer. By another way of viewing it, the *Institutes* follows the structure of the Apostles' Creed. Accordingly, book 1 treats God the Creator; book 2, Christ the Redeemer; book 3, the Holy

Spirit; and book 4, the church. Again, a discussion of the Holy Spirit in book 1 seems misplaced, an incoherent "glip" in the work's ordering of material.

This aesthetic problem, to be sure, is partially resolved if one views the first nine chapters not as properly a part of book 1 but as prolegomena in which Calvin sets forth his mode of proceeding and his source. That explanation has cogency, but it alters the structure Calvin himself provided.

More troublesome is the circular argument Calvin constructed for the activity of the Spirit in order to establish in scripture a source for the knowledge of God that is beyond all doubt. First the Spirit speaks through the writers of the Bible, and then it testifies to us internally that it has done so. Calvin acknowledges that this claim is beyond reason. He thought one could be certain only if no human element were involved. "The testimony of the Spirit is more excellent than all reason [omni ratione praestantias esse]. For as God alone is a fit witness of himself in his Word, so also the Word will not find acceptance [reperiet] in men's hearts before it is sealed by the inward testimony of the Spirit. The same Spirit, therefore, who has spoken through the mouths of the prophets must penetrate into our hearts to persuade [ut persuadeat] us that they faithfully proclaimed what had been divinely commended" (1.7.4, OS 3:70.1–8). The circle is tight, and it is arbitrary. As such, it is incoherent, that is, without argument that one who does not accept the premise can understand.

The doctrine is thoroughly formal: we are presented with what is necessary in order for scripture to be an infallible source. The Bible is not the writers' work but God's through the Holy Spirit; if we receive it as such it is not our perceptiveness but the Holy Spirit telling us that it is so. Calvin's position is clear, but by any current standards for argument, it is incoherent.

It is not that Calvin does not know the tough questions. As a matter of fact, he takes note of them: "Who can convince us that these writings came from God? Who can assure us that Scripture has come down whole and intact even to our very day? Who can persuade us to receive one book in reverence but to exclude another...?" (1.7.1, OS 3:65.24; 66.1). But he can only dismiss these questions; he cannot answer them. Nor should we think he deals with them in chapter 8, which is entitled "So Far as Human Reason Goes, Sufficiently Firm Proofs Are at Hand to

Establish the Credibility of Scripture." The "proofs" are circular, spurious, and determined by the conclusion that is known in advance. Calvin admits at the end that "of themselves" they "are not strong enough to provide a firm faith" (1.8.13, OS 3:81.20–21). He notes this not because he knows the arguments are weak but because certainty would be endangered if any element of human reason, any impulse of *intelligere* were admitted into the arena. *Intelligere* is the arena of discussion; "firm faith" is possible only when "reverence for Scripture" has been lifted "beyond the realm of controversy" (1.8.13, OS 3:81.22). The acceptance of scripture as a certain source for the knowledge of God, as Calvin takes it, is an arbitrary and thus incoherent act that Calvin removes from the human will or intellect by attributing it to the Holy Spirit. However acceptable that view may have been in the sixteenth century, it is difficult to see how it can be other than deeply troublesome in the twentieth, at least with twentieth-century persons who have something of a global perspective and a critical consciousness.

The language Calvin uses to develop his position is thoroughly consistent. Scripture, because it is the product of God through the Holy Spirit, calls for a response of obedience, assent, and docility. By this he means accepting scripture as true without question, taking upon oneself the demeanor of a child who learns from its parents what is right and true without comprehending why. The truth is given from the outside, and however much Calvin may emphasize that the testimony of the Spirit is internal and however firmly one might come to accept it as truth, it is difficult to see how this appropriation can contribute to human integrity insofar as integrity is related to coherence. But then, when Calvin proposes being an "integer" as the primal and, by implication, the salvific condition, he is writing about relational knowledge (1.2.1, OS 3:34.13–17).

What Calvin writes about the Holy Spirit in chapter 7 of book 1 is mixed in its valence. On the one side he can state that scripture "seriously affects us only when it is sealed upon our hearts through the Spirit" (1.7.5, OS 3:70.21–22). This language seems appropriate to the Spirit, but it is difficult to put together with terms, on the other side, such as "subdue" and "compel" (1.7.4, OS 3:69.23–24). These latter words correspond better to the objective character of the knowledge that is given; they do not cohere with the phrases "the secret testimony of the Spirit" (*arcano testimonio Spiritus*; 1.7.4, OS 3:69.11) and "the inward testimony of the Spirit" (*interiore Spiritus testimonio;* 1.7.4, OS 3:70.4–5). The difficulties mount.

The concentrated discussion in book 3, chapter 1, and in the ensuing material contains no such difficulties regarding the relational source for the knowledge of God. The activity of the Holy Spirit in that connection is discussed in its appropriate place (book 3). Moreover, it is not presented in an arbitrary and circular way but in coherence with the determination of life in the one who has faith. In addition, the language describing the activity and effects of the Spirit is what one would expect to go with the phrase "the secret working of the Spirit" (*arcano testimonium Spiritu;* 3.1 [chapter heading], OS 4:1.6–7). Overall there emerges a possibility for understanding (*intelligere*) that carries a good part of the discussion throughout the better part of book 3.

It should, therefore, come as no surprise that the terms "docility," "obedience," and "assent" and the kinds of sentences that go with them do not appear in this discussion of the Spirit and what it elicits. Just as docility as an effect of the Spirit seems arbitrary, mechanical, and incoherent, pointing us to what should be learned, so the terms Calvin uses to describe the activity of the Spirit in book 3, chapter 1 point us to what is descriptive of faith and thus coherent. That is, they bespeak a transformation of the self that corresponds to a pervasively effective response in the subject to the object such that one can see both why one speaks about the object in the way set forth and why one's life takes on the character that is described. In considering this "principal work of the Holy Spirit" (*fides praecipium est eius opus;* 3.1.4, OS 4:5.14; *proprium munus,* 3.1.4, OS 4:6.3; *opus eius peculiare,* 3.2.39, OS 4:49.36), we are in an entirely different arena of thought and language.

The terms Calvin uses with and for the Holy Spirit in book 3, chapter 1 are the verbs "to enjoy," "to unite effectually," "to quicken," "to nourish," "to taste," "to assure," "to make us fruitful," "to cleanse," "to purify," "to restore," "to inflame," and "to breathe divine life into us" and the nouns "sanctifier," "spirit of adoption," "guarantee and seal," "water," "oil," "anointing," "fire," and "spring." Calvin takes these terms from scripture, but he uses them here not to teach what one must learn and assent to but to show the appropriate description of that power by which the distance between God and us that still pertains in objective knowledge is overcome and Christ becomes ours. By implication the verbal tense shifts from past to present and the verbal mood from imperative to indicative. Now the talk is not about what has been written but about what is the case in the life of faith; nor is it about what one should or must know but about what one knows and is.

The 1960 translation of the *Institutes* by Ford Lewis Battles has rightly become the standard English version. It is fluent and remarkably free of errors. There is, however, a mistake in translation that is pertinent to the present point. Battles rendered the beginning of book 3, chapter 1 as follows: "We must now examine this question. How do we receive those benefits which the Father bestowed on his only begotten Son—not for Christ's own private use, but that he might enrich poor and needy men? First, we must understand that as long as Christ remains outside of us [i.e., objective to us], and we are separated from him, all that he has suffered and done for the salvation of the human race remains useless and of no value for us." And then the critical sentence: "Therefore, to share with us what he has received from the Father, *he had* to become ours and dwell within us" (emphasis added). The Latin for the last clause is *nostrum fieri et in nobis habitare opportet* (*OS* 4:1.14). By rendering *opportet* in the past tense Battles causes us to think of an event that is over and done with, an "event" objective to us by which Christ became identified with humanity in general. "It was necessary"; "Christ had to become...." *Opportet*, however, is in the present tense (and was rightly rendered in both the Allen and the Beveridge translations): "It is necessary"; "Christ must become...." Calvin is not speaking here simply of what happened in the past and thus is outside of us. On the contrary, he is speaking of what must happen now, of what must happen and does happen at any time, if salvation, the new creation of the self as an integer, takes place.[4]

There is a mystery here, but it is quite different from the mystery, if that is the right word, in the production and preservation by God of a book containing the true information about God's plan. Faith as the conviction of God's benevolence toward us is a mystery in the sense that

---

4. Cf. 1.2.1 where Calvin describes Adam's original state as being integral (*si integer stetisset Adam* [Battles translates *integer* here as "upright"]; *OS* 3:334.17). Note the relation of the Latin *integer* (unit, whole) to the Greek root *so* (unit, whole), as in *sodzein* (to save, to make whole), *soter* (savior, the one who makes whole), and *soteria* (salvation, wholeness). The salvation that, according to Calvin, becomes effectual in this collapse of the distance between subject and object is therefore not primarily an expectation of eternal life in heaven but a present reality, and meditation on the future life is an accompaniment that calls for brief treatment after he has discussed most of the effects of faith here and now.

one cannot attribute it to an ordinary cause without violating the nature of the event itself. One is speaking of a response to the proclamation of Christ that turns one outward from oneself and constitutes thereby such a radical determination of one's life that it would violate what one understands to have happened to attribute it to oneself or to any other cause within the world. The spontaneous response is gratitude that requires for its syntactical completion a prepositional phrase beginning with "to." We are grateful to God. The voice of the verb changes from active to passive, which requires for its syntactical completion a prepositional phrase beginning with "by." We have been illumined and made new by the Holy Spirit. The mystery of the object remains, but the coupling of object and subject with its accompanying language is descriptive in a way that can be understood. It is coherent. Calvin himself does not explicitly call attention to this coherence, but it is recognizable in his discussion and language in those two first chapters of book 3.

This descriptive coherence with the predominance of the indicative mode of the verbs prevails in the chapters that follow. In them Calvin tracks the effects of the relation to Christ in the life of the believer. At two points he is explicit about the coherence of what he wants to say. First, at the beginning of chapter 3: "Even though we have taught in part how faith possesses Christ, and how through it we enjoy his benefits, this would still remain obscure if we did not add an explanation of the effects we feel" (3.3.1, *OS*, 4:55.2–5). The verb "to feel" (*sentire*) should not be confused with sentimentality; it refers to what happens in the human being who is determined by faith. The indicative mode (not what we *should* feel) and the present tense (not simply what Christ *did*) are telling. One is inclined to say there is no authority operating here at all. Calvin is simply describing what happens. The logic of the human self in relation makes it persuasive. Second, later in chapter 3 he emphasizes that these effects are not derivative from faith; they are not inferences or subsequent steps. Rather they are immediately given with faith. He is describing the new creature, showing how the person determined by faith lives. "We do not imagine," he writes, "some space of time" between the occurrence of faith and its effects (3.3.2, *OS* 4:56.21–23). Again, he makes no appeal to an authority that might direct him toward what he should say.

He expresses his logic materially in the first subject he introduces after the chapter on faith. In the third chapter he deals with repentance, and he explains why. "Surely no one can embrace the grace of the gospel without betaking himself from the errors of his past life into the right way, and applying his whole effort to the practice of repentance" (3.3.1, *OS* 4:55.20–23). That is, anything else is unthinkable, incoherent.

So one is repentant because the new life in which one is turned outward from the self carries with it the memory of a life turned in upon itself and the consciousness of the residual power of that self-centeredness (chaps. 6–7). Because the new life is a being turned outward from the self, it is a life that is and wants to be lived for others and in denial of the self, bearing the cross, as it were (chap. 8). All of this, the new determination of life and its effects, is summarized in the doctrine of justification by faith (chaps. 11–19). The one who is thus justified and related in gratitude to God will speak the truth to God. That is, that person will pray (chap. 20). The elements fit together comprehensibly.

Even the polemics in these chapters fit the overall coherence and resist impulses to interject arbitrary appeals to authority. He objects to the scholastic doctrine of penance because those who teach it "are wonderfully silent concerning the inward renewal of the mind, which bears with it the correction of life" (3.4.1, *OS* 4:85.31–86.1). He objects to the scholastic insistence on satisfactions, the practice of indulgences, and the doctrine of purgatory, referring to them as "superstitions" (*superstitiones;* 3.5.10, *OS* 4:146.5). By that term he means something comparable to what we mean: a claim that a particular result follows from a particular act with no coherent connection between the cause and the effect.

In his discussion of justification he attacks Osiander and, once again, the scholastics. The basis for these criticisms is the same in both instances. He objects to Osiander because he transformed the doctrine of justification into a metaphysical theory. "In this whole disputation the noun 'righteousness' and the verb 'to justify' are extended in two directions; so that to be justified is not only to be reconciled to God through free pardon [i.e., relational] but also to be made righteous, and righteousness is not a free imputation but the holiness and uprightness that the gift of God dwelling in us inspires. Secondly, he [Osiander] sharply states that Christ himself is our righteousness, not insofar as he by expiating sins as Priest appeased the Father on our behalf, but as he is eternal God and life" (3.11.6, *OS* 4:187.9–16). Calvin's problem with this theory is that it objectifies the matter and thereby distorts justification for human beings. "We do not, therefore, contemplate [*speculamur*] him

outside ourselves from afar in order that his righteousness may be im-
puted to us but because we put on Christ and are engrafted into his
body—in short, because he deigns to make us one with him" (3.11.10,
OS 4:191.31–34).

Calvin's objection to the scholastics on this issue focuses on their having construed justification as a legal transaction. According to them, one
begins by "accepting grace" (3.14.12, OS 4:231.11–12, 16–17), and then
one's works coupled with forgiveness supplemented by works of su-
pererogation maintain the righteousness that has been granted. Again,
this legal construal objectifies what Calvin thinks can only be understood in relational terms. Only when the self is determined in relation
to the object, Christ, does one's life become characterized by gratitude
and self-denial with the consequence that all grounds for boasting are
undermined.

In this last sentence we see the coherent connections in the doctrine
of faith. Calvin resisted every attempt he knew that threatened to break
the human relational logic of what he saw. The coherence is available
not only to those who are determined by this faith but also universally.
That is, even those not determined by faith, once they understand what
the subject matter is and how it is properly expressed, can see that the
parts fit together and constitute a coherent whole.

Coherence and Incoherence
in Calvin's Doctrine of Election

The descriptive coherence of book 3 seems to break apart in chapter 21
when Calvin introduces the doctrine of eternal election, the predestination of some to salvation and others to damnation. With only a nod
or two to the doctrine of faith—and these only by application, not with
immediacy—Calvin sets forth the doctrine objectively as an explanation
of what is the case with God. Once again the discussion is pervasively
determined by what stands written in the Bible, and the proper human
response is docility and assent.

With his remarkable knowledge of scripture Calvin ranges with agil-
ity over the Bible in presenting the evidence for double predestination,
but it is clear that Romans 9–11, Ephesians 1:4-5, and accounts in the
Hebrew scriptures of the election of Israel are the driving force. He

was certain that the doctrine of double election was given with the acceptance of the authority of scripture.

He does make a gesture toward putting together an argument in support of the justice of God in eternal election. His gesture, however, is no more successful here than it was in the discussions of the natural knowledge of God, the divinity of scripture, fallen humanity and human responsibility, or divine providence. He argues that God's justice demands that God condemn and that God's mercy leads God to save, an argument no more persuasive in the *Institutes* than in the texts of many church fathers who employed it earlier. His ship of thought on this point runs aground on the principle of equity. He cannot explain why neither justice nor mercy is universal in application; nor can he propose a principle of selection that makes sense. The consideration of equity, by the way, was well-known to Calvin, and he gave it an essential place in his exposition of both ecclesiastical and civil government (see 4.20.16).

In passing Calvin acknowledges that some "falsely and wickedly" (3.23.11, OS 4:405.1) have raised the question of equity, but he responds lamely by insisting that because election has no ground in the person there is no partiality on God's side (3.23.10) and by returning to the references to justice and mercy, quoting Augustine (3.23.11). Implicitly he acknowledges that his gesture toward argument is inconclusive. In treating election, he notes, we are dealing with a mystery that is beyond all understanding. The divine plan is "incomprehensible" (3.23.1, OS 4:394.10).

Scripture dictates proper conclusions. Justice is determined not by what we think the word means but by what God does, rationality not by what makes sense to us but by what God says, and wisdom not by any human criteria but by what God thinks. God's acting, speaking, and thinking are reliably found in one place only: Holy Scripture. As he puts it succinctly, "We forget to speak well when we cease to speak with God" (3.23.5, OS 4:399.27–28). To challenge that principle is to evoke from Calvin a pass at an argument and then the question from Romans 9:20, "O homo, tu quis es qui disceptes cum Deo?" ("Who are you, O man, to argue with God?"; 3.23.4, OS 4:397.30–31 passim).

The other side of the observation that Calvin's reasoning is determined in advance by the information given in scripture is that scripture, in this doctrine as in others, plays a limiting role. Calvin insists that we can say only so much as scripture says and no more. With Lactantius,

Calvin thought we should remember that the word "religion" derives etymologically from the verb *relegere,* to keep within limits (1.12.1, *OS* 3:105.18–21). Given this premise Calvin is both consistent and moderate. Because what is given in scripture is not an intelligible concept he does not treat it as such. He refuses to use this datum of knowledge, as certain as it is, as a base from which to draw inferences. He knows that to do so is a natural human tendency, but precisely because of that fact he considers the tendency in this case one of Satan's most convenient tools. Human reason must stay clear of this doctrine. We are to accept what we are told...and do nothing with it!

Indeed, we are to do nothing with it. The doctrine of geminal predestination in Calvin is finally a purely formal doctrine, that is, a doctrine with no discernible application for human beings in the present. The only applications we can know are those documented in scripture (e.g., "Jacob I loved, and Esau I hated"). Election is God's secret and incomprehensible plan.

It is the great fault of later Calvinists that they overlooked this formal character of double election as Calvin presented it and began to explore ways by which one could determine whether or not, in God's eternal and immutable plan, one belonged to the saved. Calvin allows for nothing of the sort. Does a person show every sign of reprobation? That person may yet be converted, and even should that person die without showing any signs of change, her or his inner life is unknowable to us. Does a person show every sign of having been elected to life? That person may be like the grain of wheat that fell on shallow soil, and even should that person die before withering like the rootless plant, no one of us can know his or her inner life. ("Far be it from us to say that judgment belongs to the clay, not to the potter!" [3.23.14, *OS* 4:409.17; cf. 3.23.13; 24.1].) As presented in scripture, as a datum of knowledge to be accepted without understanding, the doctrine is purely formal.

As such Calvin recognizes that it is "horrible" (3.23.7, *OS* 4:401.28) and a "deep abyss" (3.24.3, *OS* 4:413.22–23). We can say it is horrible in more ways than Calvin thought. As assented to and defended by Calvin the doctrine is destructive of human understanding. Given a claim that a statement or set of statements is true the human mind will inevitably raise questions and attempt to explore the implications. To criticize Calvin for trying to stifle that impulse would violate the historical sense. In his age human understanding was undermined in various spheres by appeal to what a person of today can only judge to be arbitrary authority. Future generations may find arbitrary acceptance of authorities in us, but the principle has broken down for those who in any substantive way have been affected by developments since the Enlightenment. For those persons, one must say that Calvin's assault on human reason is horrible indeed.

That horror subsides in five paragraphs near the end of Calvin's treatment of divine election. There we are presented with quite a different picture of the doctrine. These paragraphs deserve our careful attention.

Calvin is aware that his representation of geminal predestination as what I have called a "formal" doctrine—that is, a doctrine with no determinable application at all—will almost invariably evoke severe unrest in the faithful. It is not enough, therefore, to rest with a purely objective exposition that glorifies God and evokes awe and docility in human beings. He must deal as well with the problem of certainty among the faithful.

He alludes immediately to the theme with which he began book 3, the illumination of the Spirit. "This inner call," he writes, "is a pledge of salvation that cannot deceive us" ("Interior igitur haec vocatio pignus est salutis quod fallere non potest"; 3.24.2, *OS* 4:412.31–32). This is an astonishing shift from the impossibility of human judgment he has just elaborated in detail. Certainty about a salvific relation to God is to be found only in the occurrence of faith, the cause of which the believer can attribute only to the secret testimony of the Holy Spirit. That sentence is nothing more than a restatement in somewhat different order of Calvin's definition of faith. Faith is "a firm and certain knowledge of God's benevolence towards us, founded upon the truth of the freely given promise in Christ, both revealed to our minds and sealed upon our hearts through the Holy Spirit." The question of certainty about oneself has already been answered.

No other answer should be sought. As a matter of fact Calvin feels obliged to enter the most serious warning against any attempt to raise the question about oneself out of the exposition to which he has just devoted more than three chapters! "We should indeed seek assurance of it [our salvific relation to God] from this [the evocation of faith in us by the Holy Spirit]: for if we try to penetrate to God's eternal ordination, that deep abyss will swallow us up" ("Certitudo quidem eius inde nobis petenda, quia si ad aeternam Dei ordinationem penetrare tentemus, profunda illa abyssus nos ingurgitabit"; 3.24.3, *OS* 4:413.21–23). Some people, he says, "to make sure about God's plan . . . perversely yearn to flit above the clouds" (3.24.3, *OS* 4:414.1–3). Note the relational form of the sentence: *nobis,* to us.

The warning continues: "Satan has no more grievous or dangerous temptation to dishearten believers [strong language for Calvin] than when he unsettles them with doubt about their election, while at the same time he arouses them with a wicked desire to seek it outside the way. I call it 'seeking outside the way' when mere man attempts to break into the inner recesses of divine wisdom, and tries to penetrate even to highest eternity, in order to find out what decision has been made concerning himself at God's judgment seat. For then he casts himself into the depths of a bottomless whirlpool to be swallowed up; then he tangles himself in immeasurable and inextricable snares; then he buries himself in an abyss of sightless darkness" (3.24.4, *OS* 4:414.10–19). Indeed! Given a piece of knowledge as certain, one will assume it is applicable and explore it. Calvin feels impelled to urge his readers not even to think about the fact of double predestination . . . lest they imperil their salvation.

Certainty is found only in being related to Christ, through whom the good things of God are extended toward us. Because these good things are received in faith as a gift we may appropriately "feel" (*sentiat*) that the benefits result from our "secret adoption" (*ex recondita illa adoptione;* 3.24.4, *OS* 4:415.4–6). That is "as much as we may lawfully know of his plan" (3.24.4, *OS* 4:415.8–10). Finally: "It is his will that we be content with his promises, and not inquire elsewhere whether he will be disposed to hear us" (3.24.5, *OS* 4:416.33–34). The shift in Calvin's mode of thought and speech in these five paragraphs is all the more astonishing when we recall that the certainty of faith, to which he now refers, is not unattended by doubt and unbelief!

A further astonishment over the shift in these paragraphs comes with the recognition that in them Calvin does not allude to double predestination at all. The certainty of faith carries with it no knowledge of another person and no inference about damnation. With confidence based on trust in God one can only count oneself an object of God's benevolence and, receiving that benevolence as a life-determining gift, hazard to think—avoiding, however, any ground for boasting—that one has been freely elected, a mystery that not only must but can be left to God.

There is in these paragraphs a coherence, a "human" logic, that renders what Calvin writes here comprehensible. It is the same coherence as the relational knowledge presented in 1.1.2 and in the first twenty chapters of book 3. Making this observation specifically with respect to election, distinguishing these few pages from the many Calvin devotes to the subject, illuminates a special difficulty Calvin faced and could not easily solve with his view of biblical authority. I refer to the difficulty of bringing a stop to all speech and thought once the twofold divine election has been affirmed. On the one hand, as long as the doctrine is represented as objective truth, the mind cannot bring itself to a halt, and it will do so only by cajoling and thus by denial of that impulse to understand, *intelligere*, that is a part of being human. On the other hand, when the starting point is the grateful consciousness of being put in relation to God, the utterance of the term "election" (single election spoken in a whisper) stands at the end rather than at the beginning of the series, and the mind as well as the mouth come to rest.

Conclusion

I have two brief and somewhat speculative points to make in conclusion.

The first has to do with Calvin's well-known aversion to superstition. So far as I know no one has yet made a careful and thorough study of Calvin's use of this word to see if he uses it consistently, to see therefore if the many things he objects to as superstition constitute a coherent set. Should anyone undertake such a study the question that should be explored is: Does Calvin consistently understand by superstition the acceptance of something as true or the adoption of certain practices on grounds that are incoherent with what is accepted or adopted? This is the ordinary meaning of superstition, as in the belief that breaking a mirror causes seven years of bad luck. It is clear that this genre of beliefs and practices is what Calvin had in mind some of the time when he spiced his polemics with the charge of "superstition."

If, however, that ordinary meaning is the key to Calvin's usage we must observe that he violated his proscription of superstition at one most critical point with immense consequences for his theology. I refer to his support of the objective knowledge of God in scripture. The structure he erects in explanation of the certainty of this knowledge and its identity with the canon is incoherent. Historically it is difficult to fault Calvin on this point. His explanation of scriptural authority and of how human beings become certain of it may be unique, but he certainly cannot be distinguished from most of his contemporaries and forebears in affirming the certain truth of scripture in all its parts. Moreover, as we have observed, scripture to Calvin was a limiting principle. We know only what it tells us and no more. In this insistence he was more moderate and modest than a good many of his contemporaries, forebears, and followers. Even so, from the perspective of our own time his (and the others') claims for the divine origin of the canon and for the divine confirmation of its divine origin must strike one as arbitrary, provincial, and incoherent, in short, as superstitious.

The second point has to do with the consequences for the doctrine of election in Calvin if the legalistic principle of biblical authority is removed. One can say only that given Calvin's warnings against saying any more about the secret recesses of God's mind (so to speak, the "abscondite" side of God) than we must by virtue of having been informed by God, all talk about double predestination would disappear. It would not be replaced by an alternate explanation of human destiny but rather by a pervasive agnosticism. If "we cease to speak well when we cease to speak with God," then in the absence of a declaration from God we can only keep silent.

Finally, one must, of course, raise the question whether the loss of biblical authority, as Calvin viewed it, would not mean the collapse of everything he said. To that question an affirmative answer could be given only if one held that the beginning of faith is an arbitrary and incomprehensible assent. No one who understands what Calvin meant by the faith that makes people new can hold to that view.

SEVEN

Randall C. Zachman

The Awareness of Divinity and the Knowledge of God in the Theology of Calvin and Schleiermacher

One of the major issues regarding the possible continuity between the theological tradition of the Reformation and nineteenth-century liberal theology, and especially between Calvin and Schleiermacher, has to do with the role of experience or consciousness in theology, especially the role of a "point of contact" (*Anknuepfungspunkt*) in the human person for the revelation of the grace of God, be it the awareness of divinity as in Calvin or the feeling of absolute dependence as in Schleiermacher. The classic argument between Brunner and Barth over this issue, which subsequently divided the dialectical theology movement itself, had more to do with the relationship between Calvin and Schleiermacher than it did with the role of Roman Catholic "natural theology" in Protestant theology.[1] And yet most of the discussion of this issue in the theology of Calvin has taken place without specific reference to the theology of Schleiermacher, for whom the *Anknuepfungspunkt* was a necessary and technical concept. In this essay I will seek to reconsider and clarify the continuities and discontinuities between the meaning of the sense of divinity (*sensus divinitatis*) in the theology of John Calvin and the feeling

---

1. See "Nature and Grace" by Emil Brunner and the reply, "No!" by Karl Barth, in *Natural Theology*, trans. Peter Fraenkel (London: Geoffrey Bles/The Centenary Press, 1946).

of absolute dependence (*das schlechthinnigen Abhangigkeitsgefuehl*), or the God-consciousness (*das Gottesbewusstsein*), in the theology of Friedrich Schleiermacher.

The formal similarities between the awareness of divinity and the feeling of absolute dependence are themselves striking and worthy of note. First, the linguistic similarities should be noted. The word *sensus* in Latin carries the same meaning as *Gefuehl* and *Bewusstsein* do in German: that is, awareness or consciousness. To speak of an awareness of divinity is quite similar to speaking of a feeling of absolute dependence that is our immediate consciousness of God. Second, the methodological similarities are striking. Both Calvin and Schleiermacher begin their *summa pietatis* with a discussion of the awareness of divinity or the feeling of absolute dependence, and claim that it is both the anthropological root of all religion and the source of the anthropological impossibility of atheism.[2] Both limit their discussion of God to human awareness of God, and close off any discussion of God in God's self (*Inst.* 1.10.2; *CF,* p. 52). Both make the awareness of God the beginning point of all right teaching about God.[3] Hence it would seem that for both theologians, the awareness of divinity or the awareness of absolute dependence provides the anthropological starting point for all right teaching of Christian piety, becoming for both the point of contact for all that follows. It is this formal similarity that may have led many scholars virtually to equate the sense of divinity in Calvin with the feeling of absolute dependence in Schleiermacher.[4]

In spite of these formal similarities, however, still greater material dissimilarities exist between Calvin and Schleiermacher, arising primarily from what each theologian considers to be the true revelation of God. For Calvin, the awareness of divinity should direct humanity to the self-revelation of God in the universe (clarified by scripture and the Spirit) and in Christ (illumined by the Spirit), for there alone do we learn who

---

2. John Calvin, *Institutes of the Christian Religion,* trans. Ford Lewis Battles (Philadelphia: Westminster Press, 1960), 1.3–4 (hereafter this work will be referred to as *Inst.*); Friedrich Schleiermacher, *The Christian Faith,* ed. H. R. Mackintosh and J. S. Stewart (Philadelphia: Fortress Press, 1976), propositions 1–6 (hereafter this work will be referred to as *CF*).

3. Calvin, commentary on Acts 17:24, in *The Acts of the Apostles,* trans. John W. Fraser (Grand Rapids, Mich.: Wm. B. Eerdmans, 1973), 2:112; *CF,* p. 247.

4. Edward A. Dowey, Jr., *The Knowledge of God in Calvin's Theology* (New York: Columbia University Press, 1952), 55, where Dowey agrees with this equation previously made by Reinhold Seeburg and Rudolph Otto.

God is and what God is like: the infinite, spiritual, and triune fountain of every good thing. Piety is possible only when one moves from the sense of divinity to the certain knowledge of God acquired from the self-revelation of God (*Inst.* 1.2.1). For Schleiermacher, the feeling of absolute dependence is the sole revelation of God, and the self-identical essence of all piety (*CF*, proposition 4). Our experience of the universe and of Jesus may stimulate and strengthen the feeling of absolute dependence, but they reveal nothing about God not already contained in that feeling. Piety is always and only a modification of feeling or awareness, and never becomes a form of knowing. This contrast can best be illustrated by first setting forth the way in which the God-consciousness functions as an *Anknuepfungspunkt* in Schleiermacher's theology, and then using that as a point of comparison for our treatment of Calvin.

The Feeling of Absolute Dependence in Schleiermacher

According to Schleiermacher, the awareness of absolute dependence is not only the starting point upon which all revelation of God must build, but is also the sum total of all that God reveals to us about God's self. Even the concept or term "God" is a description, given to us in an original way, of the "Whence" of the feeling of absolute dependence (*CF*, pp. 17–18). The original revelation of God to the God-consciousness is not only the point of contact for all further revelation of God, but is the sum total of all revelation of God. Our experience of the universe and of the Redeemer reveals to us nothing more about God than that God is the one on whom we are immediately aware of being absolutely dependent.

The doctrines concerning creation and preservation do not explicate a revelation of God that is not already contained in the feeling of absolute dependence. Rather, they describe that feeling, as abstracted from the Christian self-consciousness, in terms of what it tells us about the relationship of God to the world. In particular, Schleiermacher is concerned to demonstrate that our knowledge of the world as a complete and self-enclosed system of nature coincides with and summons forth the awareness of absolute dependence, with which it then combines (*CF*, pp. 173–74). According to Schleiermacher, the ability of the awareness of God to combine with the consciousness of the world-system makes it possible to be a pious Christian in the age of Newton. The awareness of God is not excluded but is rather stimulated by the scientific understanding of the world. But the knowledge of the world does not reveal anything to us about God not already found in the feeling of absolute dependence. In particular, this means that the doctrine of creation must be understood solely in light of the doctrine of preservation (*CF,* 142–49).

However, the *possibility* that the awareness of God may combine with any and every objective consciousness does not mean that this *in fact* happens. In the state of sin the God-consciousness is hindered from combining as easily and often as it should with the objective consciousness (*CF,* p. 54). The awareness of absolute dependence remains, however, even in the most extreme form of sin, though it is hindered from combining with many determinations of the sensible self-consciousness.

In the fellowship founded by Jesus Christ, the person experiences the overcoming of such obstruction by the enhancement of the ability of the awareness of God to combine with the consciousness of the world. This means that the consciousness of the Christian contains both the awareness of sin and the simultaneous awareness that sin has been and is being overcome in the fellowship of Jesus Christ (*CF,* p. 356). The historical condition for the possibility of this experience of the overcoming of sin by the strengthening of the awareness of God is the appearance in history of a human being who had a perfect awareness of absolute dependence, namely Jesus of Nazareth. "The Redeemer, then, is like all men in virtue of the identity of human nature, but distinguished from them all by the constant potency of His God-consciousness, which was a veritable existence of God in Him" (*CF,* proposition 94, p. 385). In Jesus Christ, therefore, the ideal (*Urbild*) with regard to the God-consciousness has become historical (*CF,* proposition 93). It should be noted, however, that Jesus reveals nothing to us about *God* that is not already contained in the awareness of absolute dependence present in *all* people, even though that awareness only reaches perfection in Jesus.

The community of the Redeemer is therefore the place where the perfect God-consciousness of Jesus is communicated to his followers, through the testimony and preaching of the community informed by the picture of Christ in the community (*CF,* p. 69). However, the God-consciousness of Jesus would not redeem us unless we already had the awareness of absolute dependence within us, constituting our original perfection, which the communicated God-consciousness of Christ strengthens. The very first movement of our conversion from the fellow-ship of sin to the fellowship of the Redeemer depends on the presence of the God-consciousness as its point of contact: "This [i.e., our original perfection] is what we regard as the first point of attachment [*Anknuep-fungspunkt*] for every operation of divine grace" (*CF*, p. 495). The grace of Jesus Christ does not, therefore, *reveal* to the feeling of absolute dependence something of which it is essentially unaware, but rather *strengthens* the awareness of absolute dependence itself. Even the dis-tinction between nature and grace has solely to do with the level of the strengthening of the God-consciousness, and not with a self-revelation of God that surpasses the awareness of absolute dependence (*CF*, p. 495).

We are now in a position to understand the way in which Schleier-macher uses the awareness of absolute dependence as a point of contact in his theology. The awareness of absolute dependence not only forms the original revelation of God to human nature, but is also the sum total of all revelation of God, in light of both our encounter with the pre-serving activity of God in the world and our experience of the perfect God-consciousness of the Redeemer in the Christian fellowship. The most that can be said about God on the basis of the awareness of ab-solute dependence is that God is the eternal cause of the whole nexus of finite causality, including both the system of nature and the appear-ance of the Redeemer in history, for only the divine causality is able to explain (*erklaeren*) the awareness of absolute dependence.[5]

However, the very causality that comprehends the whole of the nat-ural and historical order of the world prevents God from entering *into* the world, either by the Son of God becoming incarnate in Jesus of Nazareth or by the Holy Spirit revealing Christ to our hearts and minds through the preaching of the gospel. Any coming of God into the world would annihilate the awareness of absolute dependence, and so is fun-damentally excluded from consideration. It is therefore not surprising that the doctrine of the Trinity, meant to bear witness to the coming of God into the world, "is not an immediate utterance concerning the

---

5. "All the divine attributes to be dealt with in Christian Dogmatics must somehow go back to the divine causality, since they are only meant to explain [*erklaeren*] the feeling of absolute dependence" (*CF*, p. 198). The same causality is applied by Schleiermacher to his discussion of election. "Indeed, whenever we form an inclusive idea of natural causality as a self-enclosed whole and go back to its basis in the divine causality, we can reach no ground of determination for the latter except the divine good-pleasure" (*CF*, p. 555).

Christian self-consciousness," for it constitutes a direct violation of the
feeling of absolute dependence and the eternal causality of God that explains it (*CF,* proposition 170, p. 738). As we shall see, it is in this doctrine
of God, grounded in the awareness of absolute dependence, that constitutes the basis for the material differences between Schleiermacher and
Calvin.

The Awareness of Divinity in Calvin

According to Calvin, all human beings have been endowed by God with
an awareness of divinity. "There is within the human mind, and indeed by natural instinct, an awareness of divinity [*Divinitatis sensum*].
This we take to be beyond controversy" (*Inst.* 1.3.1). The awareness of
divinity makes all people unavoidably aware that there is a God who
created them, and whom they ought therefore to worship and obey.
"Since, therefore, men one and all perceive that there is a God and that
he is their Maker, they are condemned by their own testimony because
they have failed to honor him and to consecrate their lives to his will"
(*Inst.* 1.3.1). The sense of divinity consists in the awareness that there is
some God who ought to be worshiped, adored, and obeyed. As such,
the awareness of divinity is also called by Calvin the seed of religion
(*semen religionis*), which gives rise to all of the religious life of humanity
(*Inst.* 1.3.1–2).

   Scholars have long associated the awareness of divinity closely with
the conscience, especially on the basis of Calvin's statement in his commentary on John: "There are two main parts in that light which yet
remains in corrupt nature. Some seed of religion is sown in all: and also,
the distinction between good and evil is engraven in their consciences."[6]
However, scholars have also consistently *distinguished* the awareness of
divinity from the conscience, thereby making its content mysterious and
elusive and making it difficult to distinguish Calvin's position on the
awareness of divinity from those of Schleiermacher or Otto.[7] In contrast
to such a reading, Calvin's understanding of the awareness of divinity

---

6. Calvin, commentary on John 1:5, in *The Gospel according to St. John,* trans. T. H. L.
Parker (Grand Rapids, Mich.: Wm. B. Eerdmans, 1961), 1:12.
7. "It is significant that Reinhold Seeburg says that the 'essence of religion' for Calvin is
the same as for Schleiermacher, 'absolute dependence'—and further that Otto chooses this
same quality in Schleiermacher to illustrate the first element of the numinous 'creaturely

is best understood as being a function of the conscience itself. The conscience, according to Calvin, is the awareness of divine judgment (*sensus divini iudicii*) (*Inst.* 3.19.15), and it is the awareness of divine judgment that is itself the sense of divinity (*sensus divinitatis*), making us aware that there is a Maker who must be worshiped, honored, and obeyed. This connection is suggested in the *Institutes* when Calvin refutes the practical atheism of those like Caligula who attempt to deny the awareness of divinity within them; Calvin argues that the terrors of conscience that these persons experience are signs that even they are aware of what they seek to deny—that is, God (*Inst.* 1.3.2–3). Calvin also describes atheism as the denial not of the being but of the judgment of God, thereby further suggesting the identification of the awareness of divinity with the awareness of divine judgment (*Inst.* 1.4.2). However, in a sermon that he preached on Job, Calvin explicitly identifies the conscience as the awareness of divinity:

> God, then, has let men run wild, and they are completely plunged into perdition; yet there has remained some seed in their hearts, and they have been convicted, so that they cannot say, "We do not know what God is, we have no religion whatever"; since no one can be exempt from it; for *it has remained engraven on the conscience* that the world was not formed by itself; that there was some heavenly majesty to which we must be subject.[8]

The knowledge that there is some God (*esse aliquod Deum*) who created us, and whom we ought therefore to reverence, worship, and obey, is engraved on the consciences of all and forms the awareness of divinity in all people. The awareness of divinity (*sensus divinitatis*) is therefore not without specific content, but is itself the awareness of divine judgment (*sensus divini iudicii*) in the consciences of all people. The conscience as the awareness of divine judgment makes us aware that there is some God who ought to be worshiped and obeyed.

The awareness of divinity may make us aware that there is some God who is to be worshiped, but it does not tell us who the true God is or what God's nature is and therefore cannot tell us how the true God is

---

feeling.' We are here in the area of the truly numinous in Calvin's theology" (Dowey, *The Knowledge of God in Calvin's Theology*, 55).

8. Calvin, sermon on Job 32:1-3, in *Sermons from Job*, trans. Leroy Nixon (Grand Rapids, Mich.: Baker Book House, 1979), 219–20, C.O. 35:5–6; emphasis added.

to be worshiped. "For the true rule of godliness is precisely this, to have a clear grasp of who the God is, whom we worship."[9] The conscience as the seed of religion therefore holds before all people the duty and obligation to know with certainty who the true God is and what God's nature is like, in order that they might be instructed as to how God is to be truly worshiped (*Inst.* 1.3.1). The conscience cannot reveal to us who the true God is or what God is like, but rather turns us outside of ourselves to seek to know God where God has revealed God's self.

The inability of the conscience, as the awareness of divinity, to bring us to the true and certain knowledge of God becomes especially clear when we consider Calvin's understanding of the knowledge of God. According to Calvin, the true God is our Father and our Lord. As our Father, God is the fountain of every good thing (*fons omnium bonorum*), who not only wills to give us all good things in creation but who ultimately wills to give God's self to us in the Son through the Holy Spirit. As our Lord, God is the holy and righteous One who wills that our lives be brought into conformity with God's nature so that we might be the image of God by mirroring God's holiness in our lives, and thereby be united with God in eternal life.

The knowledge that God is our Father, the fountain of every good, gives birth to piety, in which we trust in, pray to, and give thanks to God for all good things (*Inst.* 1.2.1). The knowledge that our Father is the Lord, the holy and righteous One, gives birth to religion, in which we seek to conform our lives to God's will and nature, out of gratitude for all that the Father gives us (*Inst.* 1.2.2). Although Calvin insists that God cannot be known as Father without being reverenced as Lord, he clearly gives priority to knowing God as Father, the fountain of every good, without which there can be no willing reverence and fear of God.

It is now clear why the conscience as the awareness of divinity cannot reveal the true God to humanity. The conscience is aware of only the *judgment* of God, and hence only can know God as Judge. The conscience can therefore neither know God as Father *nor reverence God as Lord* on the basis of its own awareness of divinity, but must rather seek the knowledge of the Father where God has revealed God's self. "Moreover, although our mind cannot apprehend God without rendering some honor to him, it will not suffice simply to hold that there is One

---

9. Calvin, commentary on Acts 17:24, in *The Acts of the Apostles*, 2:112, C.O. 49:410.

whom all ought to honor and adore, unless we are also persuaded that he is the fountain of every good, and that we must seek nothing elsewhere than in him" (*Inst.* 1.2.1). God as Father and Lord is simply not the content of the *sensus divinitatis* rooted in the *sensus divini iudicii,* no matter how much this awareness is strengthened by God. If the conscience is to know with certainty that its Maker and Judge is also its Father and Lord, then it must be instructed by a revelation of God given *to* the sense of divinity that cannot in principle arise *from* it.

The awareness that there is some God is not the original revelation of God for Calvin, as the God-consciousness is for Schleiermacher: rather, the original revelation of God is given in the works of God in the universe (*Inst.* 1.5.1). God's essence cannot be known, but God does reveal God's self in works, and it is from them that we can come to know God. In particular, the works of God set forth and depict the powers (*virtutes*) of God, such as wisdom, goodness, mercy, righteousness, power, rectitude, and truth. "We must therefore admit in God's individual works—but especially in them as a whole—that God's powers are actually represented as in a painting" (*Inst.* 1.5.10). God represents these powers in God's works in order to bring us to an awareness (*sensus*) of those powers, which would then form the basis of the true knowledge of God in piety and religion. "For the Lord manifests himself by his powers, the force of which we feel within ourselves and the benefits of which we enjoy" (*Inst.* 1.5.9). The awareness of divinity in the conscience can make us aware of only the judgment of God. In order to become aware of the other powers of God—that is, wisdom, goodness, truth, mercy, righteousness, and power—and to know God as the source of these powers, we must turn to the powers of God depicted in the works of God in the universe, which reveal the true God to us.

Our awareness of the powers of God should first lead us to see those powers set forth in God's preservation and governance of ourselves and the world, and then to see God as the source and fountain of all the powers depicted in creation. The powers of God depicted in the works of creation thereby reveal that the God who governs and sustains the universe is our Lord and Father, the fountain of every good. In this way, the awareness that there is some God who ought to be worshiped should lead to the awareness of the powers of God set forth in creation, by which we come to know God as our Lord and Father (*Inst.* 1.2.1). The knowledge that God is our Father should in particular arise from our awareness of the powers of God that are evident in our human nature, "because by adorning us with such great excellence he testifies that he is our Father" (*Inst.* 1.5.3).

The awareness of the powers of God should teach us piety, which knows God as the fountain of every good. "For this sense of the powers of God (*Virtutum Dei sensus*) is for us a fit teacher of piety, from which religion is born" (*Inst.* 1.2.1). The knowledge of the true God in piety in turn gives birth to religion, which represents the true worship of the true God. If God our Father created us, and governs us by divine wisdom, righteousness, mercy, and judgment, then it follows that we should obey our Creator in all things: and yet we are to render our service not out of fear of judgment, but out of gratitude, in the knowledge that our Lord is our Father. Because piety knows that God is the fountain of every good, we know that we ought to trust God, to pray to God for every good thing that we lack, and to thank God for every good thing that we receive. Thus, just as piety arises out of the awareness of the powers of God, so also does religion arise out of piety: for from piety we learn that the Father wishes to be worshiped by trust, prayer, thanksgiving, and willing obedience.

Had Adam remained upright, the awareness of divinity in the conscience would have led us to seek to know God through the awareness of the powers of God depicted in the universe, which would give rise to piety and religion. "The natural order was that the frame of the universe should be the school in which we were to learn piety, and from it pass over to eternal life and perfect felicity" (*Inst.* 2.6.1). However, our fall into sin has subjected our minds to blindness and ingratitude, so that we no longer attain piety by means of our awareness of the powers of God. Our blindness is manifested by the fact that we do not seek God where God has revealed God's self, but rather seek to know God's essence directly, and judge it according to the capacity of our carnal minds. "They do not therefore apprehend God as he offers himself, but imagine him as they have fashioned him in their own presumption" (*Inst.* 1.4.1). Our blindness therefore leads us to form for ourselves carnal conceptions of deity. Our ingratitude is manifested by the way we refuse to acknowledge that the Father is the source of all the good that we receive. "For nothing is more preposterous than to enjoy the very remarkable gifts that attest the divine nature within us, yet to overlook the Author who gives them to us at our asking" (*Inst.* 1.5.6).

Our blindness and ingratitude therefore prevent our encounter with the works of God in creation from attaining to a true awareness of the powers of God (*sensus virtutum Dei*) and instead lead to a taste of divinity (*gustus divinitatis*) based on our vitiated encounter with the self-revelation of God in the universe. "For at the same time as we have enjoyed a slight taste of the divine from contemplation of the universe, having neglected the true God, we raise up in his stead dreams and specters of our own brains, and attribute to anything else than the true source the praise of righteousness, wisdom, goodness, and power" (*Inst.* 1.5.15). The taste of divinity we attain from contemplating the universe does not lead to the true and certain knowledge of God, but at worst leads to the carnal worship of idols, and at best leads to the uncertain worship of an unknown god.

Because the conscience as the awareness of divinity holds before us the duty to know *with certainty* who the true God is whom we are to worship, it will convict us when we do not attain to such certain knowledge. "However much they boast, yet because they continue to be perplexed in their consciences, they are bound to be held convicted by their own judgement of themselves."[10] Nor will the conscience as the awareness of divine judgment allow us to plead ignorance as an excuse for not knowing God; for it knows that our inability to know God is rooted in our sinful blindness and ingratitude. "And, indeed, we are not allowed thus to pretend ignorance without our conscience itself always convicting us of both baseness and ingratitude" (*Inst.* 1.5.15). At the very best, therefore, the awareness of divinity in the conscience leads to the taste of divinity from the powers of God in the universe, on the basis of which we form carnal conceptions of God and offer superstitious worship to idols.

As bad as superstition is, however, it is not the worst form of ungodliness. The limit of impiety is reached by the malicious, who not only fail to know God as Father but also deny that God is Judge. They do this by denying the judgments of God in the world and the sense of the judgment of God in the conscience. The malicious may concede the existence of a god, but because they deny that god any judgment their theoretical theism is in fact practical atheism. "Accordingly, whoever heedlessly indulges himself, his fear of heavenly judgment extinguished, denies that

---

10. Calvin, commentary on Acts 17:22, in *The Acts of the Apostles*, 2:110, C.O. 48:408–9.

there is a God" (*Inst.* 1.4.2). The malicious not only fail to come to an awareness of the powers of God in the universe, but they also deny the awareness of divinity in their consciences.

Although both the superstitious and the malicious are ungodly, Calvin still considers superstition to be the lesser of two evils, because it does not deny the awareness of divinity, that there is some God whom all ought to worship and obey. "If, however, we were to choose one of two evils, superstition is more tolerable than the gross impiety which obliterates every thought of a God [*deitatis sensum*]."[11] The clear implication of this distinction between the superstitious and the malicious is that the former, by retaining the awareness that there is a God who ought to be worshiped, can be better instructed about the truth of God, whereas the malicious are beyond all instruction.

This is why the awareness of divinity is the irreducible starting point in the order of right teaching about the true religion. "If anyone wishes to discuss religion in general this will be the first point, that there is some deity to whom worship is due from men."[12] It is for this reason that Calvin begins the *Institutes* with the claim that there is an awareness of divinity implanted by God in the consciences of all people; for only when his readers concede that there is some God whom we ought to worship can Calvin instruct them in the true religion. Such instruction (*institutio*) must then proceed to the true and certain knowledge of God the Creator as properly set forth in God's works by the testimony of scripture and the inner witness of the Holy Spirit, in order to distinguish the true God from the throng of idols (*Inst.* 1.6–9). The scriptural teaching about the infinite and spiritual essence of God annihilates all carnal gods by revealing what the true God is like; and the scriptural testimony to the works of creation and providence sets forth the true God as our Father and Lord, thereby instructing us in who the true God is (*Inst.* 1.10–18).

However, we cannot know the Creator as Father and Lord because we are no longer children of God, but are rather sinners who are destitute of every good thing that God bestowed upon us in Adam (*Inst.* 2.1–4). For this reason, God must again reveal God's self as Father and Lord to sinful creatures, not by the powers of God set forth

---

11. Calvin, commentary on Habakkuk 2:20, in *Commentaries on the Twelve Minor Prophets*, trans. John Owen (Grand Rapids, Mich.: Baker Book House, 1981), 4:129, C.O. 43:561–62.

12. Calvin, commentary on Acts 17:24, in *The Acts of the Apostles*, 2:112, C.O. 48:410.

in the universe—for they also reveal the curse of God upon us as sinners—but by the powers of God set forth in the human creature, Jesus Christ. In Jesus Christ, the eternal Son of the Father has become human in order to take every evil from us so that he might give us every good thing found in him, ultimately consisting in eternal life in union with God. Apart from this wonderful exchange, no one can know God as Father and reverence God as Lord. And no one can know and accept Jesus Christ as the fountain of every good apart from the gospel illuminated by the Holy Spirit, which engrafts us into Jesus Christ and makes us participants in him and all his blessings.

Comparison of Schleiermacher and Calvin

We are now in a position to understand the similarities and differences between Schleiermacher's use of the awareness of absolute dependence and Calvin's use of the awareness of divinity. The major similarity is that both Schleiermacher and Calvin root all religion—Christian as well as non-Christian—in the human awareness of divinity. They both also make the awareness of divinity in the minds of all the starting point in their instruction on true religion, thereby refuting atheism and establishing the existence of God on the basis of a form of human consciousness. They both refuse to discuss the true religion with anyone who refuses to concede this basic starting point.

The fundamental difference between them lies in what each considers to be the true revelation of God. For Schleiermacher, the immediate awareness that we are absolutely dependent is not only the starting point of instruction, but is also equivalent with the only revelation of God. Our consciousness of the world and of the Redeemer does not reveal to the feeling of absolute dependence anything of which it is in principle ignorant, but rather stimulates and strengthens that feeling. Even the statement that "God is love" (John 4:14) is understood in terms of this heightening of the God-consciousness: "Divine love does not reveal itself unequivocally except where it shows a generally protective and fostering care of what is highest and most specific in man, namely, his God-consciousness" (*CF*, p. 728). The most that can be said about God is that God is the eternal omnicausality underlying the system of nature and human history, including the appearance of the Redeemer (*CF*, p. 555).

For Calvin, in contrast, the awareness of divinity is the sense of divine judgment in the conscience. It can and should make us aware that there is some God who ought to be worshiped, and can hold before us the duty to know that God in certainty and truth, but it is categorically unable to reveal the true God to us. The true God is our Father and Lord, the fountain of every good, whose holiness we are to reflect in our lives so that we might be joined with God in eternal life. We can come to know God only by our awareness of the powers of God as they are depicted in the works of God in the universe. These powers include not only judgment but also wisdom, mercy, justice, righteousness, truth, and goodness. Our sinful inability to know God from our awareness of the powers of God means that God must reveal God's self to us from heaven, first by bearing witness to God's works in creation by the testimony of scripture and the Holy Spirit, and then by the gospel of Jesus Christ the prophet, who bears witness to himself as the fountain of every good set forth by the Father for sinners, illuminated to our minds and consciences by the Holy Spirit. No matter how much the awareness of divinity is strengthened, apart from Jesus Christ it can tell us only that God is our condemning Judge, and not our Father and Lord. For Calvin, if God does not come into the world as the Son in Jesus Christ and as the Holy Spirit through the gospel, then we cannot know God as Father (*Inst.* 3.2.1).

The material difference between Schleiermacher and Calvin on the role of the awareness of God in their theology is ultimately rooted in the difference in their understanding of who the true God is. For Schleiermacher, God represents the "Whence" of the feeling of absolute dependence, whose eternal omnicausality underlies the whole of the natural system but who remains outside of, yet essentially related to, that system (*CF*, p. 217). God can only be the "Whence" of the feeling of absolute dependence if there is a world that is absolutely dependent upon God (*CF*, p. 728). The pious consciousness therefore excludes thinking about God as the eternal relation of Father, Son, and Holy Spirit (*CF*, p. 739), while the feeling of absolute dependence excludes any coming of God into the world.

For Calvin, God is the Father even apart from God's relationship to the world, as the fountain of divinity in eternal relation to the

Son and Holy Spirit (*Inst.* 1.13.25). God graciously created the world in order that humanity might be brought into relation with God as their Father in the Son through the Holy Spirit, and mercifully sent the Son to become human and die so that God might again be Father of God's sinful human creatures (*Inst.* 2.6.1). God is not simply the eternal omnicausality of the world, but is the Father who wills to give us every good thing, and ultimately himself, through the crucifixion of his eternal Son and the bestowal of the Holy Spirit. The experience of piety corresponds completely with the testimony of scripture in setting forth God as Father through the Son his image and the Holy Spirit his power.[13] We do not know God when we are aware that there is some God who ought to be worshiped, but only when we know that God as our Father and Lord, who not only freely gives us all good things in creation, but gives us God's self in the Son through the Holy Spirit, so that we might live with God in eternal life.[14]

Conclusion

The task of historical theology consists of seeking to understand the unity of the theology of those theologians who precede and accompany us—to learn, as much as is humanly possible, to think as they thought—and to locate their place within the Christian tradition by means of their relationship with those who precede and follow them. In this essay, I have sought to illuminate the theology of Calvin and Schleiermacher with regard to the sense of divinity or consciousness of God, in order to discern the possible continuities and discontinuities between them. I have shown that there is considerable continuity at a formal level in the way in which the awareness of divinity functions as an irreducible first step in the order of right teaching and as an existential refutation of atheism. However, I have also elucidated a profound discontinuity at the material level between Calvin's and Schleiermacher's understand-

---

13. Calvin, *Instruction et Confession de Foy*, in *Opera Selecta* 1.396; *Instruction in Faith (1537)*, trans. Paul T. Fuhrmann (Philadelphia: Westminster Press, 1949), 46.

14. "If the Lord will share his glory, power, and righteousness with the elect—nay, will give himself to be enjoyed by them and, what is more excellent, will somehow make them to become one with himself, let us remember that every sort of happiness is included under this benefit" (*Inst.* 3.25.10).

ings of the self-revelation and nature of the one true God. Ultimately, it is the doctrine of the Trinity, attesting the self-revealing and self-bestowing love of the Father in the Son through the Holy Spirit, that distinguishes Calvin from Schleiermacher.

Part 3

Essays on
Nineteenth-Century Themes

EIGHT

Claude Welch

The Perils of Trying to Tell the Whole Story: Historiographical Issues in the Study of Nineteenth-Century Theology

The past quarter-century has seen a striking revival of interest in the development of theology in the nineteenth century, as shown both by a host of special studies and by attempts to survey the century as a whole. It is the latter efforts that will be my immediate interest here, partly because of the relative paucity of such works in the preceding half-century, but especially because of the struggle for inclusiveness and the kinds of historiographical questions these works raise: questions of the purposes of the study, of temporal, geographical, and confessional scope, of the perspective of the authors, of the selection of texts, and particularly of the role of social context in theological articulations.

I shall focus initially, therefore, on seven ambitious works, now in English, that are of special relevance: my own two volumes on Protestant thought in the nineteenth century; a three-volume work, edited by Ninian Smart et al., on religious thought in the West in the nineteenth century; Hendrikus Berkhof's survey of two hundred years of theology; Jaroslav Pelikan's fifth and final volume in his history of Christian doctrine; James Livingston's text on Christian thought from the Enlightenment to Vatican II; Gerald McCool's study of Catholic theology in the nineteenth century; and T. M. Schoof's survey of Catholic thought from 1800 to 1970.[1]

In some ways comparable to these volumes are two broad-ranging collections of sources, with introductions that provide useful overall interpretation. These are works by B. M. G. Reardon and Joseph Fitzer, the latter being especially valuable for the Catholic scene.[2]

Further, though still prescinding largely from the many works on individual figures, we may identify several special studies that either illumine or illustrate the historiographical problems: B. M. G. Reardon on British theology from Coleridge to Gore; Owen Chadwick on secularization in the nineteenth century; B. A. Gerrish on the Reformed tradition; Thomas F. O'Meara on early nineteenth-century Roman Catholic thought, and on German Catholic theology from 1860 to 1914; Marilyn Massey on the political meaning of Strauss's *Life of Jesus;* David S. Pacini on the "cunning" of modern religious thought; R. W. Franklin on some Catholic developments in Germany, France, and England; Bruce H. Kirmmse on Kierkegaard in the nineteenth-century Danish setting; and Charles D. Cashdollar on positivism and Protestant thought in Britain and America.[3]

---

1. Claude Welch, *Protestant Thought in the Nineteenth Century,* 2 vols. (New Haven: Yale University Press, 1972, 1985). Ninian Smart et al., eds., *Nineteenth Century Religious Thought in the West,* 3 vols. (Cambridge: Cambridge University Press, 1985). Hendrikus Berkhof, *Two Hundred Years of Theology: Report of a Personal Journey,* trans. John Vriend (Grand Rapids, Mich.: Wm. B. Eerdmans Publishing Co., 1989); originally published as *200 Jahre Theologie: Ein Reisebericht* (Neukirchen-Vluyn: Neukirchener Verlag, 1985). Jaroslav Pelikan, *Christian Doctrine and Modern Culture (since 1700),* vol. 5 of *The Christian Tradition: A History of the Development of Doctrine* (Chicago: University of Chicago Press, 1989). James C. Livingston, *Modern Christian Thought: From the Enlightenment to Vatican II* (New York: Macmillan Co., 1971). Gerald A. McCool, *Catholic Theology in the Nineteenth Century: The Quest for a Unitary Method* (New York: Seabury Press, 1977); a revised edition (with more appropriate title) was published in 1989 as *Nineteenth-Century Scholasticism.* T. M. Schoof, *A Survey of Catholic Theology: 1800–1970,* trans. N. D. Smith (New York: Paulist/Newman Press, 1970); originally published as *Aggiornamento* (Baarn, Holland: Het Wereldvenster, 1970). See also Claude Welch, "The Problem of a History of Nineteenth-Century Theology—Welch Reconsidered," *Journal of Religion* 70, no. 4 (October 1990): 606–17, an essay on which I have drawn at several points in the present discussion.

2. Bernard M. G. Reardon, *Religious Thought in the Nineteenth Century: Illustrated from Writers of the Period* (Cambridge: Cambridge University Press, 1966). Joseph Fitzer, ed., *Romance and the Rock: Nineteenth-Century Catholics on Faith and Reason* (Minneapolis: Fortress Press, 1989).

3. Bernard M. G. Reardon, *From Coleridge to Gore: A Century of Religious Thought in Britain* (London: Longman Group Ltd., 1971). Owen Chadwick, *The Secularization of the European Mind in the Nineteenth Century* (Cambridge: Cambridge University Press, 1975). B. A.

I

Even a casual inspection of the most inclusive studies noted above reveals some striking commonalities as well as differences.

1. All of these writers, in most cases explicitly, find motivation for their work in the special dependence of theology or religious thought in the twentieth century on developments in the previous century. For example, I contended that the nineteenth century "remains most important for us to understand because of the way in which it has shaped our most disturbing questions";[4] hence it cannot be coincidental that the problems and themes on which we concentrate for the nineteenth century should be primary in the theological agenda of the last half of the twentieth century. Berkhof's central concern is to trace a dialectic of thinkers' efforts "to build a bridge between the gospel and their secularized cultural environment," a problem that he finds distinctively different after Kant and continuing into the present.[5] Fitzer avers that "to understand present-day Catholicism we must study Catholicism in the century stretching from 1800 up to 1914."[6]

Although the point is less widely represented in the individual essays in the volumes of Smart et al., the editors begin by calling attention to the fact that each of the currently debated issues in religious thought "was either initially raised or significantly recast during the nineteenth century" and find there "those thinkers who in the main have determined the direction of modern religious thought in the West"; thus "twentieth century religious thought is very much the child of the nineteenth."[7] Pelikan, though like Karl Barth tending to emphasize the

---

Gerrish, *Tradition and the Modern World: Reformed Theology in the Nineteenth Century* (Chicago: University of Chicago Press, 1978). Thomas F. O'Meara, *Romantic Idealism and Roman Catholicism: Schelling and the Theologians* (Notre Dame, Ind.: University of Notre Dame Press, 1982); and idem, *Church and Culture: German Catholic Theology, 1860–1914* (Notre Dame, Ind.: University of Notre Dame Press, 1991). Marilyn Chapin Massey, *Christ Unmasked: The Meaning of "The Life of Jesus" in German Politics* (Chapel Hill: University of North Carolina Press, 1983). David S. Pacini, *The Cunning of Modern Religious Thought* (Philadelphia: Fortress Press, 1987). R. W. Franklin, *Nineteenth-Century Churches: The History of a New Catholicism in Württemberg, England, and France* (New York: Garland Publishing, 1987). Bruce H. Kirmmse, *Kierkegaard in Golden Age Denmark* (Bloomington: Indiana University Press, 1990). Charles D. Cashdollar, *The Transformation of Theology, 1830–1890: Positivism and Protestant Thought in Britain and America* (Princeton, N.J.: Princeton University Press, 1989).

    4. Welch, *Protestant Thought*, 1:17.
    5. See Berkhof, *Two Hundred Years*, xi passim.
    6. Fitzer, *Romance*, 3; see Schoof, *Survey*, 12, 16.
    7. Smart et al., *Nineteenth Century*, 1:1, 2.

continuity of the eighteenth and nineteenth centuries more than the others, also finds the time from 1700 to the present to be an intelligible and continuous period of "modern theology."[8] What we see here, I think, with the waning of the dialectical theology after the 1950s and in the wake of the Second Vatican Council, is almost a rediscovery of the nineteenth century and a new appreciation of its continuity with the twentieth.

2. In contrast to the conventional late nineteenth-century and early twentieth-century writing on the nineteenth century,[9] these studies that seek to cover the whole century represent a new style, which is intentionally and explicitly transnational in scope. At the outset of my own survey of the Protestant scene, I argued strongly that we ought at least to ask whether there were common problems and common directions, even important unities, in the Protestant community as a whole;[10] and I sought in the structure of the work to show that, as regards the North Atlantic theological world, the answer to this question was affirmative. This contention has been widely welcomed in subsequent discussion. The essays in the volumes edited by Smart et al. range broadly over the European, British, and American scenes. Berkhof, while focusing especially on the Continent (including a distinctive report on the Netherlands), finds it necessary to take serious and sympathetic account of British and American thinkers. Pelikan casts the widest net of all, interpreting the whole modern Christian world (except Asia and Africa) and blending the discussion of Roman Catholic, Protestant, and Eastern Orthodox doctrine.

Livingston's excellent selection of materials illustrating Christian thought from the Enlightenment to Vatican II is similarly transnational. Fitzer's work on nineteenth-century Catholic thought incorporates continental, British, and American sources. Franklin's impressive study of the emergence of new styles in Catholicism brings together Württemberg (the Tübingen school), England (the Oxford movement), and France (the Benedictine liturgical revival). Gerrish treats both German and American figures in the Reformed tradition in the nineteenth century. And even Reardon's 1966 collection of sources, though Reardon

---

8. Pelikan, *Christian Tradition*, 5:vii–ix.
9. See esp. Welch, *Protestant Thought*, 1:8–14.
10. Ibid., 1:14–18.

believes the best mode of interpretation is by way of national groups, includes British and American as well as European thinkers.

3. With the exception of Pelikan's work, which seeks explicitly to deal with the *church's doctrine* (i.e., "what the church of Jesus Christ believes, teaches, and confesses on the basis of the word of God"),[11] all these inclusive works (and most of the special studies) are oriented mainly to individual thinkers, to what Pelikan calls the soloists rather than the chorus. Partial exceptions to this pattern might be claimed for some of the essays in volume 3 of the Smart series, for the structure of my own second volume, and for Franklin's study. In all of these cases, though, the emphasis is on the distinctive or the novel (the "cutting edge") rather than the commonplace or the routine.

This pattern raises the hermeneutical question in a different form than it takes, say, for the biblical texts, where the corpus has some generally recognized limits. For the historian of the nineteenth century faced with hundreds of texts, a primary question is: *What is* the text? or rather *Which* texts should be chosen? As part of his attempt to hear the chorus rather than only the theological soloists, Pelikan is most inclusive, drawing on liturgy, poetry, and music as ways in which the church's teaching and belief are expressed. But even among those who concentrate on the theologians, there are significant differences. For the most part, Smart's authors focus on the recognized great thinkers. Berkhof's work, and mine especially, seek to widen the scope to include a number of those who are infrequently referred to in the theological classroom, in the interest of offering a more fully illuminating vision of the century.

4. The almost complete absence of women from the discussions is noteworthy, and is an important illustration of the problem of deciding which are the texts to be interpreted. With the partial exception of Pelikan, the attention of the historians is directed mainly to the professional elite, and the theologians and church leaders of the nineteenth century were almost entirely male. But the authors do not even bother to take note of this fact, or to speak of the cultural and historical obstacles to women's writing and thinking, or to identify important texts from female authors, especially in the genre of the novel, that might be important in other ways than the writings of professional theologians

---

11. Pelikan, *Christian Tradition*, 1:1.

and philosophers who worked out of the particular social contexts of the theological and philosophical faculties.

II

Given these general similarities there are at the same time important differences that point to basic historiographical problems.

1. One is the question of temporal scope. Reardon, Smart, Fitzer, and I (also McCool, though with an epilogue on the twentieth century) focus strictly on the development from Kant or Schleiermacher, or the French Revolution, to the end of the century—that is, to the First World War. Berkhof and Schoof extend the story to the mid–twentieth century. Livingston seeks to include the whole period from the early Enlightenment to Vatican II. And Pelikan deals with the entire "modern" period, which he counts as extending from about 1700—a judgment not unlike that of self-styled postmodernists who define modernity as beginning with the Enlightenment and extending to some point in the twentieth century.

At one level, these differences do not represent significant historiographical disagreements, but only matters of convenience in the choice of starting and ending points. One has to begin somewhere and end somewhere, and every historian recognizes that all thinkers and movements have antecedents and that we always look at the nineteenth century from some standpoint in the twentieth and thus with a view to the consequences of the former century.

Yet at another level we do see here far-reaching conflicts of views. Is the development of theology in the nineteenth century to be considered as essentially a continuation of the eighteenth century (or even the Enlightenment as a whole), or are the new beginnings sufficiently distinct that a real turning point can be found at the end of the eighteenth century (with Kant, or the French Revolution, or Schleiermacher)?

The latter view is explicit in my work and in that of Berkhof and Fitzer (also McCool and Schoof), and it is at least implicit in the volumes edited by Smart et al. and in Reardon. The contrary view has classic expression in Karl Barth's history of nineteenth-century theology, in which over half the volume is devoted to the eighteenth-century "prehistory" and the supposed novelty of the nineteenth century is really to be understood as a continuation of Enlightenment ideas.[12] This judgment also seems to be reflected in Pelikan's work, where the "modern period in the history of Christian doctrine" (i.e., from 1700) is treated as a whole and defined "as the time when doctrines that had been assumed more than debated for most of Christian history were themselves called into question."[13] In both cases we have a largely negative judgment as to the distinctiveness of the nineteenth century. Barth sees it as continuing the wrongheaded anthropologizing that has now to be corrected, and Pelikan views it as a further time of threat to authentic Christian doctrine by forces of modern culture.

2. In relation to such questions, and perhaps underlying some of the disagreements, is the problem of the kind of historical theology, relative to interest, perspective, and subject matter, that is being pursued. None of these interpretations represents what might be called "theological history," or "theology of history," in which the story is told explicitly from the viewpoint of the historian's own theological commitments, whether with a view to showing how the past establishes the present view or with the purpose of pointing out the errors that need correction. Examples of that sort of history might be Augustine's *City of God* or some of the modern works that Karl Barth criticizes, like Schaeder's *Theocentrische Theologie,* Herrmann's *Geschichte der protestantischen Dogmatik,* Brunner's *Mysticism and the Word,* and even Troeltsch's essay reviewing a half-century of theology, where "the authors are not guiding us in a shared investigation of what the men of the past may be saying to us; rather the one who has already made his discovery, who has done with listening, directs us with vigorous gestures to the position where he is now standing (not to say, sitting!)."[14] The goal of this kind of history, we might say, is subsumed wholly under the interests of systematic or constructive theology.

It can be argued, of course, that despite his intentions the story Barth actually tells of the nineteenth century, as a continuing wrongheaded

---

12. Karl Barth, *Die protestantische Theologie im 19. Jahrhundert, ihre Vorgeschichte und ihre Geschichte* (Zürich: Evangelischer Verlag, 1956). A partial English version (eleven of the twenty-nine chapters) was issued by Alasdair MacIntyre and John McIntyre under the title *From Rousseau to Ritschl* (London: SCM Press, 1959). The full text was published as *Protestant Theology in the Nineteenth Century: Its Background and History* (Valley Forge, Pa.: Judson Press, 1973). Page references in footnotes are to the latter edition.

13. Pelikan, *Christian Tradition,* 5:viii.

14. See Barth, *Protestant Theology,* 20–21.

anthropologizing that has now to be corrected, has some of these characteristics. And aspects of this tendency, I believe, may be found in Pelikan's account. His effort at a history of Christian *doctrine,* as distinguished from theology, depends on his assurance that he knows what the church "teaches," rather than just what theologians assert. Yet the notion of what is taught by the church remains vague, except when we are dealing with dogmatic definitions, and Pelikan is unable to tell us clearly how to distinguish, from the eighteenth century on, between church teachings (or the voice of the chorus) and voices of theological soloists. Appeals to such symposia as *Foundations* (1912) or the collection *Fundamentals* (1910ff.), as well as to the Lambeth Quadrilateral (1888), but with the omission, for example, of *Essays and Reviews* (1860) and *Lux Mundi* (1889), do not help much. One is left with more than a suspicion, particularly from the kinds of sources Pelikan likes to cite, that his determining (though unacknowledged) commitment is to a quite conservative tradition, thus the emphasis on the reception given to ancient doctrines and the presumption of a unified "orthodoxy" whose crisis begins in the eighteenth century and continues in the nineteenth. (It may not be irrelevant that John Henry Newman, in the essay on development of doctrine, seems to have become Pelikan's primary mentor, rather than Adolf von Harnack, in the history of dogma.) It certainly cannot be charged that Pelikan is unfair to the data; on the contrary, he is scrupulously fair to the texts he chooses to cite. But as we shall see, the development of doctrine is not really set forth as a dialogue with culture.

"Historical theology," as represented in most of the works we have in view, is an enterprise no less "interested" than is a theology of history. It eschews historicism. The viability of the Christian theological enterprise is for these historians an important issue (though not necessarily a settled issue), hence the concern with how the past illumines and contributes to the present, with *why* a movement or thinker needs to be treated (thus, in the particular case we are considering, it involves the question of continuity/discontinuity of the nineteenth and twentieth centuries), and with the dialogue between a thinker or movement and a culture whose voices must be granted their own integrity. (One might suggest a parallel to the task of philosophical theology, as distinguished from systematic theology.)

To put it another way, the historical theologian stands in some sense within the community of faith/concern and wants to know what the past can teach us, but without the confidence of a theology of history in either the continuity or the success of the theological enterprise. There is an interest in theological construction, but it is not determinative of the historical investigation. The historian's theological and historical judgments must be openly acknowledged, so that they can be judged by the reader. Yet figures of the past must be fairly treated and allowed to speak for themselves, including those for whom the interpreter sees no current theological value. A classic instance of historical theology, then, is Ernst Troeltsch's history of Christian social teachings.

Among the recent histories we are considering, my own work and that of Fitzer are plainly of this sort (and implicitly also the works of Livingston, Reardon, and Schoof). Berkhof's intriguing study is an especially good example. He writes candidly from the standpoint of a theologian deeply concerned with the possibilities and problems of theology in the late twentieth century. With Kant as the point of departure, he orients the whole book to the dialogue of theology with its cultural environment, seeing the most inclusive and pervasive problem of the past two centuries as the question of gospel and culture, or theology in a secularized world, and thus tracing especially the theological efforts at mediation with changing cultural situations. But while as a theologian he wants to be committed to the validity of the gospel, he recognizes that the question of the *meaning* of the gospel is precisely the problem of the dialogue. Hence in asking at the end if the whole search means anything, he is not pessimistic, yet he is conscious that the dialectic will continue in ways we cannot now define.[15]

"History of theology" (or of religious thought) is a caption that is surely often used to refer to what I have here called historical theology. But we may also use it to denote another sort of enterprise—one that largely prescinds from the question of validity and that seeks to bracket any commitments of the interpreter. This stance may be illustrated by the three volumes edited by Smart et al. Even though the purposes and intentions of the authors of the twenty-seven individual essays vary widely, the stated task and subject matter of the collection, as suggested by the title, *Nineteenth Century Religious Thought in the West,* are not historical theology but rather a history of religious ideas or thinking about religion (and its critique) in the nineteenth century. "History of religious

---

15. Berkhof, *Two Hundred Years,* 308–12.

thought," as represented here, is a species of intellectual history or history of ideas, which can (in principle) be quite detached from theological commitments of the historian, though it may also represent other interests (e.g., those of a "historicist" program), and in the case of the Smart volumes the pattern of independent essays precludes the whole from having a really inclusive perspective.

3. A third major historiographical question raised by all these works is whether it is possible to write a history of *Christian* theology in the nineteenth century, or whether the histories of Catholic and Protestant theology must be done separately. With the exception of Pelikan, whose work embraces not only Roman Catholicism and Protestantism but also Eastern Orthodoxy, all the attempts to give an inclusive interpretation of the nineteenth century have been content to focus on either Protestant or Roman Catholic thought. Except for brief discussion of some Roman Catholic modernists in the second volume, my own work was restricted to the Protestant development. Berkhof similarly adheres to the Protestant scene, except for a page on Newman and a chapter on the Catholic "bridge" from the time of Blondel.[16] McCool, Schoof, and Fitzer deal only with Catholic thinkers and developments. To be sure, in the volumes edited by Smart et al., three of the chapters are devoted to the Catholic voices, including Newman, the Tübingen school, and Roman Catholic modernism (plus a chapter on Russian religious thought). But no attempt is made to integrate these discussions with the course of Protestant thought in the century (and it is of course a defect in the three volumes as a whole that there is no unified vision that holds together the essays by the individual authors). The books of Livingston and Reardon, especially the former, likewise include some important Catholic figures, but once again without setting their work in clear relation to the non-Catholic developments.

In no small part, the reasons for such restrictions have to do with the competence of the authors. One can write only about what one knows, and not many of us have the extraordinary breadth of knowledge and linguistic competence of a Pelikan. But substantive reasons have also been proffered. I felt at the outset that "the responses of Roman Catholic and Protestant thinkers [to the cultural influences from the French Revolution on] were sufficiently diverse ... that it would be artificial to try to

---

16. Ibid., 229–55; de Lubac and Rahner are the chief figures discussed.

combine them in a common scheme of interpretation."[17] The reactions of Protestants and Catholics in the nineteenth century to romanticism and German idealism, and the wrestlings with Darwin and the new "historical consciousness," seemed to rest on vastly different grounds and to take place on the opposite sides of high walls, by persons largely oblivious of each other's work, so that mutual neglect or polemic was the rule. The Protestant story seemed best susceptible to interpretation by reference to individual thinkers and their impact; Catholic theology, however, particularly given the increasing centralization in the century, had to be seen far more in terms of the voice of the church and authoritative pronouncements. Considerations of this sort seem to have been operative also in most of the other works on the nineteenth century (with the notable exception, again, of Pelikan's book, though that proceeds from a different perspective).

Now, however, particularly in view of the post–Vatican II situation and the appearance of significant Catholic reconsiderations of the nineteenth century, this separation of the Protestant and Catholic stories can be sharply questioned. I have suggested elsewhere that with the employment of a different kind of image for organizing the central theological themes or problems of the century, a primary image of concentric or overlapping circles rather than temporal or linear development, Catholic and Protestant theology in the nineteenth century can indeed be seen together.[18]

III

1. If one identifies the most inclusive and pervasive circle of concern for the nineteenth century as the problem of church and society, or Christianity and culture—that is, the problem of coming to terms with what Chadwick calls the secularization of the Western mind in the nineteenth century, with the post-Enlightenment secular reason, with bourgeois culture, and with developing industrial society—then it is clear that Protestant and Catholic theology can be placed within the same framework of analysis. I have suggested, and I still think not wrongly, that this problem of the relation of church and society comes especially to

17. Welch, *Protestant Thought*, 1:1n.
18. See Welch, "The Problem."

focus in the latter part of the century.[19] But it is surely present throughout the century—and is just as germane to Catholic as to Protestant
thinking, and as much to conservative as to liberal—all the way from
Schleiermacher's *Speeches* and Chateaubriand's *Genius of Christianity*
at the beginning of the century down to the work of Troeltsch and
Rauschenbusch and of the Catholic modernists and Leo XIII and Pius X
at the end of the century.

Significantly, both Berkhof and Pelikan organize their work around
this theme. But they do it in quite different ways, Berkhof by stressing mediation with philosophical views, Pelikan in terms of response
to a cultural critique whose lineaments, to the astonishment and bewilderment of the reader, are left almost entirely unspecified. And both
are far too narrow in the depiction of the culture to which response is
made. A more adequate analysis would have to take account, for example, of such matters as the following: (*a*) the early nineteenth-century
romanticist influences on both Catholic and Protestant thought; (*b*) the
revolt against the anticommunal, individualistic spirit that Franklin documents in Möhler, in Guéranger, and in the Oxford movement; (*c*) the
concerns with the relations of church and state, not only in the Catholic reaction to the French Revolution and Napoleon's reforms (e.g.,
in the developing ultramontanism), but also in German Protestantism
(in Schleiermacher's political activities and in the later, much different, Throne and Altar theme of Lutheranism), in Britain (in Coleridge's
idea of the clerisy and in the origins of the Oxford movement), and in
the radical American experiment with separation of church and state;
(*d*) the fortress mentality of Pius IX after 1848 and the mid–nineteenth-
century upsurge of conservatism and denominationalism in Protestant
theology; (*e*) the varying responses to Marx, as well as to Schopenhauer
and Nietzsche; (*ff*) the importance of Arnold and of British agnosticism; (*g*) the intricate relations of late nineteenth-century Protestant
liberalisms and the emergent Catholic modernism; (*h*) the responses to
socialism in the social encyclicals of Leo XIII and in the Protestant social
gospels in Switzerland, Britain, and America; and (*i*) the condemnation
of Catholic modernism and the growth of Protestant fundamentalism.
The list could be greatly extended, but it suggests interesting and viable
ways of viewing Catholic and Protestant thinking in the same context.

---

19. Welch, *Protestant Thought*, 1:6–7, 2:x.

2. Somewhat smaller in circumference than the preceding would be the circle of concerns with what I have called the possibility of theology,[20] or with the forms of mediation, particularly with philosophy, that lie at the heart of Berkhof's account. This is the problem of the restatement of the nature of the theological enterprise after the shocks to traditional theology from pietism and the Enlightenment. The historians of Catholic theology focus on a comparable problem, put mostly in the language of the relation of faith and reason—in the Tübingen school; in Günther, Froshammer, and Lamennais; in Newman; in Scheeben; in the growing dominance or revival of Thomism through Kleutgen, Vatican I, and Leo XIII; and in the modernist movement.

For the most part—with the exception of modernists like Tyrrell and perhaps some representatives of the Tübingen school—Roman Catholic thinkers did not have the same sense as the Protestants of having to make new beginnings. Yet the discussions of faith and reason reflect a kind of theologizing that is explicitly post-Enlightenment. And this focus in Catholic theology can be interestingly and productively related to the new theological starts in Schleiermacher, Hegel, and Coleridge; to the vast array of mediating theologians in mid–nineteenth-century Protestantism; to the development of "liberal theology" in Germany and America and of "liberal catholicism" in Anglicanism; to the "critically orthodox"; to the struggles (both Catholic and Protestant) with evolutionary theory; and to the continuing conservatisms and the emergence of fundamentalism at the end of the century (paralleled by the reaction of Pius X in the condemnation of modernism).

3. The innermost circle, then, would embrace the new considerations of the role of Jesus Christ, and more broadly the problem of faith and history. Here the matter of chronology comes prominently to the fore. This specific problem arises forcefully in the Protestant scene with the work of David Friedrich Strauss in 1835, though almost simultaneously in Emerson, and a little later in Britain in the translation by Mary Ann Evans (George Eliot) of Strauss (1846), and in *Essays and Reviews* (1860). But it did not really emerge in Catholicism until after Renan's *La Vie de Jésus* (1863) and more particularly in the modernist controversy. It was thus a problem less pervasive throughout the nineteenth century, though by the end it had come on all sides to a critical focus, which

---

20. Ibid., 1:5, 57–126.

was also to be generalized in the form of the question of faith and the new historical consciousness, in Troeltsch above all, and which on the Catholic side was reflected in the work of Loisy, Tyrrell, and Blondel, in the condemnation of modernism, and in the papal establishment of the Biblical Commission.

4. An analysis of the forms of the historical problem leads us back again to the question of the social context for theology, which raises the most intriguing and subtle methodological questions for interpreting nineteenth-century theology. It is important that most of the inclusive works we have noted make a point of calling attention to the social context. Berkhof, as we saw, orients his whole work to the question of the relation of modern theology to its cultural environment. Pelikan's title of volume 5 is *Christian Doctrine and Modern Culture*. In my own work, the historical/cultural context is always at least implicitly—and more explicitly in the second volume—in the background as essential to understanding Protestant thought. The Smart et al. volumes note the importance of "non-intellectual factors—whether social, economic or political—which conditioned the course of religious (and other) thought in the nineteenth century."[21] At the outset, Fitzer proposes as an overview that Vatican I was "the center point of Catholic response" to "the *many* revolutions affecting the nineteenth century," including the French and American revolutions and the industrial and scientific revolutions.[22] And for a briefer time period, O'Meara intends to write a "history of the interplay between faith and culture in the first half of the nineteenth century"—though the ensuing survey relates almost entirely to the impact of Schelling's philosophy on Catholic thinkers.[23] O'Meara's later volume is explicitly oriented to "church and culture," as seen in the work of five German Catholic thinkers in the latter part of the century.

Finally, it may not be amiss here to recall that Karl Barth advised the students in his 1932–33 lectures on nineteenth-century Protestant theology to have "some first-hand idea of the atmosphere, the trends and the feel of the time[s]," even to compile "a synchronous chart for every single year of the period with which we are occupied," with five columns: "the first for entering the most important dates of world history in gen-

---

21. Smart et al., *Nineteenth Century*, 1:4.
22. Fitzer, *Romance*, 5.
23. O'Meara, *Romantic Idealism*, ix.

eral; the second for the most noteworthy events in the history of culture, art and literature; the third for church history in general; the fourth for the dates of birth and death of the most prominent theologians of the period; and the fifth for the years in which their most important books were published. Anyone who does this will see a mass of connexions which I shall rarely be able to go into here."[24]

The problem here is that so seldom are the implications of these assertions about the importance of social context followed up. Although some connections appear in the individual essays, Smart and his associates explicitly disclaim any effort to produce a "social history of religious thought," which "would be a worthwhile project, but a nonetheless separate exercise from that which has been undertaken here."[25] Berkhof, in accord with a long tradition in (especially) German histories of theology, concentrates heavily on the philosophical developments in the cultural environment. He does believe "that social-economic relationships are much more culture-conditioning than we often thought (for thinking was the privilege of the well-to-do classes)," but also "that fundamentally they are not more influential than so many other elements which together form the infrastructure of our society—like heredity, eroticism, nationality, etc."[26] My two volumes have been criticized for lack of attention to how developments in theology were responses to the relevant social changes. This is a legitimate complaint, for I would much prefer to be identified with Troeltsch's type of history, which stresses the historical circumstances (or is, as Troeltsch put it, "essentially sociological-realistic-ethical"), rather than with Harnack's type (or Pelikan's?), which focuses on the dogmatic and on the influences of contemporary philosophy and is thus an "essentially ideological-dogmatic" presentation.[27] I do regard the cultural-historical context as essential for understanding Protestant (and Catholic) thought, but I did fail to provide adequate clues about *how* this thinking is a response to its specific contexts.

Pelikan's study is especially disappointing in this respect. He proposes to deal with Christian thought and modern culture. He judges that the modern period as a whole is characterized as the time when

---

24. Barth, *Protestant Theology*, 25–26.
25. Smart et al., *Nineteenth Century*, 1:4.
26. Berkhof, *Two Hundred Years*, xvii.
27. See Welch, *Protestant Thought*, 2:292–93.

doctrines that had been assumed throughout the preceding centuries
were called into question, with "a growing attack by modern culture and
secular thought,"[28] and he records many of the doubts about areas of
Christian belief. But where is modern culture in the discussion? At best,
the sociocultural context seems to be only a stage on which the story of
doctrine is played. And the stage is not even described: Kant appears,
but as far as I can find, there is no mention of Hume, Herder, Hegel,
Feuerbach, Marx, Nietzsche, and Freud—or even of Darwin, though
the threat of the "evolutionary hypothesis" to the traditional ideas of
creation in the divine image and of original sin is discussed. In other
words, the shape and texture of modern culture and the particular character of the challenges from natural or social science never come into
focus. And one gets no picture of the impact of the democratic mind
or political individualism on the notions of biblical and ecclesiastical
authority; one gets no powerful sense of the growth of nationalisms,
imperialisms, and industrialism, or of world wars and the Holocaust
(the "Nazi regime" appears only in connection with the Barmen Declaration's "polemic against the politicization of the church's preaching
and teaching").[29]

What is wrong here is that Pelikan has been unwilling to learn from
Troeltsch. In the first volume, in a comment on Troeltsch's *Social Teachings,* he speaks of that work as "the most articulate statement of the
thesis that Christian doctrine cannot be interpreted—as it has been interpreted in our work—in isolation from its social and cultural setting."[30]
But however the attempt to treat Christian doctrine in such isolation
may have worked in earlier volumes, for the modern period the weakness is evident. Surely, for example, one cannot deal responsibly with
the *Syllabus of Errors* or the decrees of Vatican I, which figure fairly large
in Pelikan's account, without an exhibition of the sources and the kinds
of thinking in the nineteenth century to which these were a response.

One immediate consequence of the preceding argument is this: at a
minimum, proper regard for the social dimensions of theology, particularly when one looks at Protestant and Catholic scenes together in terms
of the problem of church and society, requires attention to social teachings, ethics, and so on. One must reckon with "Life and Work" as well as

---

28. Pelikan, *Christian Tradition,* 5:9.
29. Ibid., 5:291.
30. Ibid., 1:360.

with "Faith and Order," and the social context of both must be considered. The errors relating to the rights of the church, in Pius IX's *Syllabus*, are just as much part of the theological story as the errors regarding the nature of reason. Pope Leo's social encyclicals are just as germane as *Providentissimus Deus* and *Aeterni Patris*. The social gospel belongs in the picture (and it is usually there) as much as does Herrmann or Harnack. Schleiermacher's *Sittenlehre* needs to be dealt with in conjunction with the *Glaubenslehre*. And so on. In short, historical theology must become more like social history, at least in the sense that social teachings are understood as part and parcel of the theological story.

The central question, however, is not whether the social context (however defined) must be clearly brought into view in any study of modern theology or doctrine (or ethics)—it must be—but whether that context is to be understood essentially as *background*, that is, as the stage setting in front of which the drama of theological discourse is played out, or as in some ways *constitutive* for the enterprise, that is, as essentially involved in the content, the shape, and the motivation of the drama (here the stage setting is as much a part of the drama as the script). I am persuaded that both sorts of interpretation are necessary, but the ways in which both are important need to be articulated. And *none* of the inclusive works we have examined does that, though Chadwick's *The Secularization of the European Mind in the Nineteenth Century* significantly points in the right direction.[31] Chadwick insists that social history and intellectual history cannot be separated: "Without the intellectual enquiry the social enquiry is fated to crash; as fated as was the intellectual enquiry when historians asked no questions about the nature of the society in which ideas were propagated or repudiated."[32]

Among the special studies of particular nineteenth-century movements, those by Cashdollar and by Franklin take small steps in the right direction.[33] Much more interesting and important, however, as full-

---

31. One might also think of Pacini's *The Cunning of Modern Religious Thought* as looking in this direction, though Pacini has a quite different program, arguing that the whole course of modern thought ought not to be viewed as secular but really as religious: "What postured as the antireligious proceeded from what was, at bottom, a religious frame of reference" (p. 59)—specifically, the "rational life-form of self-preservation" (p. 18).

32. Chadwick, *Secularization*, 14; see also 11–14.

33. Cashdollar, *Transformation*; Franklin, *Nineteenth-Century Churches*, e.g., 21–27 on the "cultural dynamic."

scale attempts to show the real interdependence of social context and theological articulation, are the works by Kirmmse and by Massey.[34]

Kirmmse's study involves an intensive analysis of the social and political views of Kierkegaard, focusing on the writings after 1846 (i.e., after the completion of the "literature"), and setting these against the background of a detailed study of the social, religious, cultural, economic, and political history of Denmark from the late eighteenth century through the mid–nineteenth century.[35]

He eschews the common psychological-biographical approach, which has tended to psychological reductionism or elusive "explanations" of the relation between Kierkegaard's private life and his public literary career, dealing instead in detail with the "historically specifiable forces working in SK's environment and in particular the various religious and political-cultural alternatives which he could choose or reject."[36] Thus, for example, he outlines the contrasts between the rural and the urban culture, the peasant and the cultural elite, the Mynsterian and the Grundtvigian forms of Christendom.

In particular, he notes the great importance of the events of 1848 and following, whose impact is shown in a detailed examination of the later writings of Kierkegaard.[37] Kirmmse concludes that Kierkegaard was in fact a populist and an egalitarian rather than an elitist with respect to the locus of culture and an agnostic with respect to the significance of history—in contrast both to the Mandarin Golden Age romanticism of Denmark, with its kind of liberalism, and to the populist romanticism of a Grundtvig. Thus Kierkegaard can be understood as presenting a "genuinely modern, post-1848 alternative to the *ancien régime* world view of the Golden Age."[38] And it is apparent how the social context is genuinely constitutive for Kierkegaard's writing and is responded to in myriad ways down through the culmination in the *Attack on Christendom*.

An especially interesting example of the subtlety and difficulty of the problem of social context as constitutive or background is Marilyn Chapin Massey's study of the meaning of Strauss's *Life of Jesus* in German politics. She sets out to "recover dimensions of human experi-

---

34. Kirmmse, *Kierkegaard*; Massey, *Christ Unmasked*.
35. Kirmmse, *Kierkegaard*, 9–247.
36. Ibid., 509 n. 1.
37. Ibid., 265–481.
38. Ibid., 247.

ence and meaning that historical traditions have excluded," notably the relationship between the roles of the 1835 *Life* in the history of Christian thought and in political and social history, roles that have been acknowledged but "never adequately explained."[39] A principal device in the explanation is the comparison of the *Life* with a contemporary feminist novel, *Wally the Skeptic* (1836), which was also banned by the authorities, and for the same sorts of reasons, namely, that they both disturbed the sleep of Germany in the mid-1830s.[40]

Strauss plainly did not have the sort of political motivation expressed in a letter by Feuerbach (1843) that asserted that "theology is for Germany the only practical and successful vehicle for politics, at any rate for the moment."[41] And Strauss did not count himself among the political and social reformers—the "Young Germans," publicly condemned by the Frankfurt Diet of 1835—yet he could defend them in the context of the powerful politicization of religious allegiance, with the weeding out of the rationalists from the theological faculties and the union of Throne and Altar in the minds of both political and ecclesiastical authorities (e.g., Friedrich Wilhelm III, Hengstenberg, and Gerlach).

While Strauss was not politically motivated in the *Life*, the structure and style of his criticism did in fact support democratic protest, as did *Wally the Skeptic* in another (more pathological) way. We cannot deal here with the subtleties or details of Massey's argument. But three aspects of the argument about Strauss may be summarized. At one level, Strauss's attack on the traditional interpretations of the Gospels could not but weaken a political authority that associated itself with the dogmas of Protestantism. More directly, Strauss's argument in the conclusion of the *Life* that the divine could not be wholly resident in an individual but only in the race as a whole, together with the shift from Jesus to the popular consciousness of the first century in accounting for the creation of the Gospels, supported a move toward democratic consciousness as well as weakening the favor for Hegelianism by indicating that Hegel's theory of monarchy involved democratic elements.[42] Further, the light-heartedness of Strauss in criticism of the reliability of the Gospels, almost casually throwing away deeply held beliefs, was a style of comic irony

---

39. Massey, *Christ Unmasked*, vii, 3.
40. Ibid., 42.
41. Cited in ibid., 38–39.
42. Ibid., e.g., 54–55, 81, 103.

(not tragic irony or satire): "It is the work's ironic inversion of what is considered reality that defined its overall structure and carries political meaning."[43]

Massey's interpretation of Strauss is a good illustration of how social context can be both background and constitutive. Insofar as the *Life* was directed to the theological question, the political and social situation of Germany in the 1830s is background for a radical step forward in Gospel criticism and for Strauss's development of a Hegelian view. But the importance of the work is also determined by the support that it gave, positively in the 1835 edition and negatively in the 1838 edition, to the revolutionary political forces of the 1830s; thus its *meaning* is also constituted as political.

In her argument, Massey maintains a delicate balance between authorial intention and the "meaning" of the work. She associates herself with Michel Foucault's question "whether the subjects responsible for their scientific discourse are not determined in their situation, their function, their perceptive capacity, and their practical possibilities by conditions which dominate and even overwhelm them," and thus seeks to identify "general cultural configurations that dominated Strauss and others of his generation."[44] Yet in exposing so vividly the political meaning of the *Life*, Massey is attentive to Strauss's conscious intentions and does not minimize the enormous importance of his work in the history of biblical interpretation and theology.

Here I suggest we have, at least for modern history and the kinds of texts we mostly deal with in the nineteenth century, an appropriate way of handling the now vexed hermeneutical question of authorial intention. Given the nature of such sources as these, we cannot neglect the stated purposes of an author, and a first responsibility of the historian is to try to see the work from within those conscious intentions and in relation to the community an author is directly addressing. Yet a "hermeneutic of suspicion" must also come into play with respect to the text as such, and levels of meaning can legitimately be found beyond (or below) the reflective consciousness or self-consciousness, so that one may understand more fully than the author what the work finally means, and perhaps more fully why it said what it did.

---

43. Ibid., 72.
44. Ibid., 8–9.

This consideration of the problem of dealing with the social context of theology leads to a final conclusion or observation about the ways of doing history of nineteenth-century theology.

It may well be that the best way, and perhaps the only practical way, to deal effectively with the interrelation of explicitly theological endeavors and their social contexts is in terms of relatively limited geographical and temporal analysis, as in the case of *Christ Unmasked* and *Kierkegaard in Golden Age Denmark*. In principle, one could seek to apply comparable procedures for the theologies and contexts of a whole century, but this is unlikely to be feasible for any one person, or perhaps even for a team of interpreters working together. The case for "national" histories might seem to be strengthened by such difficulties—but those histories that have actually been written have not in fact been noticeably better in vitally setting theological developments in the larger social setting,[45] and one would have to take account of the social changes within the national boundaries (many of which are not in any case restricted to single nations, any more than are theological shifts). Thus the future of the history of nineteenth-century theology lies with many different kinds of studies. And those historians who have the temerity to try to tell the "whole" story will have to be particularly sensitive to the kinds of social connections that can be adequately exposed only in studies whose scope is smaller.

---

45. Among recent works see, e.g., Reardon, *From Coleridge to Gore.*

NINE

Marcia Bunge

Herder and the Origins of a Historical View of Religion: An Informative Perspective for Historical Theology Today

In contrast to many thinkers of the Enlightenment, Johann Gottfried Herder (1744–1803) made a radical turn to history. He emphasized the historical character of human existence, believing that all aspects of culture take shape only within concrete historical settings. He also called for an appreciation of the uniqueness and integrity of diverse cultures and historical periods and warned against judging them according to European standards. His ideas played a significant role in the emergence of historical consciousness in the nineteenth century, securing for him a place in the development of historicism and the philosophy of history.

The significance of Herder's ideas about history is not confined, however, to the philosophy of history alone. Herder was also a theologian and exegete who applied his historical ideas to religion, theology, and the Bible. He viewed religion, like all aspects of culture, as a historical phenomenon. He therefore paid attention to the unique historical contexts in which various expressions of faith emerge, and he studied the ways that they change and develop over time. His emphasis on the historical dimension of faith led him to appreciate the diversity and uniqueness of religious beliefs. Unlike many of his contemporaries, he encouraged his readers not to judge these beliefs in relation to one another or according to European ideas but rather to study them "on their own terms" and in relation to their unique historical contexts.

Herder's historical view of religion contributed to the development of several disciplines. His conviction that all peoples possess religion and his respect for the diverse religions of various cultures helped to inspire the modern discipline of the history of religions.[1] His historical view of religion also lifted up the relation between religion and culture, contributing to the development of the fields of anthropology, archaeology, and the sociology of religion.

In the realm of biblical criticism he prompted a historical examination of the texts and an appreciation of their individuality. In Hebrew Bible studies, this approach inspired a new appreciation of Hebrew language and poetry.[2] In his writings on the New Testament, he discussed the theological and historical diversity of the Gospels, the oral traditions behind them, and the priority of Mark. He is therefore regarded as a founder of literary-historical criticism.[3]

Major histories of Protestant thought, such as those by Karl Barth, Emanuel Hirsch, and Claude Welch,[4] also recognize the importance of Herder's historical insights for theology. Karl Barth, for example, claims that Herder's penetrating understanding of the concrete reality of history opened the way to central theological developments of the nineteenth century. Barth believes that Herder was "the inaugurator of typical nineteenth century theology before its inauguration by Schleiermacher"[5] and states his significance in these bold terms:

---

1. Ulrich Faust, *Mythologien und Religionen des Ostens bei Johann Gottfried Herder* (Münster: Aschendorff, 1977), 228–29; Claude Welch, *Protestant Thought in the Nineteenth Century* (New Haven, Conn.: Yale University Press, 1985), 2:104–5; Gustav Mensching, *Geschichte der Religionswissenschaft* (Bonn: Universitäts-Verlag, 1948), 53–55, 66.

2. See, for example, *Die Religion in Geschichte und Gegenwart*, 3d ed., s.v. "Bibel-Wissenschaft des AT."

3. Erhardt Güttgemann, *Offene Fragen zur Formgeschichte des Evangeliums* (Munich: Kaiser, 1970), 120. Werner Kümmel claims, "Herder was the first to recognize problems that much later were to concern that branch of gospel research known as form criticism" (*The New Testament: The History of the Investigation of Its Problems*, trans. S. McLean Gilmour and Howard Kee [New York: Abingdon, 1972], 82).

4. Karl Barth, *From Rousseau to Ritschl*, trans. Brian Cozens (London: SCM Press, 1959), 197–224; Emanuel Hirsch, *Geschichte der neuern evangelischen Theologie im Zusammenhang mit den allgemeinen Bewegungen des europaischen Denkens* (Gütersloh: Gerd Mohn, 1952), 4:224ff.; Welch, *Protestant Thought*, 1:41, 54.

5. Barth, *From Rousseau*, 223.

Herder's significance for those theologians who came after him can scarcely be rated highly enough. Without him the work of Schleiermacher and de Wette would have been impossible, and also the peculiar pathos of the course of theology in the nineteenth century. Without Herder there would have been no Erlangen group and no school of religious history. But for Herder, there would have been no Troeltsch.[6]

Although scholars recognize the importance of Herder's historical approach for the development of these various fields in religion and theology, they tell us little or nothing about it. He is often simply mentioned as a thinker who played a significant role in viewing religion and theology from a historical perspective. If more is said about him, he is characterized as a "romantic" who emphasized the individuality and the unique historical contexts of particular religions, biblical texts, and periods of church history and who discovered this individuality through an act of "empathy" (*Einfühlung*). In other words, he is presented as one who attempted to abandon prejudice and concern for the present and to understand a text or a past age by creatively entering its unique world and by reconstructing the spirit of an age or the intentions of the author.

Hans-Joachim Kraus, for example, in his discussion of Herder's interpretation of the Bible, contrasts Herder's "romantic-intuitive" approach with the "rational-critical methods" of the Enlightenment. Kraus depicts Herder's hermeneutics as a form of experience and empathy.[7] Despite his discussion of ambiguities in Herder's interpretation of the Bible, Hans Frei also seems to support the opinion that Herder's approach to the Bible is one of "total surrender" or "direct *Einfühlung*" into the spirit of an age or the experience of an author.[8]

Klaus Scholder, who attempts to outline Herder's importance for the development of historical theology, also characterizes Herder in this

---

6. Ibid., 200.

7. Hans-Joachim Kraus, *Geschichte der historisch-kritischen Erforschung des Alten Testaments* (Neukirchen: Neukirchener Verlag, 1956), 121, 128. Even Thomas Willi's extensive study of Herder's interpretation of the Old Testament concludes that Herder's approach is best characterized as *palingenesie*—"a creative act" through which the interpreter is able to read the text through the soul of the author; see Thomas Willi, *Herders Beitrag zum Verstehen des Alten Testaments*, Beiträge zur Geschichte der biblischen Hermeneutik, 8 (Tübingen: J. C. B. Mohr, 1971).

8. Hans Frei, *The Eclipse of Biblical Narrative* (New Haven, Conn.: Yale University Press, 1974), 184–86, 189.

way. He claims that Herder attempted to discover the individuality of periods in Christian history through an "aesthetic-empathizing" process.[9] Although Scholder recognizes the contribution of Herder's radical historical insights to Protestant thought, he contrasts his approach to a true historical-critical method and concludes that it was naive and uncritical.

This view of Herder as one who emphasized individuality and empathy is being criticized in recent studies of Herder's early writings on history in general. Hans Dietrich Irmscher claims, for example, that Friedrich Meinecke's typical characterization of Herder as a virtuoso of empathy who attempts to lose his connection to the present is incomplete.[10] Irmscher argues that although Herder does pay attention to the individuality of a period and attempt "to place himself" in it, he also attempts to understand the past from the standpoint of the present. On the one hand, he recognizes that the interpreters of history are also part of a particular historical context and cannot transcend it. They cannot therefore lose themselves completely in the past but are rather informed by it. On the other hand, Herder recognizes that the past can be a resource for shaping the future. Thus, for Irmscher, in Herder's early writings on history, he relates to the past in three ways. He recognizes not only its difference from the present but also its influence on the present and its power to shape the present and the future.

Hans-Georg Gadamer also criticizes the characterization of Herder as one who sought to discover the individuality of past ages through empathy.[11] Gadamer claims that Herder's early work on history, *Auch eine Philosophie der Geschichte* (1774), did not merely aim to reconstruct the past. Rather, it was also a critique of the present age and, more significantly, a "contribution for the future."[12] Gadamer's work also points out that Herder's view of history included much more than merely a respect for the individuality of each period. Herder also recognized that each age has its own presuppositions and limitations. Further, his view

---

9. Klaus Scholder, "Herder und die Anfänge der historischen Theologie," *Evangelische Theologie* 22 (1962): 433.

10. Hans Dietrich Irmscher, "Grundzüge der Hermeneutik Herders," in *Bückeburger Gespräche über Johann Gottfried Herder* (Bückeburg: Grimme, 1973).

11. Hans-Georg Gadamer, "Herder und die geschichtliche Welt," *Kleine Schriften* (Tübingen: J. C. B. Mohr, 1972), 3:100–117.

12. Ibid., 102.

of history included a critique of skepticism and a belief in God's ordering activity within history.

Such critiques of the common perception of Herder's early writings on history and the significance of his historical understanding of religion for Western religious thought prompt a reevaluation of his work. This essay has a dual aim and dual thesis. Its initial aim is to present a more accurate account of Herder's historical understanding of religion and theology. The thesis of the first part of the essay is that Herder's historical approach to religion and theology is more complex than has been recognized and can best be characterized through the principle of *Bildung*.

This examination of Herder's historical approach to religion helps to uncover the nature and scope of his significance for the development of religious thought. More significantly, a clearer understanding of his historical approach reveals its value for the historical study of religion today. The second aim of the paper is to focus on the ways that his approach provides insight for one such area: historical theology.

The term "historical theology" has been used in a variety of ways. Friedrich Schleiermacher used it, for example, to indicate a radical shift in the nature of dogmatics. For him, dogmatics was no longer mainly a deductive, biblical science but rather a historical task that "offers historical knowledge of the (then) present condition of the Evangelical Church."[13] He called this new form of dogmatics "historical theology" and distinguished it from "philosophical" and "practical" theology, claiming that its aim is to study the life of the Christian community both in the past and in its present condition and to recognize that this present condition "can be adequately grasped only when it is viewed as a product of the past."[14]

Other theologians, such as F. C. Baur, Adolf von Harnack, and Ernst Troeltsch, who were indebted to Schleiermacher, have also been designated "historical theologians."[15] They do not, however, use the term

---

13. Brian Gerrish, *The Old Protestantism and the New* (Chicago: University of Chicago Press, 1982), 209.

14. Friedrich Schleiermacher, *Kurze Darstellung des theologischen Studiums zum Behuf einleitender Vorlesungen*, ed. Heinrich Scholz, 3d ed. (Darmstadt: Wissenschaftliche Buchgesellschaft), secs. 26–28. English translation by Terrence Tice, *Brief Outline of the Study of Theology* (Atlanta: John Knox Press, 1977), 26.

15. See, for example, Wilhelm Pauck, *Harnack and Troeltsch: Two Historical Theologians* (New York: Oxford University Press, 1968); and Scholder, "Herder," 425.

"historical theology" in Schleiermacher's specific sense. Their designation as historical theologians stems from their study of the development of Christian doctrine and from their unique attempts to reflect the presuppositions of modern historical consciousness in their theological claims.

Today historical theology is most often understood as a distinct field of study situated between church history and systematic theology. Jaroslav Pelikan defines historical theology as "the genetic study of Christian faith and doctrine."[16] He understands it as a discipline that serves but does not replace systematic theology.

If, for the purpose of this essay, we understand the term in Pelikan's sense of "the genetic study of Christian faith and doctrine," then we find that Herder's historical approach not only inspired this field but also provides guidance for the nature of this task today. The scope of this essay does not allow me to attempt to trace more precisely either Herder's influence on the origins of historical theology, although such a study is needed, especially in the English-language literature,[17] or to chart the influence of other thinkers on Herder's work, for he united tendencies found in thinkers before him. Rather, I will focus on ways that Herder's work might serve as a guide for historical theology today. The thesis of the second part of this essay is that Herder's historical approach, as characterized by *Bildung,* provides an informative perspective on the complexity of examining Christian faith and doctrine historically.

I

Herder wrote no history of religions or Christian dogmatics, but he did discuss religion in several fragments and in his major works on history;[18] he wrote several complete and influential interpretations of the

---

16. Jaroslav Pelikan, *Historical Theology: Continuity and Change in Christian Doctrine* (New York: Hutchinson, 1971), xiii.

17. Pelikan does not mention Herder in his chapter on the evolution of historical thinking (*Historical Theology,* 33–67), and Welch only mentions him as one of several thinkers who prepared the way for a historical understanding of the development of dogma (*Protestant Thought,* 2:176).

18. See *Auch eine Philosophie der Geschichte zur Bildung der Menschheit* (1774) and *Ideen zur Philosophie der Geschichte der Menschheit* (1784–91).

Bible;[19] and he discussed the task of theology most directly in his later theological writings and in works addressed to theological students.[20] His historical approach to religion in these texts cannot be understood without first recognizing certain presuppositions underlying them all.

Herder assumes, first of all, that religion is *sui generis*. At a time when religion was easily equated with either morality or doctrine, Herder lifted up the uniqueness, intricacy, and power of religion. As early as 1774, years before Schleiermacher's *Speeches* (1799), Herder warns preachers that morality cannot be equated with religion,[21] and throughout his writings he distinguishes religion from doctrine.[22] He believes that religion is more deeply rooted in human experience than either science or morality; it touches and guides all aspects of our being. At the same time, he points out the intricate and influential role of religion in every area of culture.

Herder also assumes that religion is an essential part of human nature. He believes that all peoples possess religion and that it is the highest expression of our humanity (*SW* 13:161–65). It reveals the human attempt to discover order and meaning in the world. It also directs human beings to that which they are meant to be: "Religion touches all human tendencies and desires in order to harmonize them all and guide them to the right path" (*SW* 20:135). It is "the innermost consciousness of what we are as parts of creation and what we ought to be and to do as human beings" (*SW* 20:159). His view of religion is based on his conviction that God has worked throughout history, guiding and directing human beings in various ways, and that all people are created in God's image (*SW* 13:394–95).

These presuppositions helped to restore a central place to religion and theology in the late eighteenth century. Yet Herder's view of religion was even more significant in the history of Western religious thought because he also viewed all religions as historical phenomena. As

---

19. His most important interpretations of the Bible are *Älteste Urkunde des Menschengeschlechts* (1774, 1776); *Erläuterungen zum Neuen Testament* (1775); *Lieder der Liebe* (1778); *Vom Geist der ebräischen Poesie* (1782–83); *Vom Erlöser der Menschen* (1796); *Vom Gottes Sohn der Welt Heiland* (1797).

20. See *An Prediger: Fünfzehn Provinzialblätter* (1774); *Briefe, das Studium der Theologie betreffend* (1780–81); *Briefe an Theophron* (1808); *Christliche Schriften* (1794–98).

21. Johann Gottfried Herder, *Sämmtliche Werke* (hereafter *SW*), ed. Bernhard Suphan (Berlin, 1877–1913), 7:250.

22. See, for example, his *Christliche Schriften*.

we have seen, most studies depict his approach as an attempt to grasp the individuality of religious beliefs within their particular historical settings through empathy. Yet Herder's approach is more complex and can best be characterized through the notion of *Bildung*. This is a detailed concept that has been interpreted in many ways. In German it can mean "formation," "cultivation," or "education" and has been used in many ways to speak about how we develop as human beings. In his *Ideen zur Philosophie der Geschichte der Menschheit,* however, Herder presents two basic elements of *Bildung,* and these can help us understand some of its general characteristics.

The first element of *Bildung* is "tradition" (*SW* 13:343–53). Tradition underscores the limited historical nature of human beings. It is a way of saying that the thoughts and actions of human beings are shaped both by immediate historical circumstances and by all that has come before them. No one, for Herder, becomes a human being alone. We are connected with parents, teachers, and friends, with all the circumstances of our life and with our culture. Herder recognizes that this culture has been, in turn, influenced by its history and by other surrounding cultures and their pasts.

Beyond tradition, the process of *Bildung* has a second principle—"organic powers." These are the powers that human beings possess to receive and to convert into their own natures what has been transmitted by tradition to them. These powers apply tradition to the needs of the present situation. Without such powers, history would be an endless imitation of what has already been.

Herder also claims that *Bildung* is guided by a universal purpose—"humanity" (*Humanität*) (*SW* 14:235–52). This is a broadly defined and significant term in his writings. It expresses the notion that all human beings share a common purpose and direction and is based on the conviction that all human beings are made in God's image. Herder often equates humanity with religion, claiming that it gives direction to human development in all its diversity (see, e.g., *SW* 13:154, 161).

Herder believes that the process of *Bildung,* through which human beings are both formed by tradition and transform tradition anew, is universal. This does not imply that all human beings are the same. For Herder, they are shaped by *different* traditions and possess *different* gifts. No one person or culture is the same as another. Nevertheless, Herder believes that all human beings undergo this process of *Bildung*.

If we focus on "tradition" and "organic powers," then we find they are taken into account in four ways in Herder's historical approach to religion and can help us to characterize it more accurately. First, in his historical approach we see Herder taking "tradition" into account by studying the historical context of forms of religious expression. He does this in two ways. On the one hand, he studies the immediate historical circumstances in which religious beliefs are developed and expressed. He demands that they be understood in relation to the cultural and intellectual environment in which they emerge. On the other hand, he insists that the historical study of religion must also involve a study of the surrounding traditions that have influenced a particular religion. When he discusses the historical context of early Christianity, for example, he speaks about the influence of Hellenistic, Jewish, and even gnostic thought on it.

His attention to "tradition" was especially important in his interpretation of the Bible. In his study of the New Testament, he looks "behind" the text not only to the immediate historical context of each book but also to the oral and written traditions in which it is embedded. He tells students of theology not only to read the Bible in its original languages but also to study the Near Eastern languages that have influenced the Greek and Hebrew of the Bible (*SW* 10:7–11). He also looks at the influence of Near Eastern literature and religions on the Bible. He points out, for example, the influence of Jewish and Hellenistic thought on the New Testament. He is also intrigued by the similarities between the New Testament and Zoroastrian thought, as expressed in the *Avesta*,[23] and he discovers the influence of gnostic images and beliefs on the Gospel of John (*SW* 19:285–300).

Second, in his historical approach to religion, Herder pays attention to the "organic powers" of human beings by studying the individuality of various religions and religious texts. He studies the new and unique ways that people appropriate what has been handed down to them. This appreciation for the individuality of religious expression leads him to insist that religions and religious texts be studied without prejudice and without judging them according to foreign standards.

In a fragment on mythology, for example, he criticizes those who

---

23. See Herder's *Erläuterungen zum Neuen Testament* (*SW* 7). Herder used the French translation of Anquetil Duperron, published in 1771.

judge ancient Greek and Eastern myths as mere superstitions or teachings about false gods.[24] He says that these myths were "activities of human reason," for they express ways that human beings have attempted to understand their world and to express their feelings about it. He claims that we can learn much about a people's thoughts and culture from these myths and that we should treat them with humanity and examine them without prejudice or hatred. In a late dialogue written by Herder entitled "Über National-Religionen: Erstes Gespräch" (1802), the two partners of the dialogue say that the human race is one family with a diversity of characteristics and religions, and that religions should strive to be the best of their kind without measuring and comparing themselves to others (SW 24:48–49).

Herder's attention to the "organic powers" of human beings also plays a role in his interpretation of the Bible. He says we must allow each text to speak on its own terms and recognize its individuality (see, e.g., SW 11:165–70, 176–81). He looks at the characteristics of the text that reflect the unique gifts of the author, the specific audience the author addresses, and the particular purpose for which the text was written. He also says that we should not compare the text to forms of literature from other cultures and periods. Rather, we should study the literature in its own historical context and read the Bible in its original languages. Herder is especially critical of those in his time who attempted to evaluate the Hebrew Bible according to the standards of Greek and Roman literature. He emphasizes that Hebrew is a very different language than Latin or Greek and that the literary forms of the Bible, such as the Psalms and parallelisms, should not be compared to the poetry of Pindar or the odes of Horace (see, e.g., SW 12:207–11). He also warns that the Gospels of the New Testament should not be compared to Greek or Roman styles of writing history (SW 19:194–95), and he lifts up the differences between the four Gospels, saying that they are understandable in the light of the diverse gifts of the Gospel writers, their particular audiences, and the specific contexts in which they wrote (SW 19:207–17, 416–24).

A third aspect of Herder's historical approach is his attention to the influence of tradition on the interpreter of religion. He recognizes that religious traditions continue to inform us today—whether we acknowl-

---

24. The fragment is entitled "Fragment einer Abhandlung über die Mythologie" and was published for the first time from Herder's Nachlass by Ulrich Faust in Mythologien, 43–46, 154–55.

edge it or not. In particular, he notes the deep influence of Christianity on Western culture. He claims that even those who are not Christians are deeply influenced by the language of the Bible and by Christian beliefs. Christianity is, for Herder, a central part of the tradition that the West has inherited, and we are not to deny its effect on our lives today.

This insight is grounded not only in Herder's conviction that human beings are historical creatures and are shaped by all that comes before them. It is also informed by his recognition of the complex relationship between religion and culture. In an early essay, he speaks about the social and political role of religion (*SW* 32:145–57). Later, in his *Ideen,* he says that religion introduces the first elements of culture and science to a people and that often the earliest forms of science are nothing more than a kind of religious tradition. He also says that Europeans received their sciences "in no other way but in the garb of religion" (*SW* 13:390–91).

In addition to disclosing the complex interrelationships of religion and culture, Herder's attention to the "tradition" and thereby to the historicality of the interpreter also led him to recognize that the task of the interpreter is both necessary and limited. The difficult work of interpretation is necessary because the particular language and situation of the interpreter differ from people of the past or people of other cultures. The interpreter cannot understand other religious beliefs "immediately," through some act of empathy alone, but must use all available critical tools. Interpretation is limited, however, because the interpreter will never, despite the use of all these tools, be able to understand a text or a past age completely. The interpreter can never transcend the historical and linguistic horizon of his or her own understanding.[25]

A fourth aspect of Herder's historical view of religion is his emphasis on our own powers to transform tradition. He believes that the study of religions in their historical contexts can be a resource for the present. For him, the study of the religious expressions of the past is not an empty exercise. Rather, the past can be used to transform the present. The study of the history of Christianity can, for example, uncover new insights that we can apply in the present. This conviction is grounded in Herder's appreciation of the "organic powers" of every generation's interpreters of religion who do not simply repeat the tradition handed down to them

---

25. One central area of Herder scholarship is the study of his conviction that language and thinking are integrally related and his role in linguistics and the philosophy of language.

but appropriate it in new ways according to their own particular historical circumstances. Religious traditions are, for Herder, dynamic and continually in the process of change because of the powers that human beings possess to transform tradition in their own unique ways.

We see his emphasis on the application of tradition for today throughout his interpretations of the Bible and in his discussion of dogmatics (SW 10:276–81, 314–23). Like many theologians before him, he believes that dogmatics is a science that is based on the Bible and that shows the relation between doctrines of the church. It is a "sacred philosophy," "a system of the noblest truths for the human race concerning the happiness of the human spirit and its eternal salvation" (SW 10:277). Yet Herder adds a historical dimension to dogmatics that changes its shape. He says that dogmatics should include an understanding of the *history* of dogmatics. He wants theologians to study the development of particular doctrines in their historical contexts so that they can understand the meaning of the terms in the context in which they arose. The theologian must then determine if these terms should still be used in the present situation or if they should be changed so that they are more intelligible today. If they are changed, then the theologian must have a very keen sense of both the content of the doctrine and the use of contemporary terms. In one passage, he desires that a history of dogmatics be written that has a section at the conclusion of each doctrine about how this doctrine could best be presented to people in our time (SW 11:5–6).[26]

Herder's strong emphasis on application is also apparent in his understanding of the goal of dogmatics and the study of the Bible. For him, this goal is preaching and the formation of the soul (SW 11:5–10, 16–23). In other words, it is the proclamation of the truth and the transformation of the ways that we think and act. He questions the value of the study of the Bible and dogmatics if they are not applied to our lives (SW 11:5–6). He also says that the best kind of preaching relates the biblical text to our situation today (SW 11:16–23). This can be done in a variety of ways. It requires, however, much preparation. The pastor must use ever-new and fresh materials and have a clear understanding of the situation of the listeners.

From this brief outline of components in Herder's historical ap-

---

26. He believes that Johann Salomo Semler's writings have paved the way to this kind of history but does not think it has yet been written.

proach to religion and theology, it is clear that the view of Herder as a "romantic" who attempted to grasp the individuality of the biblical texts and of past religious beliefs through empathy is inadequate. In addition to embracing the individuality of a text or period, his historical approach also examined the influence of both the immediate historical context and surrounding traditions; it took into account the influence of religious tradition on the present and the complex relation between religion and culture; and it emphasized the importance of appropriating the past in new ways for the present. In other words, it took into account the "tradition" and the "organic powers" of both those who have expressed religious beliefs in the past and those who study them today.

Herder does say that the discovery of these aspects of religion requires empathy. One must be able to enter imaginatively the spirit of a past age or of a text. At the same time, he recognizes that a historical view requires much more. It demands knowledge of original languages, the literature of other surrounding cultures, the historical context, and other religions. This requires the use of all available critical tools and historical data. Further, historical interpretation for Herder also applies the past to the present and therefore demands an understanding of the questions, concerns, and language of one's own time.

II

With this more complete picture of Herder's historical approach to religion, theology, and the Bible, it becomes easier to appreciate the nature and scope of his impact on religious thought in the nineteenth century in the many fields of study mentioned above. We can also more clearly understand his role in the development of historical consciousness in general. With the help of his ideas a historical view not only of religion but also of all aspects of culture became unavoidable. This historical consciousness created a new appreciation of the diversity between cultures and within history. At the same time, it challenged theology and all areas of human inquiry regarding the status of universal truth claims. If all aspects of culture are shaped by their historical context, then can we speak any longer of truths that are valid for all peoples?

Such challenges, prompted by the rise of historical consciousness, provided the ground for the emergence of historical theology in the nineteenth century. Indeed, Ernst Troeltsch called the development of a historical view of the world one of the most central characteristics of modern thought and believed that theology must address it.[27] He and others sought new forms of theological method that could take historical consciousness and thereby the historical nature of Christianity and the Bible into account.

The task of historical theology today has been made more challenging, in part, by the growing awareness in twentieth-century thought of the interpreter's own embeddedness within history. Historical theologians must confront not only change in Christian doctrines, and all the questions this raises about their status as truth claims, but also the interpreter's own historicity. Their task has also been made more exciting and yet more difficult through the burgeoning research about the past and about other religions provided by those in disciplines that developed in the nineteenth century—for example, social and economic historians, archaeologists, and historians of religion.

Faced with such challenges, the historical theologian can be tempted to simplify the task of historical theology rather than deepen and strengthen it so that it might more adequately address them. The historian might attempt, for example, to focus attention exclusively on the past, aiming to provide a "purely historical account," and skirt the issues of truth and the limitations of one's own presuppositions. His or her research might also tend to focus on ecclesiastical sources and avoid references to the wealth of historical work done in fields outside theology.

Herder's own historical approach to religion does not solve the difficult challenges that it helped to create. Ironically, however, it can provide historical theology with some guidelines for facing them today. The four aspects of Herder's approach, as outlined in part 1 of this essay, can help steer us away from tendencies to simplify the task of historical theology and can remind us of the complexity and richness of its task today.

First, if we keep in mind the "tradition" of the object of study, then we are reminded that thinking historically means studying both the immediate historical context of a particular period of Christianity and the traditions that have influenced it. In other words, awareness of "tradi-

---

27. See, for example, Ernst Troeltsch, *The Absoluteness of Christianity and the History of Religions* (Richmond: John Knox Press, 1971), 45; idem, *Writings on Theology and Religion*, ed. Robert Morgan and Michael Pye (Atlanta: John Knox Press, 1977), 129–37.

tion" demands the study of both immediate historical circumstances and the influence of other religions and cultures on Christianity. This approach requires both detailed historical research and reference to the resources of biblical scholarship and the history of religions.

Troeltsch insisted long ago that a theology that is historically informed must include comparisons to other religions.[28] Yet historical theologians, who very often emphasize the necessity of exact historical research, have, at times, neglected and even intentionally ignored the influence of other religions on Christianity. Harnack, for example, did not incorporate the insights of the history of religions into his work and failed to recognize the influence of Judaism on early Christianity. According to Pelikan, the relation of Judaism to Christianity is still being neglected today. He reminds his readers that the task of historical theology must include a deeper understanding of the role of Judaism in the early church and throughout the church's history.[29]

Second, Herder's eye toward the "organic powers" of a particular period can remind us that thinking historically also means taking into account the uniqueness and rich variety of Christian expressions of faith, even within one period of history. This requires an eye for the unique contributions and talents of particular thinkers as well as for the particular concerns and questions of their unique audiences. Attention to individuality of expression within the history of Christian thought can help the historical theologian avoid generalities that hide the complexity of history and that often serve only to highlight the historian's own prejudices.

This aspect of thinking historically is often missing in the work of historical theologians of the nineteenth century. The desire to discover the "essence" or "origin" of Christianity often drove out attention to its intricacy. This lack of appreciation for the complexity of religious history could also be seen in the tendency to schematize religions according to broad and often empty generalities. Although the history of religions was still in its infancy in the early nineteenth century, Herder's historical approach gave him a much more sophisticated treatment of other religions and their relation to Christianity than we find, for example, in either Georg Wilhelm Hegel or Schleiermacher.

---

28. Gerrish, *Old Protestantism*, 210–11.
29. Pelikan, *Historical Theology*, 75.

Although historical theologians today are not generally tempted to dismiss the wealth of unique expressions of faith in search of a Christian essence or a grand scheme of history, they do ignore this wealth on other grounds. Eagerness to support one's own theological convictions can, for example, cloud one's understanding of the complexity of a particular period. As Pelikan observes, "Historical theology is still to a large degree dominated by confessional interests" in such a way that "party spirit often prevails over historical interests."[30]

Indifference to questions other than our own can also cut us off from an appreciation of the intricacy of the past. The questions of women today and in the past were, for example, long ignored. Recent attention to them has, however, opened up rich, new perspectives on history. One way to foster an openness to the questions of others is to keep in mind Herder's radical appreciation of individuality and that aspect of his historical approach that uses empathy to help discover it.

The recognition of Herder's third element—the "tradition" of the interpreter of history—has two implications for the task of historical theology today. On the one hand, more broadly, it calls for an appreciation of the complex relation between Christianity and Western culture. Neither Christianity nor Western culture can be studied in isolation, for they are integrally related. Thinking historically requires, then, an open exchange of ecclesiastical and secular historical research. The historical theologian is to use the resources of intellectual, social, and political history.

On the other hand, the "tradition" of the interpreter suggests, more narrowly, that historical theology requires a keen awareness of the limitations of interpretation. The interpreters of the history of doctrine should recognize that they, like all historians, do not approach history without presuppositions. They themselves have been conditioned by the questions and concerns of their own particular cultures and religious traditions.

Although the discussion of the limitations of interpretation, which was prompted especially by the work of Hans-Georg Gadamer, has reached sophisticated levels in philosophical, literary, and theological debates today, the issue is at times not even mentioned in the work of historical theologians. Troeltsch certainly confronted the prob-

---

30. Ibid., 77.

lem squarely throughout his writings. In his essay on the essence of Christianity, for example, he says that the decisions about this essence can never be "absolutely presuppositionless and impartial."[31] Yet few historical theologians since Troeltsch have taken up the subject seriously.

Awareness of the limitations of interpretation is demanding and raises the issue of relativism. Nevertheless, it is necessary to the task of historical theology and has several positive benefits. It can invite a more honest appraisal of the interests and questions that drive one's research. This not only helps provide critical reflection on possible limitations of one's research and changes that might address them but also gives insights into its strengths and specific contributions. Moreover, awareness of limitations of interpretation can prompt a fuller account of the philosophical and theological presuppositions underlying one's work. It is precisely through such reflection that one understands more clearly one's own convictions about history and can thereby contribute more fruitfully to debates about relativism.

Investigation of not only one's own presuppositions but also those of others helps us understand their work and the possible resources they offer for responding to the challenge of relativism. Troeltsch's metaphysical presuppositions, for example, play a major role in his understanding of historical theology, even though, as Walter Wyman has shown,[32] he did not make explicit the relationship between them. These presuppositions give us clues for understanding the ways that Troeltsch attempted to avoid both absolutism and relativism. Herder's own radically historical viewpoint also does not end in relativism. Yet we can understand his position only with reference to his assumptions about humanity and to his belief, stemming from the Judeo-Christian tradition, that God is active throughout history, uniting its vast course within a common plan that we can never fully understand (*SW* 5:558–61). Even the development of historicism[33] and historical theology[34] cannot be understood without reference to underlying presuppositions about God's providence.

---

31. Troeltsch, *Writings*, 159.

32. Walter Wyman, *The Concept of Glaubenslehre: Ernst Troeltsch and the Theological Heritage of Schleiermacher* (Chico, Calif.: Scholars Press, 1983).

33. Georg Iggers, *The German Conception of History* (Middletown, Conn.: Wesleyan University Press, 1986), 36.

34. Scholder, "Herder," 437–40.

These ways of recognizing limitations of interpretation do not necessarily lead either to relativism or to a simple solution to it. They do provide, however, avenues for a sincere and fruitful discussion of relativism. A more honest view of one's own beliefs and the resources that others have used to address relativism can only strengthen one's participation in the discussion. Current philosophical debate on the nature of interpretation is not, of course, the central subject matter of historical theologians. Their focus must remain the development of doctrine. If they have taken seriously a historical perspective, however, then their work must also reflect an awareness of the limitations of interpretation and the issues this raises.

If we take into account the fourth element of Herder's historical approach, the "organic powers" of the interpreter, then we are reminded that the task of historical theology should include the application of the past to the present. Historical research and a keen awareness of today's questions and concerns are to work together to offer not only a rich understanding of the past but also new possibilities for the present. In other words, historical theology is to be done for the present.

This conviction has been a major component of historical theology since its beginnings. Harnack, for example, believed that the study of history must prepare us for the present.[35] Troeltsch too believed that historical study is carried out for the sake of the present.[36] He also says that theology has the task of reappropriating the tradition for one's own age[37] and that the definition of the essence of Christianity, which is sought through detailed, historical research, is an "ideal thought" that "provides the possibility of new combinations with the concrete life of the present."[38]

Although central to historical theology from the beginning, the application of the past to the present is not always understood to be the task of the historical theologian today. Instead, the task is sometimes more simply understood as the description of the formation of past doctrine alone. Yet without reference to questions of the present, the past

---

35. Pauck, *Harnack and Troeltsch*, 18–21.
36. See, for example, Ernst Troeltsch, *Protestantism and Progress* (Philadelphia: Fortress Press, 1986), 18. He says here that the chief aim of history is "the understanding of the present."
37. Ernst Troeltsch, *Glaubenslehre* (Munich: Duncker and Humbolt, 1925), 38–39.
38. Troeltsch, *Writings*, 162; also 156–63.

does not speak to us. It can no longer provide us with new insights that challenge us and perhaps even prompt us to reformulate our own beliefs.

An emphasis on the present might not only allow the past to speak more clearly to us but also serve to narrow the gap between historical theology and systematic theology. Classic systematicians of the twentieth century, such as Karl Barth and Paul Tillich, have paid attention to the history of dogma and given lectures and written books on the subject. In the past few years, however, the relation between systematics and historical theology has appeared to be less fruitful than that between systematics and philosophy. Renewed application of the past to the present on the part of historical theologians might remind systematicians that the study of the past is not only essential for an understanding of the church but also provides new possibilities for the present. As Herder recognized, a precise history of the formulation of doctrine can provide guidance in expressing these doctrines more clearly in our own context. It can also raise insightful questions that open up new ways of thinking in our own time.

Herder's attention to the "tradition" and "organic powers" of both past religious expressions and present-day interpreters reminds us that the task of historical theology is complex. It is not limited to the study of the immediate historical contexts in which doctrines were formulated. It also involves an awareness of the influence of other religious traditions on them and therefore calls for reference to resources in biblical studies and in the history of religions. Thinking historically demands an eye for the individuality and diversity of unique expressions of Christianity found throughout its history. Historical theology also requires a solid understanding of the complex relation between religion and culture and thus eagerly uses the insights of intellectual, social, and political historians. Moreover, it calls for reflection on the questions that direct one's research and the examination of one's own theological and philosophical presuppositions. Finally, historical theology is carried out for the present and requires an understanding of the questions and concerns of one's own time.

Although recognition of the complexity of the task of historical theology presents many difficulties, it also creates new perspectives on Christianity and makes the study of its past much more vibrant and rewarding. Reference to other religions and attention to Christianity's relation to culture promote, for example, a lively dialogue with academic fields outside historical theology; such dialogue can help to uncover the intricate complexity of religious faith. Deeper reflection on one's own assumptions and theological convictions provides self-knowledge and can foster critical reevaluation of one's research. It is precisely through this kind of reflection that one can contribute more fully to the present discussion of relativism. Finally, applying the past to the present makes thinking historically a vital, vibrant enterprise that has meaning for today.

CONCLUSION

This brief examination of Herder's writings has shown that his historical perspective on religion and theology cannot be characterized as a romantic appreciation of the individuality of past religious beliefs that is discovered through empathy. Rather, his historical perspective involves the detailed study of a particular historical context and the influence of other religions and cultures on it. It also involves an awareness of the influence of religious traditions on one's own culture, the complex relation between religion and culture, and the limitations of one's own perspective. At the same time, thinking historically involves application of the past to the present. This approach was grounded in a belief in the uniqueness and importance of religion and in a conviction in the meaning of history and God's activity in it.

These elements of Herder's historical approach were informed by his own tradition and by the wealth of ideas about history in eighteenth-century Europe. Herder took up these ideas and transformed them through his own keen appreciation of the richness and diversity of human history and cultures. His ideas, in turn, shaped the development of historical consciousness and religious thought in the nineteenth century. The field of historical theology has attempted to take into account the historical view of the world that Herder's ideas helped to create. By looking back at Herder's own complex approach, historical theology can not only learn more about its own history but also gain insight into its complex yet vital task today.

TEN

Michael J. Himes

Historical Theology as Wissenschaft: *Johann Sebastian Drey and the Structure of Theology*

Within Catholic theology at the beginning of the nineteenth century, church history served either as an allied field providing precedents for and illustrations of ecclesiastical doctrine and discipline or as a source of ammunition for interconfessional polemics. The emergence of historical theology as an intrinsic moment within the whole Roman Catholic theological enterprise is an accomplishment of a group of important scholars who either taught or studied with the Catholic theology faculty at the University of Tübingen. The foundation for that accomplishment is the creative rethinking of the structure and method of theology by Johann Sebastian Drey (1777–1853). Two related elements stand at the root of that rethinking: the creative appropriation of the *wissenschaftlich* method that Drey learned from Friedrich Wilhelm Schelling and the central role that Drey accorded to the church as a living community of shared experience.

The Coherence and Necessity
of the Structure of Theology

In 1812, a Catholic seminary was founded at Ellwangen whose imposing title, the Katholische Friedrichslandesuniversität, was not matched
by imposing resources.[1] Drey became the first professor of dogmatic
theology and apologetics and moved with the fledgling theologate
when it was joined to the distinguished University of Tübingen in
1817. As a member of the founding faculty, he shared the responsibility
for organizing the curriculum. This gave him the opportunity to consider the relationships of the fields within theology and the method of
their organization. In 1819 Drey published his ideas on these issues in
*Kurze Einleitung in das Studium der Theologie mit Rücksicht auf den wis-
senschaftlichen Standpunkt und das katholische System,*[2] which illuminates
not only the direction of its author's thinking but the early course of the
Catholic Tübingen school generally.

In the preface to this ground plan for the study and teaching of theology in accord with the demands both of Catholic doctrine and practice
and of the "scientific standpoint," Drey distinguished his goal from that
of his predecessors in the task of writing a theological encyclopedia.
Previously one delimited the various branches of the science, gave a
brief history of each subdiscipline, noting the major figures and their
contributions, discussed the current state of the field and the rules of
procedure generally observed by its practitioners, and listed the best
authorities of the time. The alternative that Drey preferred was to demonstrate that the science is an organic whole out of which the various
branches develop naturally. One can do this formally, showing how
the chief subdisciplines emerge from a shared perspective, tracing their
interconnections, illustrating their rootedness in the positive foundation

---

1. For a brief account of the founding of the faculty at Ellwangen and its subsequent move to Tübingen, see Rudolf Reinhardt, "Die Katholisch-theologische Fakultät
Tübingen im ersten Jahrhundert ihres Bestehens: Faktoren und Phasen der Entwicklung," in *Tübinger Theologen und ihre Theologie: Quellen und Forschungen zur Geschichte der
Katholisch-Theologischen Fakultät Tübingen,* ed. R. Reinhardt (Tübingen: J. C. B. Mohr [Paul
Siebeck], 1977). Also, F. X. Funk, *Die katholische Landesuniversität in Ellwangen und ihre Ver-
legung nach Tübingen: Festgabe zum 25. jährigen Regierungsjubiläum Seiner M. des Königs Karl
von Württemberg* (Tübingen, 1899).

2. Drey, *Kurze Einleitung in das Studium der Theologie mit Rücksicht auf den wissenschaft-
lichen Standpunkt und das katholische System,* ed. Franz Schupp (1819; reprint, Darmstadt:
Wissenschaftliche Buchgesellschaft, 1971).

of the science, and comparing their usefulness in attaining one or another practical result of the science. As an example of this formal laying out of a science, Drey cited[3] Friedrich Schleiermacher's *Kurze Darstellung des theologischen Studiums zum Behuf einleitender Vorlesungen.*[4]

Schleiermacher had begun his outline of theological studies by defining theology as "a positive science, whose parts are bound into a whole only through their common reference to a definite mode of faith, i.e. a definite form of God-consciousness." He had explained that

> Generally, a positive science is an ensemble of scientific elements which belong together not because, by the very idea of science, they form a necessary part of the organization of the sciences, but only because they are required for the performance of a practical task.[5]

But Drey did not consider such an approach fully adequate. He too described theology as a positive science, but by this term he meant a science "whose content is empirically or historically given."[6] For Schleiermacher the unity of theology consisted in the cooperation of all its subdisciplines in the accomplishment of its goal, whereas for Drey the unity of theology was grounded in the nature of human knowing. Nothing, he insisted, is more likely to dampen the ardor of beginning students than the idea that their discipline is an accidental collection of topics or an arbitrary repertoire of professional skills. If students are to become enthusiastic about their subject, they must be led to see the intrinsic connection between it and their own innermost nature. They must be shown that knowledge of the field is "originally identical with the human spirit, arises out of it and so asserts itself in an independent

---

3. Ibid., iv.
4. Schleiermacher, *Kurze Darstellung des theologischen Studiums zum Behuf einleitender Vorlesungen* (Berlin, 1811), critical edition by Heinrich Scholz (1910; reprint, Hildesheim: Georg Olms Verlagsbuchhandlung, 1977). (Footnotes in what follows refer to Scholz's critical edition of the text.) John E. Thiel has an excellent study of Drey's indebtedness in the *Kurze Einleitung* to Schleiermacher's *Kurze Darstellung,* especially with regard to Drey's treatment of doctrinal development: "J. S. Drey on Doctrinal Development: The Context of Theological Encyclopedia," *Heythrop Journal* 27, no. 3 (July 1986): 290–305. See also Thiel, "Orthodoxy and Heterodoxy in Schleiermacher's Theological Encyclopedia: Doctrinal Development and Theological Creativity," *Heythrop Journal* 25, no. 2 (April 1984): 142–57; and idem, "Theological Responsibility: Beyond the Classical Paradigm," *Theological Studies* 47, no. 4 (December 1986): 573–98, esp. 579–85.
5. Schleiermacher, *Kurze Darstellung,* 1.
6. Drey, *Kurze Einleitung,* vi.

guise as a special science, as a special but necessary function of human knowledge in general."[7]

But Drey's position was formed by graver considerations than simply good pedagogy. He was convinced that theology had gone into decline when it lost its sense of connectedness to life. In 1812 he had published an article maintaining that a thorough rethinking of the teaching and the doing of theology within Catholicism was necessary.[8] A renewal of theology was essential for the life of the church in that it must have a profound effect on the clergy, who, whether they recognize it or not, always act on the basis of some sort of theological principles rooted in their understanding of religion. Theology, according to Drey, is the systematic expression in self-conscious terms of what lies at the heart of religious living, an expression that clarifies religious experience and so furthers it.

To illustrate what was wrong with the arid theology taught by many of his contemporaries, Drey invited comparison with the theology of the Middle Ages. This had been the product, according to Drey, of a culture marked by the interpenetration of religion and life. Christianity was neither a historical recollection nor the conclusion of a line of reasoning, but a positive fact of current experience. Experience, not reason, grounds religion. It is a matter of *Gemüt*, not *Verstand*. Scholastic theology had understood this because, contrary to the image of it that the Enlightenment had promulgated, it had been formed in a mystical and contemplative spirit; it was "the impress of [the scholastics'] spiritual sensitivity."[9] This great medieval synthesis of life and religion, of *Verstand* in service of *Gemüt*, fell apart because of the divorce of reason and life. The attempt had been made to erect philosophy independent of theology and, in reaction, theologians had tried to build on the foundation of a purely intellectual process, *Verstand*. But such an intellectual process cannot grasp experience, Drey warned, and consequently appreciation of the church as a community of common experience dimmed until it had virtually disappeared in his own day. Tradition, the concrete

---

7. Ibid., v.
8. Drey, "Revision des gegenwärtigen Zustandes der Theologie," *Archiv für die Pastoralkonferenzen des Bistums Konstanz* 1 (1812): 3–26; reprinted in J. R. Geiselmann, ed., *Geist des Christentums und des Katholizismus: Ausgewählte Schriften katholischer Theologie im Zeitalter des deutschen Idealismus und der Romantik* (Mainz: R. Oldenbourg, 1940), 85–97. (Footnotes in what follows refer to the original [1812] text.)
9. Ibid., 9.

living reality of the community, no longer served as the norm for theology. Rather, the norm became institutionalized authority expressed in
one member of the community, the pope. The reformers had rejected
this authority, but they appreciated even less than their contemporaries
who remained Catholic the importance of the living community and so
raised up individual experience and understanding as the norm. In an
attempt to balance this extreme subjectivity, they had placed scripture as
the concomitant objective element in Christianity. And so the living tradition of the community, which preserves the past while transforming
it to meet the needs of the present, had been replaced by the dead letter. Scripture was the only objective ground left on which theologians
could concentrate in order to avoid wandering off into an ever-more
fantastic subjectivity. Theology was reduced to philology and grammar.
Rather than the magnificent, organic unfolding of a positive, spiritually
enlivening reality across time, this dry erudition had rendered the history of salvation a series of discrete events that could be explained either
by a supernaturalist appeal to the will of God or by purely contingent
causes. The lifeless analyses of discursive reason (*Verstand*) overcame the
living insights of intuitive reason (*Vernunft*) and the concrete data of history. Tradition had come to mean only the inherited weight of decisions
and decrees. This did not mean that tradition was dead, Drey hastened
to point out, for if it were, there would be no life left in the church at all.
Tradition lived, but unfortunately apart from theology. The task, Drey
announced, was to bring theology back to this vitalizing source.

Thus it was essential that theology be shown to be rooted in the living experience of Christians and that its various branches answer to
necessary aspects of that experience. Drey found support for this effort in the understanding of science that he received from Schelling,
especially in the latter's *Vorlesungen über die Methode des akademischen
Studiums.*[10] Drey specifically noted in his program for theological stu-

---

10. Schelling, *Vorlesungen über die Methode des akademischen Studiums* (Tübingen, 1803),
republished in *F. W. J. Schellings sämtliche Werke*, ed. K. F. A. Schelling, 14 vols. (Stuttgart and
Augsburg, 1856–61), 5:209–352 (footnotes in what follows refer to this edition); Otto Weiss's
1911 edition of the text has been reedited by Walter E. Ehrhardt (Hamburg: Felix Meiner,
1974). Drey's indebtedness to Schelling and the latter's influence on many Catholic theologians of Drey's generation in the German-speaking world have been ably explored
by Thomas Franklin O'Meara, *Romantic Idealism and Roman Catholicism: Schelling and the
Theologians* (Notre Dame, Ind.: University of Notre Dame Press, 1982); on Drey, see esp.
94–108.

dents that "various comments, very much to be taken to heart, on a
scientific formulation of Christianity and a scientific treatment of theology" are contained in this work on the interrelation of academic
disciplines, especially in the eighth and ninth lectures.[11] Schelling had
written that

> knowledge of the organic whole of the sciences must precede spe-
> cialized education for a particular profession. Whoever devotes
> himself to one special field must learn to know the place which
> it occupies in the whole and the particular spirit which animates
> it as well as the manner of education by which it is related to the
> harmonious structure of the whole. He must also learn the way by
> which he can approach his science so that he can think not as a
> slave but as a free man and in the spirit of the whole.[12]

Science, *Wissenschaft*, organized knowledge, rests on one crucial assumption: the identity of the real with the ideal.[13] Schelling's *Iden-
titätsphilosophie* is predicated on the claim that the ideal finds concrete
expression in the real and the real is intelligible because of the ideal. Pure
ideality is mere abstraction; pure reality is unknowable. One knows the
ideal only in and through the real; one grasps the real only when it is
seen as the embodied ideal.

> The nature of the absolute is that the absolutely ideal is also the
> real. In this claim lie two possibilities, that as ideal, [the absolute]
> fashions its essence into form as the real, and that, because this
> [essence] can only be absolute, it forever likewise dissolves form
> again into essence, so that it is essence and form in perfect fusion.[14]

This is the touchstone of all knowledge, and it perfectly coincided
with Drey's determination to ground theology in the living experience
of Christians. Theology was to be understood as that reflection on experience that shows the formative power of the ideal on the real and the
realization of the ideal in history. Theology was not merely a collection of

11. Drey, *Kurze Einleitung*, 57.
12. Schelling, *Vorlesungen*, 5:213.
13. Ibid., 5:215.
14. Ibid., 5:219.

professional skills united by their orientation to a common task. Theology, insofar as it was *Wissenschaft,* had to evidence its intrinsic necessity. And so it did in Drey's definition:

> Theology, as pure intellectual response to religion, arises necessarily in man; i.e., it arises according to necessary laws of man's whole nature, specifically according to those by which he seeks to clarify his experience, obscure in itself, and to maintain that which is in itself transient; through concepts man renders permanent what his heart produces in him as fleeting inclinations and disinclinations, so that by means of these concepts, he can freely awaken and, as often as he chooses, renew what he originally experienced as external or alien stimuli. As man deals with all his experiences generally, so must he do with his religious experiences, which are of supreme interest to him.[15]

Theology seeks to preserve the reality of concrete experience by discerning the ideal that informs it, and to grasp the ideal by being faithful to the concrete experience.

The description of theology as *Verstand* in service of *Gemüt,* the conceptualization of religious experience, seems to place Drey squarely in the mainstream of nineteenth-century, liberal Christian thought. It might serve as a nearly perfect example of what has been described as the "experiential-expressive" understanding of Christian doctrines.[16] As such, it lays itself open to a charge of subjectivism, dissolving all doctrinal and theological statements into symbols of an experience of transcendence deeply rooted in all human persons. Drey would have rejected this charge, however. For the principle at the heart of the *wissenschaftlich* method was that the ideal is neither temporally nor logically prior to the real, but rather that each conditions the other. Thus, as Drey applied this principle, life shaped by the doctrines, practices, and worship of the Christian community leads to Christian religious experience

---

15. Drey, *Kurze Einleitung,* 23.
16. The term is from George A. Lindbeck, *The Nature of Doctrine: Religion and Theology in a Postliberal Age* (Philadelphia: Westminster Press, 1984), 16: "[Experiential-expressivism] interprets doctrines as noninformative and nondiscursive symbols of inner feelings, attitudes, or existential orientations. This approach highlights the resemblance of religions to aesthetic enterprises and is particularly congenial to the liberal theologies influenced by the Continental developments that began with Schleiermacher."

just as truly as that experience finds expression in those forms of life. The actually existing Christian community and its history are therefore central to Drey's laying out of the system of theology. Further, one misses Drey's point completely if one fails to notice that the locus of the transcendent experience that he called "the kingdom of God" is the community of believers, not the individual. The individualism of much of liberal theology was totally foreign to the ecclesiocentric perspective of Drey and the Catholic Tübingen school.

The concrete experience—that is, the living experience of the Christian community—will differ as communities differ, and so, Drey concluded, different churches must have different theologies. And the differences among those theologies are not exhausted by the differences in doctrinal formulas, but extend to their organizations, foundations, divisions, and the uses to which they are put. Drey agreed with Schleiermacher on this point, although for different reasons. In accord with his description of theology as a collection of disciplines and skills united by their common purpose, equipping leaders for the church, Schleiermacher held that a church would have to develop a theology suited to its own spirit and needs.[17] For Drey, each Christian community must evolve its own theology because it is the church that provides the phenomenal material for the ideal construction of Christianity; it is the church whose history is shown to be the working out of that ideal; and it is the church that is the arena for the praxis born of ideal knowledge of scientific Christian theology. All scientific theology is in fact ecclesiology, for the church is the concretization of Christianity, the ideal having taken on reality, "the concrete expression of the science itself." Thus, Drey could summarize his own theological encyclopedia:

> We give an outline of *Catholic theology,* and it is as follows: the construction of the Christian religious faith through knowledge based upon the Catholic church and in its spirit, with the goal of working with this knowledge in a way suited to that church and in accord with the plan of Christianity.[18]

---

17. See Schleiermacher, *Kurze Darstellung,* 30, specifically referring to "philosophical theology": "So long as Christianity is divided into a plurality of church communities which lay claim to the same title, that is to be Christian, so too the same tasks arise with reference to them. And there is then, besides the general, a special philosophical theology for each of them.... Our particular philosophical theology is consequently Protestant."

18. Drey, *Kurze Einleitung,* 33.

Historical Theology: Grasping the Ideal in the Real

Because Christianity is "a particular positive religion with a definite content of religious ideas which, once received within human hearts, ground there a religious faith,"[19] its organized self-reflection, theology, is also a "positive" science—that is, it arises out of experiences that are always determined by the cultural development of the subject and their translation into concepts that stand in relation to other systems of concepts expressive of other experiences and perceptions. Because the subject exists in community and both experiences and interprets experiences within the context of a historical community, theology must include in its study the historical, communal expression of religious ideas. The externalization of ideas, the forms that Christianity took with its "definite content of religious ideas," the development of those ideas reflected in the developments of their externalizations in doctrine and cult, all must be included in the study of theology. It should be noted that "the religious ideas" of Christianity are "received within human hearts," not generated there. Being a positive religion, Christianity comes to believers from outside themselves. The individual believer's experience is formed by living within the believing community.

Historical theology then is an extremely important discipline within the science of theology. But the very fact of its importance raises a question. There is a history, a development of the expressions of the determination of religious feelings that is Christian faith. These expressions change, grow, and deepen. They are never fully adequate. The feelings that are the subjective aspects of experiences are raised to ideas and are lived out in history but are never perfectly expressed. At a later time one may interpret earlier expressions wrongly. Furthermore, the concerns and culturally determined forms of one stage of development may become so intimately interwoven with religious faith that it becomes difficult to separate them. Faith may be expressed badly, may on occasion be distorted. One cannot simply take the history of Christianity and abstract from it to the ideas that are the content of Christian religion. Historical study is necessary for theology but not sufficient. It cannot by itself assure real knowledge, yet Christian theology is "a construction of this faith through knowledge." Scientific theology must find a way

---

19. Ibid., 30.

of mediating the ideas of Christian faith and the history of Christian living.

Happily, Drey believed that this mediation was provided precisely by the thoroughgoing attempt to do theology as a science. The *wissenschaftlich* method of Schelling on which Drey relied dictated a double-pronged approach to theology: "The construction of Catholic theology, like all theological construction in general, can be pursued in two distinct ways: purely historically through investigation, or scientifically through construction from ideas."[20] All science is the holding together of the idea, which cannot be attained by mere abstraction from phenomena but which nevertheless explains them, and the visible, tangible realities, which incompletely embody the idea and yet have intelligible existence only because of the idea. To do theology in a rigorously scientific way is to take full account of both its positive and its ideal aspects. Science is the construction of the ideal a priori and the uncovering of that ideal in the phenomenal evidence a posteriori. Whether one does theology as an empirical a posteriori study or as an ideal a priori study should not affect one's conclusions. For obviously if the real is the embodied ideal and the ideal is the intelligible essence of the real, then as starting points each leads to the same end. Indeed, each acts as both an illumination and a verification of the other. For Drey, then, historical theology and speculative theology should be in mutually fruitful conversation.

Unfortunately, Drey's vocabulary obscures the relationship between the ideal and the real that the first section of the *Kurze Einleitung* rehearses at such length. He classified theological specializations under three headings: (1) historical theology in the broad sense, embracing both the study of scripture and historical theology in the narrow sense of what he called church history; (2) scientific theology, embracing foundational studies (i.e., apologetics and polemics) and specialized scientific theology (i.e., doctrinal systematics [dogmatics and ethics] and ecclesial systematics [liturgics, sacramentology, and canon law]); and (3) practical theology, which returns to the life of the church with the scientific knowledge attained in the first two "constructions," embracing church order and church administration. But historical investigation and scientific construction of ideas, the two prongs of

---

20. Ibid., 33–34.

true *wissenschaftlich* knowing, do not simply correspond to historical theology and scientific theology. Both prongs are moments in
both historical theology and scientific theology. Drey's multiple uses
of the terms historical (*historisch*) and scientific (*wissenschaftlich*) confuse his presentation. On the one hand, they describe complementary
approaches in any positive branch of study and so in theology, approaches that must be evidenced in any and every division of theology.
On the other hand, they also name particular divisions of theological study, and in the case of historical theology, the term "historical"
designates both a division and a subheading of that division. Drey intended that the two complementary approaches be present in every
branch of theological study because, as he had learned from Schelling,
without both there is no true and rigorous—that is, scientific—knowledge.

In Drey's classification of theological specializations, apologetics is
the crucial area. It is the study of the essence of Christianity. Because the
church is the embodiment of Christianity, the study may be conducted
by examining Christianity as a pure concept or as a living, embodied
power. The first approach seeks to answer the question, "What is the
essence of the system of Christian religion?" The second approach attempts to answer the question, "What is the essence of the Christian
church?"[21] Both presume the material supplied by biblical and historical studies. Those studies show that the Christian religion is a collection
of particular religious ideas and that the Christian church has a history
of particular forms.[22] To answer the questions concerning essence, it is
necessary to find the grounding idea beneath all the religious ideas of
Christianity, the fundamental doctrine behind all Christian doctrines,
and to show that it is the idea embodied in the church that remains constant in all its historical expressions. This search for the principle that
gives unity to the whole system of Christian doctrines and the entire
course of church history is required not only for the fulfillment of the
demands of rationality, a need experienced by the theologian, but also
for the justification of the claims of Christianity as a religion. By locating
that grounding idea of Christianity, it becomes possible to show how
this essence lies behind all religions but is fully worked out only in the

---

21. Ibid., 150.
22. Ibid., 151.

Christian religion as idea and in the Christian church as fact. This search for unity is apologetics.[23]

But this crucial division of theological science is a problem. In fact, Drey admitted, as a worked-through, rigorously performed specialization, it did not exist because a genuinely scientific historical theology in the broad sense had not yet been done. Drey mentioned three reasons why this was so: (1) the first of its two divisions, biblical theology, was underdeveloped up to the point at which Drey was writing; (2) its second division, historical theology in the narrow sense, was deficient in its presentation because it had not been pursued in a rigorously *wissenschaftlich* fashion; and (3) both biblical theology and historical theology in the narrow sense were thoroughly imbued with confessional positions.[24] Scientific theology properly so-called is built on the assumption that the data are supplied by the two divisions of historical theology, which assumption had proven false. Those who would engage in scientific theology had therefore to turn their energy and attention to the preliminary investigations and thus could not engage in their own proper pursuits, and so scientific theology was compromised.

Drey's suggested remedies for the threefold failure of historical theology relied heavily on Schelling's treatment of history in his lectures on academic studies. Schelling had warned against "pragmatic" historical study—that is, using history to illustrate social or political positions.[25] But he had also warned that history should not be done from an "absolute" standpoint, not because such a standpoint is wrong or unavailable, but because to do so is to abandon historical study and to engage in philosophy or theology.[26] History, like nature, is the synthesis of the real and the ideal. Such a synthesis, when effected by human creativity, is a work of art.

23. Ibid., 152. Drey's principal published work was in this theological specialization, *Die Apologetik als wissenschaftliche Nachweisung der Göttlichkeit des Christentums in seiner Erscheinung*, 3 vols. (1838–47; reprint, Frankfurt am Main: Minerva Verlag, 1967). Especially useful on Drey's apologetics are Wayne L. Fehr, *The Birth of the Catholic Tübingen School: The Dogmatics of Johann Sebastian Drey* (Chico, Calif.: American Academy of Religion/Scholars Press, 1981), chaps. 2 and 3; Josef Rupert Geiselmann, "Die Glaubenswissenschaft der katholischen Tübinger Schule in ihrer Grundlegung durch Johann Sebastian Drey (1777–1853)," *Theologische Quartalschrift* 111 (1930): 116–30; idem, *Die Katholische Tübinger Schule: Ihre theologische Eigenart* (Freiburg: Herder, 1964); and Josef Rief, *Reich Gottes und Gesellschaft nach Johann Sebastian Drey und Johann Baptist Hirscher* (Paderborn: F. Schöningh, 1965).
24. Drey, *Die Apologetik*, 167.
25. Schelling, *Vorlesungen*, 5:307–8.
26. Ibid., 5:307.

True history thus consists of a synthesis of the given and real with the ideal, but not through philosophy, since this transcends the real and is wholly ideal, whereas history is wholly real and yet at the same time ideal. This is possible only in art which is entirely immersed in the real, as the stage presents concrete events or histories but with a fullness and unity through which they become the expression of the highest ideas.[27]

History, like art, is the counterpart to nature; it is the concrete expression of the ideal through human action. The study of history is then the discernment of the ideal in the real. So, of course, are theology and philosophy, neither of which is simply identical with history, for history discerns the ideal without being able to account for it. It therefore remains thoroughly the study of the real.[28] Schelling advised historians that they must undertake their study "as a kind of epic poem which has no clear beginning and no clear end: one should begin at whatever point one regards as the most interesting or important and develop and expand in all directions from that point to the whole field."[29]

But Drey knew that theology, like philosophy, claims to treat in some way of the beginning and end of the epic about which history must be agnostic. Consequently, historical theology in all its branches is engaged in history with a difference. Schelling himself had recognized that Christian religious history occupied a unique position. Pre-Christian religion, especially Greek religion, had centered on the existence of the infinite in the finite as a simply given fact. The expression of the infinite in the finite was not a task to be accomplished, but was *there* to be uncovered. It was always a religion of nature. Christianity broke through this purely natural religion, according to Schelling, by means of its primary image, the God-man. In the incarnation, the fullness of the ideal, God, becomes a human being. That human being is not a classical hero, however, but an unsuccessful itinerant prophet who dies as a condemned criminal and blasphemer. Christianity has thus united extremes: the fullness of God with the most rejected of humanity. Christ "stands forth as a phenomenon decreed from all eternity but taking place in time, as boundary of the two worlds."

---

27. Ibid., 5:309–10.
28. Ibid., 5:310.
29. Ibid., 5:311.

He goes back into the realm of the invisible and promises in his
place not the principle which comes into the finite realm and
remains in the finite, but the Spirit, the ideal principle which instead leads the finite back to the infinite and, as such, is the light
of the new world. In this basic idea all the characteristic marks
of Christianity are linked together. According to its ideal orientation, to posit the union of the infinite and the finite objectively
through a symbol, like Greek religion, is impossible. All symbolization falls back upon the subject, and so the resolution of the
opposition which is not to be perceived externally but purely
internally remains a mystery, a secret. The antinomy of the divine and the natural, which permeates everything, is overcome
only through the subject's distinctive ability to think both, in an
incomprehensible fashion, as one.[30]

The concretization of the ideal is no longer simply *there*. Now it is an
achievement, a task to be performed. The achievement of the subject, to
think the infinite and the finite as one, does not remain subjective; it demands objectification. But that objectification remains the activity of the
subject; the subject's task is not to discover some objective expression of
that incomprehensible unity already out there now. No longer is nature
the sole objectification of the ideal and infinite; now there is history.

The ideas of a religion directed toward the intuition of the infinite
in the finite must be expressed preeminently in existing reality,
whereas the ideas of the opposite [kind of religion], in which all
symbolization belongs to the subject alone, can be made objective
only through action. The original symbol of any intuition of God in
[the latter] is history. But this is endless and immeasurable. It must
accordingly be represented through a phenomenon at once infinite and yet limited, which is itself not simply real, like the state,
but ideal, and which expresses the unity of all in the spirit under
the condition of separation into individuality as immediate presence. This symbolized intuition is the church as a living work of
art.[31]

---

30. Ibid., 5:292–93.
31. Ibid., 5:293.

The church is the visible expression of what is true of secular history but not always observable there, the unification of the ideal and the real, the infinite and the finite. And so Christian history is the key to secular history. Thus Drey could conclude that the historical theologian, precisely by being a theologian, is not less rigorously historical but more so. Schelling provided him with a deep foundation for the insistence that the lived experience of the church, critically examined in light of the ideal that it embodies, provides the norm for all theology.

"The Catholic View of Historical Theology"

The first division of historical theology, according to Drey, is biblical studies with its two specializations, biblical history and biblical theology. The first of these specializations was especially underdeveloped in Drey's opinion. The problem, he lamented, was that biblical history was done under the rubric of an inadequate notion of history. It is true that the theologian—and the biblical historian is or should be engaged in a subdiscipline of theology—"grasps world history, and so much the more biblical history, from the standpoint of religion."[32] What for others is "the chaotic confusion of the world is for him the drama of providence."[33] But this is not to claim exemption from the usual method of historical study. Christian theology rests on a historical foundation and is itself an important part of the history of the world. Consequently, sacred history becomes unintelligible if it is isolated from profane history.[34] But biblical historians have too often missed the significance of historical study and so the true method of doing history.

Historical theology in the narrow sense can be distinguished from biblical theology to the extent that "in the historical treatment of Christianity the point in time of its inception and original form may be distinguished from the period of its further spread and development."[35] Because the realized expression of Christianity throughout this period can be called the church, this branch of theological study can be designated church history. Drey noted that the distinction between the origin

---

32. Drey, *Kurze Einleitung,* 77.
33. Ibid.
34. See ibid., 60–61.
35. Ibid., 117.

and subsequent course of Christianity is artificial because together they form one history, and he further noted that for a truly historical grasp of the essence of Christianity, the later history is even more important than the earlier. This conclusion, which Drey calls "the Catholic view of historical theology,"[36] follows from his organic notion of history as the unfolding of the self-expression of the ideal in the real: in an organism later stages of growth are more fully revelatory than earlier stages as what was latent becomes apparent and what was present as a potentiality is actualized. Thus the ongoing life of the Christian community, its tradition, is the norm that allows for the true understanding of the Bible. Tradition is not a source of revelation in addition to the scriptures. Rather it is the whole experience of the church, the foundational moment of which is recorded in the scriptures. This "Catholic view" later provided Drey's most famous student, Johann Adam Möhler, the basis for his rejection of the principle of *sola scriptura* in favor of *scriptura in ecclesia*.[37]

According to this organic "higher concept of history," the course of Christianity's history must be understood as "the striving and straining of a single principle, of one spirit,"[38] which forms under the conditions of time and place its own forms and institutions and incorporates into itself whatever in its surroundings it finds suitable to itself. This is not a plea for a privileged position for the church historian, for Drey maintained that this "higher concept" was not unique in Christian history: "All the great phenomena of history must be so viewed."[39] The single principle whose development is to be traced through the history of the church and that gives that history its coherence is the kingdom of God, which Drey had introduced in the general introduction to his *Kurze Einleitung* as the principle of unity opposed to the egoism that attempts to cast humanity and the world as separate and independent realities.

---

36. Ibid., 118.
37. See Johann Adam Möhler, *Neue Untersuchungen der Lehrgegensätze zwischen den Katholiken und Protestanten: Eine Vertheidigung meiner Symbolik gegen die Kritik des Herrn Professors Dr. Baur in Tübingen* (1835, 2d ed.; reprint, Frankfurt am Main: Minerva Verlag, 1976), 453ff. See also Josef Rupert Geiselmann, *Lebendiger Glaube aus geheiligter Überlieferung: Der Grundgedanke der Theologie Johann Adam Möhlers und der katholischen Tübinger Schule,* Die Überlieferung in der neueren Theologie, 1–11, 2d ed. (Freiburg: Herder, 1966.)
38. Drey, *Kurze Einleitung,* 118.
39. Ibid.

This idea thus appears as supreme, as that idea of Christianity to which everything else leads and from which everything else flows. And Christ who brought about its universal recognition is accordingly the *visible head of the kingdom,* just as its visible manifestation and sensible expression is the *church.*[40]

Drey here brought together the three central and interrelated elements that he understood to characterize Christianity: the idea of the kingdom of God, the person of Christ, and the church. Christianity can be viewed from three perspectives. Philosophically, its significance lies in its recognition that the human attempt to alienate the self and its world from God is meaningless, its acknowledgment of God's perfect overlordship, and its celebration of an atonement with and effected by God. Historically, the importance of Christianity is its summation of the inchoate desire for redemption that is evidenced again and again in human history and that finds expression in Christ. Theologically, Christianity introduced new religious expressions and ideas, reawakened others, and radically altered still others either by exposing their deficiencies or reinterpreting them. This makes Christianity "a particular religious institution of a specific character," which viewed from within is seen to be "a unique system of religious doctrines," and from without is discovered to be "a uniquely unified phenomenon for the purpose of preservation of those religious doctrines and of a religious life of true worship to God—or a church."[41]

These three elements were all developed by Drey in accord with the *wissenschaftlich* model. As the pinnacle of revelation, Christianity sets forth anew the original unity between God and the universe, the revelation of God, but does so by raising that original unity to a new level. In the ideas of the incarnation and the God-man that original unity becomes free, conscious, and personal. That union of God and creation was revealed first in the universe itself, lay at the root of all religious feeling, was obscured by human egoism, and has now been revealed once again as the kingdom of God.

Drey's understanding of primordial revelation has obvious affinities with Schleiermacher's *Bewusstseinstheologie.* In both, religion is the sense of being posited with and in all that exists. This sense—which accom-

40. Ibid., 19.
41. Ibid., 18.

panies and cannot be separated from consciousness and which arises with the consciousness of self—is the primordial revelation of God.[42] For revelation is God's "expression of his essence in that which is not God and consequently other than himself. Other than God is the universe and this alone; all revelation of God can take place only in the universe, and indeed the latter is nothing other than the former."[43] But if this consciousness of oneness with the universe necessarily accompanies self-consciousness, it also is obscured by it. For when the universe divides into subject and object, the human being casts himself or herself over against everything else that exists, and the primitive consciousness of identity recedes. Nature is thus stripped of it revelatory power.[44]

Acceptance of revelation, which Drey equated with faith, is then no longer immediate through sense or intuition, but mediated through reflection. A new level of revelation is necessary. Not that God acts in a new fashion, but rather the divine action is received by human beings in a new way. Now the divine action is perceived as a work that cannot be explained as a human product or an effect of nature's intrinsic laws. For nonbelievers such an event is unnatural; for believers it is supernatural. Gradually the human race was led to the point at which the division between the universe, including humanity, and God could be overcome—that is, to the idea of the kingdom of God. "This turning point in the religious history of humanity under the guidance of revelation is called *Christianity*."[45]

It is of the essence of Christianity that this idea of the union of the divine and creation is also real. Drey insisted that the central idea of the kingdom of God, like Christianity itself, is of an "entirely *positive* kind."[46] It is grasped in a particular, concrete, and historical instance, the person of Christ, and develops in a particular, concrete, and historical community, the church. The idea is inseparable from these concretizations; the histories of this person and this community are unintelligible apart from this idea. In accord with the idea that enlivens it and that it embodies, the kingdom of God, Christianity is engaged in an ongoing struggle with the divisive, egoistic spirit of the world. That struggle has in part shaped

---

42. Ibid., 3.
43. Ibid., 10.
44. Ibid., 11.
45. Ibid., 17.
46. Ibid., 20.

the Christian spirit and so has affected the forms, doctrines, and institutions that give expression to that spirit. In consequence, the history
of the church can be studied from two perspectives: the internal history of Christianity traces the unfolding of the Christian *Grundidee* as it
has developed and expressed itself "immediately"—that is, without the
give-and-take of the constant tension between it and the worldly principle of disintegration—and the external history of Christianity deals with
the "mediate" expressions of the *Grundidee* that have been shaped by the
interaction of the church with the world.[47]

Thus the combination of the method of rigorous "scientific" knowledge drawn from Schelling with a stance toward theology that views it
as essentially positive led Drey to accord the church a central position
in his theological outline.

> The church is the true basis of all theological knowledge. From it
> and through it the theologian receives the empirically given ma-
> terial of that knowledge. Through the connection with it, all its
> concepts first attain reality; without it, they end up in airy, ground-
> less speculation. Within it, knowledge must issue again in practice
> or else knowledge remains idle, aimless daydreaming.[48]

The *wissenschaftlich* method drawn from Schelling served Drey's
Catholic sensibility well. It allowed him to place the church at the center
of his theological studies. Ecclesiology became the touchstone by which
theology is judged to be "real." Apart from the concrete life of the church,
theology is mere abstract speculation.

This was not by any means ecclesiolatry. Drey was far too astute a
critic of the church polity of his time to canonize every form and action of the church. But he insisted that the standard by which church
structures were to be criticized was provided by the church itself. He
compared the theologian's situation with that of students of law and
medicine. "The church is for the theologian what the state is for the law,
what the animal organism is for the science of medicine—the concrete
expression of the science itself through which every positive science
exists."[49] The scientific study of law proceeds by the construction of

---

47. Ibid., 119.
48. Ibid., 33.
49. Ibid.

the idea of the state out of the phenomena of the state, which idea is then uncovered in the existing reality of the state. Thus the ideal is demonstrated to be real and the existing reality is shown to be intelligible, not merely the product of historical accidents.[50] The scientific study of medicine constructs the healthily working organism on the basis of the data of existing organisms, and that ideal is then shown to explain the data.[51] In both spheres, the knowledge of the ideal thus achieved is employed to solve the imperfections of the real existents, in the one case to resolve the inequities of the de facto state, in the other to cure malfunctioning organisms. So in theology, the study of the church allows the scientific theologian to construct the ideal of the Christian faith, to explain the history and present existence of the church by the unfolding of that idea, and so to move into church reform, bringing the present church into accord with the ideal of its faith.

Drey certainly did not intend to hold to a "whatever is, is right" position that would simply identify the church as it is with what it ought to be, the concrete realization of the kingdom of God under the current historical conditions. Although he sought the "unifying point at which all the manifold phenomena, in manifold contradictions as to their externals, come together,"[52] sometimes the data do not admit to easy coincidence with the explanatory idea that raises them to ideality. Instead they remain stubbornly un-ideal. The *wissenschaftlich* method does not subsume the existing church into the ideal church. Describing the role of specifically scientific theology, under which he included dogmatics and ethics, he wrote:

> In this examination of particular historically derived concepts within the idea (or ideas) of Christianity, it cannot fail that much historical data must be uncovered which do not correspond to the Christian idea to which they ought to correspond. Such data appear then as malformations in the development of Christianity and so must be regarded as errors or mistakes and be excluded from the system.[53]

---

50. See Schelling, *Vorlesungen*, 5:313–14.
51. See ibid., 5:341–42.
52. Drey, *Kurze Einleitung*, 145–46.
53. Ibid., 167–68.

This is properly the work of the specifically scientific divisions of the theological enterprise and of polemics, not of historical theology. This scientific theology "in the strong sense" is concerned with the conceptual formulations of Christianity and the relations among those formulations. This distinguishes it from church history, which deals with the historical data and seeks historical truth. As such, church history is "unconcerned whether what is found to be historically true is also historically formed in a genuinely Christian fashion, derived from the idea of Christianity, and is in accord with this idea and with all the other Christian formulations."[54] But because so little truly scientific theology "in the pure state" had previously been done, Drey acknowledged that historical theologians had frequently had to overstep the bounds of their field in order to engage in the work that properly belongs to those in polemics and dogmatics. He was not concerned to erect watertight bulkheads between branches of theology, because both historical theologians and scientific theologians are guided by the *wissenschaftlich* method of mediating the ideal through the real. Consequently, any attempt to distinguish the two areas by simply allotting the real to historical theologians and the ideal to scientific theologians is both a fundamental misunderstanding of Schelling's and Drey's meaning of *Wissenschaft* and unworkable in practice. The emphasis in historical theology is on the data of history, but as Drey was at pains to make clear to his students, the data are unintelligible without some intuition of the ideal that forms them. The emphasis in scientific theology is on the conceptualized formulas—for example, dogmas, doctrines, and moral codes—that give expression to the fundamental idea of Christianity, the kingdom of God, but that idea is a historical reality and Christianity remains "positive." Thus the line between the two fields, while real, is fine. Drey's concern was not so much that no one should ever cross the line but rather that, when the line has been crossed, one should know that one is in a new field with new responsibilities, tasks, and procedures.

Drey's appropriation of key elements of the early philosophy of Schelling, especially the *wissenschaftlich* method, was a remarkable effort to bring Catholic theology into fruitful conversation with post-Kantian thought. In his theological encyclopedia Drey attempted to do for Cath-

---

54. Ibid., 166.

olic theology what Schleiermacher had done for Reformed theology in his *Kurze Darstellung,* and for similar reasons. Although he disagreed with Schleiermacher on the basic nature of theology, convinced that an inherent connection exists between the various components of the science and not merely an extrinsic one created by the need of providing leaders for the church, Drey held that in fact theology is also necessary for the service of the Christian community. Indeed, his efforts to reform the method and content of Catholic theology were expressly undertaken because of his conviction that the church's good required that its leaders be intellectually equipped to meet the challenges of their time. "For all the theologian's knowledge and work is for the sake of the church and its best interests."[55]

Drey's influence on subsequent historical theology is not direct. He neither taught nor wrote in the discipline of historical theology himself, although his lectures in dogmatics and his three-volume work in apologetics are frequently concerned with what he would have considered the proper work of the historical theologian. But he did shape the direction of the Catholic theological faculty at Tübingen. The centrality of the church as not only the carrier of Christian revelation but also the embodiment of that revelation in its life, liturgy, and structures deeply marked the subsequent development of Roman Catholic theology in Germany. The emphasis on tradition as the lived experience of the believing community rather than as the deposit of truths not recorded in scripture provided an immensely fruitful alternative view to the propositional understanding of doctrine that marked much of Catholic theology in the nineteenth and early twentieth century. Drey's "Catholic view of historical theology" stood in sharp contrast to the ahistorical neo-scholasticism that dominated Catholic thought in the ninety years between the two Vatican councils. Within Catholic theology he established a vision that prevented history from being reduced to the mining of proof texts for a polemically shaped dogmatic theology. His appropriation of the *wissenschaftlich* method from Schelling grounded the insistence that historical data could not be disregarded in favor of "timeless" doctrinal formulas. This permitted other Catholic theologians—Möhler, Staudenmaier, Döllinger, Hergenröther—to treat historical research not as a problem but as a resource and to engage

---

55. Ibid., 148.

in historical theology as a vital part of the theological enterprise. That within Catholic circles in the nineteenth century the term "historical theology" did not become an oxymoron was in no small part the legacy of Johann Sebastian Drey.

ELEVEN

William Madges

Johannes Kuhn: The Nature of Christian Doctrine and the Theological Task

John Henry Newman believed that in the Roman Catholic Church the historical development of doctrine was regarded as natural and necessary. But he held that the Protestant churches, with their emphasis upon scripture as theological and ecclesiastical norm, were antithetical to historical development. He thus declared: "To be deep in history is to cease to be a Protestant."[1] Friedrich Schleiermacher, as well as many of his Protestant contemporaries, held an opposing view; he maintained that development was a purely Protestant question because the Roman church claimed to rest upon immutable truth and unchanging norms.[2] And Ferdinand Christian Baur thought that the Roman Catholic understanding of doctrinal development was quite similar to the older Protestant view. As he saw it, both denied any change "by which the substantial forms of the church might be essentially altered"; the Catholic conception, moreover, held that "everything has existed from the

---

1. John Henry Newman, *An Essay on the Development of Christian Doctrine* (1878; reprint, Westminster, Md.: Christian Classics, 1968), 8. Extolling historical change, Newman proclaimed (p. 40): "In a higher world it is otherwise, but here below to live is to change, and to be perfect is to have changed often."

2. Friedrich Schleiermacher, *Christliche Sitte*, in *Sämmtliche Werke* (Berlin: Georg Reimer, 1834–64), 1/12:72–73. See B. A. Gerrish, "Schleiermacher and the Reformation: A Question of Doctrinal Development," in *The Old Protestantism and the New* (Chicago: University of Chicago Press, 1982), 193.

beginning just as it appears in the course of subsequent development."[3] To Baur this meant that the Catholic position ultimately acknowledged no real change from one age to the next.

Johannes Evangelist von Kuhn (1806–87), theologian in the Catholic faculty at Tübingen, addressed this issue of doctrinal change. The issue was important to him not merely historically, but also theologically. For only if real change in the church's teaching were possible could Kuhn justify new theological programs such as his own. The challenge that Kuhn faced confronts every creative theologian: how to utilize the latest insights into the nature of reality and humanity while maintaining fidelity to the Christian tradition. In what follows I intend to sketch Kuhn's understanding of the nature of Christian doctrine and to describe how Kuhn found the justification for his model of theology in this particular understanding of doctrinal development.

Kuhn's Theological Context

Kuhn conceived his specific theological task in the middle of the nineteenth century to consist in identifying and defending a theological position median between rationalism, on the one hand, and biblicism, on the other. Rationalism was inadequate because either it rejected the category of revelation or it spoke of revelation as an incomplete stage in the unfolding of Absolute Spirit within the consciousness of human beings. Biblicism was also theologically inadequate because it merely repeated the words of the Bible without adapting them to the time, needs, and context of its audience. Both rationalism and biblicism were one-sided, respectively emphasizing the power of human reason alone or denying it any significant role in the comprehension of revelation. In this respect, Kuhn concurred with Schleiermacher that the two movements, demonstration of the agreement of present doctrinal statements with those of primitive Christianity and demonstration of agreement with rational and philosophical investigation, could be utterly opposed only when the church exists in a diseased condition.[4] Despite some

---

3. Ferdinand Christian Baur, "The Epochs of Church Historiography," in Peter C. Hodgson, ed., *Ferdinand Christian Baur on the Writing of Church History* (New York: Oxford University Press, 1968), 96 and 115.

4. See Schleiermacher, *Brief Outline of the Study of Theology,* trans. Terrence N. Tice (Atlanta: John Knox Press, 1977), §181, p. 68.

shifts between 1832 and 1859 in his understanding of revelation and doctrinal development, Kuhn consistently maintained a balance of the natural and the supernatural, the philosophical and the theological in his description of revelation and its development.

In his earlier as well as later work, Kuhn insisted that reason and revelation are not opposed. Although revelation is a work of God and not the product of human powers, it still is not an action through which God gives human powers a direction different from their natural one. Supernatural revelation presupposes natural revelation; the former is nothing other than the extension and the interiorization of the latter. Kuhn followed his predecessor in dogmatics at Tübingen, J. S. Drey, in an attempt to overcome the dichotomy of the natural and the supernatural by conceiving historical revelation as a continuation of natural revelation.[5] In the *Uroffenbarung* (original revelation), divine power is revealed in the creation of the natural order and the divine will is revealed in the moral nature of humanity. In special or supernatural revelation, God's inner being as the Father of the Christ as well as the divinity of Christ and of the Holy Spirit is revealed. The two types of revelation are distinct, yet intimately related. Supernatural revelation occurs not merely as the completion of the revelatory function of creation, but primarily as a special act of divine love that enables human beings better to achieve their spiritual purpose, "a life of the spirit in unity with God through knowledge of God and love for God." Yet the revelation of God in Christ is immediately connected to the purpose of original revelation itself.[6]

Divine revelation in Christ, then, is both the confirmation and fulfillment of the pre-Christian revelation of God as well as its end and completion. In explaining why this revelation did not occur all at once, Kuhn appealed to an idea that was common currency in the wake of the Enlightenment, namely, the educational character of revelation. In Kuhn's words, truth can be communicated to the person of sense "only gradually and only in a sensible husk; the life of the spirit can be mediated only in those forms which speak to him or her."[7] Because the forms

---

5. See Wayne L. Fehr, *The Birth of the Catholic Tübingen School: The Dogmatics of Johann Sebastian Drey* (Chico, Calif.: Scholars Press, 1981), 31–35.

6. Johannes Kuhn, *Einleitung in die katholische Dogmatik,* 2d ed. (1859; reprint, Frankfurt: Minerva, 1968), 17, 19.

7. Ibid., 20. Like Drey, however, Kuhn too was critical of Lessing's suggestion that revelation did not give us anything human reason could not discover on its own. See p. 123.

in which revelation is expressed must be suited to humankind in its various stages of development, the presentation of Christian revelation in doctrines must change and develop.

Kuhn's Conception of Development

Kuhn believed that development is both possible and necessary. It is possible subjectively speaking because we progress in our comprehension of the truth, and it is possible objectively speaking because revelation can be represented in infinitely diverse ways. Development is necessary if the proclamation of the apostolic kerygma is to succeed in awakening faith today as it did in the days of the early church.

Kuhn articulated his position on development in distinction from alternative theories of Catholic colleagues and Protestant opponents. Against fellow Catholic and Tübingen scholar Anton Staudenmaier, Kuhn insisted that divine revelation had reached its culmination in the Christ and that this revelation was purely and completely proclaimed by Jesus' apostles. Thus, the theological task since the time of the apostles was the preservation, comprehension, expression, and application of this truth in a manner appropriate to culture at any given time. Kuhn rejected Staudenmaier's contention that new Christian truths could be proclaimed in the course of time under the inspiration of the Holy Spirit.[8] Against Tübingen theologian and Protestant opponent F. C. Baur, Kuhn insisted that Catholic theology recognized and admitted that doctrine had truly developed over time; further, he argued that Catholic theology understood that development was not simply the repetition of the old truths over and over again.

In the years between the publication of the first and second editions of his *Dogmatics* (1846 and 1859), Kuhn sharpened his presentation of doctrinal development. Baur's characterization of the Catholic conception of development was partly responsible for getting Kuhn to develop more thoroughly and explicitly his thoughts on the subject. Kuhn worked out some of these thoughts in an 1850 essay in which he endeavored to correct Baur's assessment of the seventeenth-century Jesuit historian Denis Petavius, and to refute Baur's presentation of the

---

8. Ibid., 12–13, esp. 13 n. 1.

"authentically Catholic" position on doctrinal development.⁹ The second, expanded edition of Kuhn's *Introduction to Catholic Dogmatics* (1859) presents a summary of the fruit of Kuhn's debate with Baur, augmented by some further historical research.

In the first edition of his *Introduction to Catholic Dogmatics* (1846), Kuhn stated that revelation developed but did not expand. His point was that there was indeed change over time, but change did not add substantially new truths to faith's content.¹⁰ Revelation's "infinite capacity for development" meant an infinite capacity for being presented and expressed in diverse ways. Kuhn held that these different expressions would parallel the intellectual and spiritual development of humankind.

In his 1850 response to Baur, Kuhn contested Baur's characterization of the Catholic understanding of doctrinal development as well as Baur's identification of his own position. Baur held that there were three principal ways in which the process of the history of doctrines could be understood. According to the first, the content of the church's doctrines remains substantially the same over time; there is no real movement. This "dogmatic conception" of history explained all differences in teaching from one period to the next as mere differences in form. According to the second perspective, there is nothing but movement and change in the history of doctrines; there is no abiding, substantial reality that perdures through all the periods of the church's life. The third perspective, which Baur declared the best since it transcended the one-sidedness of the previous two, perceives both continuity and change in the historical process; movement or development is the necessary mediation of the content of doctrines with itself. Baur stated that the authentically Catholic position corresponded to the first perspective, and that his own

---

9. Kuhn, "Ehrenrettung des Dionysius Petavius und der katholischen Auffassung der Dogmengeschichte," *Theologische Quartalschrift* 32 (1850): 249–93; see in particular 250. Kuhn also engaged with Protestant opponents in his 1858 article, "Die formalen Principien des Katholizismus und Protestantismus," *Theologische Quartalschrift* 40 (1858): 3–62, 185–251, 385–442. For a summary sketch of Kuhn's concerns in the period 1850–59, see Franz Wolfinger, *Der Glaube nach Johann Evangelist von Kuhn* (Göttingen: Vandenhoeck & Ruprecht, 1972), 160–63.

10. Kuhn believed that if the truth of Christian revelation could only be partially and deficiently comprehended at any given time, then revelation could not fulfill its purpose, that is, to make humanity happy and blessed in possessing the *full* truth about God. See Kuhn, *Einleitung in die katholische Dogmatik* (Tübingen: H. Laupp, 1846), 109; see also 102–3, where Kuhn rejects Strauss's contention that no one time fully possesses the truth, but all times taken together.

position corresponded to the third. Kuhn responded by arguing that Baur's position actually coincided with the second perspective, and that the authentically Catholic position was the median position between the first two—that is, it was the very position that Baur hoped but ultimately failed to occupy.[11]

The key point of dispute between Baur and Kuhn was not whether the history of dogma moves forward by real changes. On this point Kuhn was in agreement with Baur. The key question was whether these changes necessarily constituted a change in "the substantial truth of the dogma." On this point Kuhn differed from Baur. Kuhn claimed that the historical changes discernible in the church's teaching did not involve a truly *essential* difference in what was taught.[12] Although his denial of essential change appears to vindicate Baur's characterization of the Catholic position (i.e., all change is only apparent or merely a change in expression), Kuhn insisted that formal change involves real differences from one understanding or presentation of a doctrine to another. Kuhn's point was that there is real change in what the church teaches from one age to the next, but that there is also real continuity. A true understanding of the history of doctrine shows "neither mere movement and change without substantial reality, nor a substantial content without movement." Kuhn wrote:

> The movement in the historical process involving doctrines is, however, not merely of a relative kind. It consists not only in the changing opposition of dogma to different heretical conceptions, but also in the multiplicity of individual attempts to probe, mediate, and make comprehensible to others the content of faith that has been handed on.[13]

The content of faith is *substantially* the same, but what that content means and how it is to be expressed and applied are different from age to age.[14]

It must be noted, however, that Kuhn seems to have been convinced of this faithful continuity of the church's teaching largely on dogmatic rather than historical grounds. For Kuhn explicitly assumed not only

---

11. Kuhn, "Ehrenrettung," 251–52, 255, 286, 293.
12. Ibid., 286–87.
13. Ibid., 288.
14. Ibid., 291.

the absoluteness of Christianity, but also the infallible communication of the message of Jesus and the apostles through the ages by the leaders of the church.[15] Consequently, Kuhn made the bald statement that "the church never subordinated the tradition to its authority" and that the leaders of the church so perfectly renounced their own subjective opinions and were so unconditionally faithful to what had been objectively revealed that this fact constitutes "the strongest human guarantee of the preservation of the tradition, against which no exception can be raised."[16] Kuhn's presupposition that the Roman hierarchy had the special assistance of the Holy Spirit meant that his theological task was to demonstrate historically the truth of this dogmatic conviction by showing how change in the church's teaching did not mean deviation from the message of Jesus and the apostles, but rather its development in essential continuity.

Knowledge of the history of the church required Kuhn to acknowledge real changes in its teaching. Thus, he adamantly rejected Baur's characterization of the Catholic conception of development as the monotonous repetition of the same sentences, "in which all teachers of the church again and again say the same thing only with different words and with the same disdain reject as godless heresy everything that does not chime in the same tone."[17] In contrast, his dogmatic

---

15. After noting that divine revelations are not in need of proofs of their truth, Kuhn adds that this assertion is not altered by the fact that we receive these revelations today through the medium of the church. He writes: "And even when we do not immediately perceive the self-revealing God, but rather receive from the mouth of God's agents the truth revealed to them (*fides ex auditu*), this does not change the essence of faith as the unconditional and indubitable act of accepting something as true—insofar as this mediation is also divine, and insofar as we see in the apostles the agents inspired by God's Spirit and in the church founded by Christ the immediate teaching authority for us which has been animated and led by his Spirit" (*Einleitung* [1859], 202–3).

16. Ibid., 87–88.

17. Kuhn (ibid., 152–53) citing Baur's characterization of the Catholic position in his *Lehrbuch der christlichen Dogmengeschichte* (1858). This disagreement notwithstanding, Kuhn and Baur shared some assumptions and conclusions. They include: a high estimation of the importance of the history of dogma as the inner life of the church; a conception of the task of the historian of dogma (or systematic theologian) as consisting in moving backward along "the same course by which the subject matter had come down to him [i.e., the historian or theologian], in order to complete in his own consciousness the movement which the subject matter had completed objectively" (Baur, "Introduction to Lectures on the History of Christian Dogma" [1865–67], in Hodgson, *Ferdinand Christian Baur*, 270); and the view that the history of dogma was the story of the process by which the one fundamental dogma of Christianity developed distinctions within it, thus producing other doctrines. See ibid., 276–77; Kuhn, "Über den Begriff und das Wesen der speculativen Theologie," *Theologische Quartalschrift* 14 (1832): 432; see also idem, *Einleitung* (1859), 289–

conviction about the unfailing fidelity of the hierarchical magisterium to the kerygma compelled Kuhn to use only historical evidence that highlighted continuity in the church's teaching. In his second edition of the *Dogmatics* (1859), Kuhn clarified what he meant by true change without alteration of the essential content of faith. Drawing on Vincent of Lerins, Kuhn proposed the analogy of human growth as follows:

> The human being grows with the years, his or her members develop and grow larger, while he or she nevertheless remains essentially the same and does not degenerate into an ape. And even if one or another aspect of a human being's form and essence only becomes visible in later years, still even this was present in seed in that person already from the beginning.[18]

Applied to doctrinal development, the analogy suggests that the essential or substantial content of Christian revelation does not and cannot change, whereas the form in which it is expressed and the way in which it is understood do and must change.[19] Kuhn's dispute with Baur, however, impelled him to add the clarification that these formal changes were not *merely* formal in the usual sense of the word. They were not simply "other expressions of the same truth or rather of the same presentation of this truth—that is, really only translations of the truth's original formulation into the different languages and idioms of the peoples." Rather, the changes were different conceptions of the same truth, albeit different conceptions resting upon the same *fundamental* percep-

---

90. Despite his criticism of the Catholic conception of development, Baur did not reject it wholesale. In fact, Baur held that a theologically adequate conception of doctrinal development required a dialectical appropriation of the Catholic and the Protestant perspectives. Whereas the Catholic perspective held to the unity and "objectivity" of the church's history, the Protestant grasped the diversity and "subjectivity" of that history. Baur regarded both perspectives as they currently existed deficient: the Catholic, since it did not "permit freedom of movement to a great deal of material that has emerged from the substantial foundation of dogma"; the Protestant, since it lost "the substantial unity of dogma by dissolving it into the endless multiplicity of individual representations and beliefs," whereby "the whole of the history of dogma appears to fall into subjectivity" (Baur, *Lehrbuch der christlichen Dogmengeschichte*, 3d ed. [1867], cited in Hodgson, *Ferdinand Christian Baur*, 363 n. 44).

18. Kuhn, *Einleitung* (1859), 154.

19. Ibid., 20–21.

tion of things, or the result of moving from a pictorial to a conceptual comprehension of that truth.[20]

In clarifying what doctrinal development means, Kuhn began to go beyond the romantic framework of his predecessors. Although he himself used organic metaphors to explain doctrinal development, Kuhn came to perceive their inadequacy. He thus turned to Hegel's conception of dialectical development.[21] Although Kuhn thought that Hegel's position was also in need of some correction, he agreed with Hegel's basic argument that knowledge moves dialectically from immediate consciousness to mediated consciousness to the speculative concept.[22] Development, when interpreted from a dialectical perspective, is more than the natural, effortless, unconscious blossoming of a flower from a seed. Development results rather from the juxtaposition of opposing conceptions; it requires conscious thought and struggle. Kuhn reasoned that if one understands dogma as Christian truth conceived in mental images and expressed in words, then "an objective dialectic of the truth, which advances in different mental images

---

20. "The history of dogma must be viewed as true history; there must be talk of a real and progressive becoming and, to that extent, of changes (*Veränderungen*). But the history of dogma must not be conceived and defined as the history of the changes or transformations (*Wandlungen*) of dogma. The changes... concern dogma, but they do not touch its substance or essential truth, but leave them unchanged to remain the same. The changes, however, are not merely formal in the usual sense, that is, that they are supposed to be simply other expressions of the same truth or rather of the same presentation of this truth—that is, really only translations of the truth's original formulation into the different languages and idioms of the peoples, which Christianity assumes with the passage of time. Rather, they are either different presentations and conceptions of the same truth, all of which, however, rest upon the same fundamental perception, or they denote progress from the pictorial to the conceptual comprehension of this truth. For example, the pre-Nicene trinitarian teaching stands in the latter relation to the teaching of Nicea, whereas the former relation, for example, occurs in the dogma of soteriology (cf. §9)" (Kuhn, *Einleitung* [1859], 301).
21. See Herbert Hammans, *Die neueren katholischen Erklärungen der Dogmenentwicklung* (Essen: Ludgerus-Verlag Hubert Wingen, 1965), 36–39. See also Donald J. Dietrich, *The Goethezeit and the Metamorphosis of Catholic Theology in the Age of Idealism* (Bern: Peter Lang, 1979), 180, 189. Kuhn sometimes combined the organic and the dialectical conception of development. See, for example, his *Einleitung* (1859), 219–20.
22. Kuhn criticized Hegel and others for failing to acknowledge that thinking is not the source of truth, but only a means of knowing truth. Moreover, he denounced the claim that the object of philosophical and theological knowledge, Absolute Spirit, itself develops by means of conscious human reflection. And he rejected philosophical attempts to establish the concept (*Begriff*) as the essential form of consciousness. See *Einleitung* (1859), 238–39, 241–42; see also Josef Rupert Geiselmann, *Die lebendige Überlieferung als Norm des christlichen Glaubens* (Freiburg: Herder, 1959), 213–21, esp. 220; Hammans, *Dogmenentwicklung*, 36–37; and Dietrich, *Goethezeit*, 179–81.

and concepts, is thinkable, and the history of this progress...is the history of dogma." The history of doctrine therefore describes those changes (*Veränderungen*) by which the doctrinal content is "objectively further developed or turned over, represented, and comprehended from different sides."[23] Thus St. James confronts St. Paul on the question of justification, and Pauline soteriology contrasts with Augustinian soteriology. These confrontations represent not fundamental contradictions, but contrasts necessary to the proper development of Christian teaching.[24] Insofar as every entity consists of a dynamic relation of aspects, *Gegensätzlichkeit* (contrariness) belongs to the very character of a being. Kuhn concurred with Möhler that everything finite needs contrast for its development. Kuhn held that these various, contrasting elements constituted the entity itself, and he concluded that knowledge of the entity must be dialectical. Referring to the relation of pre-Nicene to Nicene teaching concerning the Trinity, Kuhn declared:

> These are changes which, of course with reference to the essential truth, are mere changes of its form, but, insofar as they do not leave the content untouched and unmoved, they are not simply formal changes.... Rather, they are forms that grow out of the dialectical further determination of this content and they express this truth.[25]

It is at this point that theology, according to Kuhn, plays a significant role in the life of the church. Theology determines the meaning of past doctrinal statements; it examines whether the current teaching of the church is in essential agreement with the teaching of Christ; and it helps to reformulate the basic content of faith in a way appropriate to the needs of contemporary culture. In its critical and creative functions, theology contributes to the dialectical development of Christian doctrine itself.

---

23. Kuhn, *Einleitung* (1859), 157.
24. Ibid., 159–65.
25. Ibid., 301–2.

The Theological Task
in Light of the Development of Doctrine

Kuhn's basic premise was that theology is vitally necessary to the life of the church. Its general significance resides in its contribution to a mature, critical comprehension of faith. Since faith cannot dispense with understanding, the Christian community cannot dispense with theology. In addition to this general function of theology, Kuhn also identified several specific tasks for theology. The task of some theological disciplines (e.g., apologetics) is to attend to the source and medium of revelation; the task of others (e.g., dogmatics) is to attend to the content of revelation.[26]

Kuhn's own area of expertise was dogmatics, and he identified three important tasks for this branch of theology. First, dogmatics has to demonstrate that the church's contemporary teaching is in essential agreement with the teaching of Christ. Second, it has to investigate the relation of the church's doctrines to truths of reason. Insofar as it attempts to understand faith in academic fashion, theology has to transform the empirical consciousness of God into appropriate "speculative" concepts. Third, dogmatics has the task of demonstrating the connection and unity of all the elements of Christian truth. Specifically, it has to explain all the facts of revelation from its most basic principles or ideas.[27] In executing these tasks, theology is alternately constructive and explanatory (with regard to the present formulation of the tradition) and historical and apologetic (with regard to past formulations of revelation).

Kuhn assigned the first of these dogmatic tasks to "positive dogmatics." This discipline relies heavily upon historical research and historical

---

26. The principal task of apologetics, to establish Christianity as the absolute religion and the church as the teacher of truth, is the first of all theological tasks since what Christians believe has come to them through the mediation of the church. In order to know that their faith is in continuity with the teaching of Christ and the apostles, Christians, therefore, must be assured of the trustworthiness of the church. See *Einleitung* (1859), 202–3.

27. In an 1832 essay, Kuhn identified the incarnation as the essence of God's revelation. But he reminded his readers that the incarnation was not to be considered an isolated divine act. See "Über den Begriff," 432. In the second edition of his *Dogmatics*, he identified two ideas as the principles according to which the entire dogmatic system was to be organized: the idea of a personal God, and the idea of God's self-revelation in Christ. See *Einleitung* (1859), 290.

understanding of the tradition.[28] From the beginning of his career, Kuhn had insisted that history is "the fundamental characteristic and simultaneously the primordial element of Christianity."[29] Consequently, history provides the raw data of theological reflection. Without detailed knowledge of the historical tradition, theology could not fulfill its explanatory and apologetic roles. Only familiarity with the entirety of doctrinal development guarantees a full grasp of the truth. Once the theologian has a basis in this doctrinal history, he or she can then approach the task of critically authenticating the teaching of the church. In executing this task, that is, in attempting to demonstrate that a particular doctrine is grounded in scripture and tradition, the theologian is to interpret scripture or tradition "scientifically"—that is, historically, not dogmatically.[30]

Kuhn assigned the second and third dogmatic tasks to "speculative dogmatics." This theological discipline is built upon three premises: that divine revelation is given to us in forms of human thought and knowledge; that the content of divine or supernatural revelation is in essential agreement with the content of "natural revelation"; and that the acceptance in faith of the truth of divine revelation occurs not through abandoning or neglecting reason, but through activating it. The conclusion that Kuhn drew from these premises was that speculative dogmatics must critically use reason without imagining that divine revelation might be reduced to mere truths of reason. The positive contribution of speculative dogmatics to the church's life is its elevation of the content of doctrine to a conceptual level (speculative concept) and the demonstration of the acceptability (credibility) of this content to human reason.[31]

Kuhn believed that to complete its assigned tasks, speculative dog-

---

28. Concerning the difference between positive and speculative dogmatics, see *Einleitung* (1859), 205.

29. Kuhn, "Über den Begriff," 299, 264. In the same essay, Kuhn defined theology as "the scientific presentation of Christian revelations as something utterly historical" (see p. 423). In his earlier debate with Strauss, Kuhn had labeled Strauss's construal of faith a philosophical construct of ideas precisely because it made faith's connection to the Jesus of history tenuous at best and irrelevant at worst. See William Madges, *The Core of Christian Faith: D. F. Strauss and His Catholic Critics* (New York: Peter Lang, 1987), 45–73, esp. 65–66.

30. Kuhn, *Einleitung* (1859), 144, 214–15, 217–28. See Wolfinger, *Der Glaube*, 141–42, esp. n. 105. As was noted earlier, Kuhn's historical reading of the tradition was in practice guided, and in some cases distorted, by his dogmatic convictions.

31. Kuhn, *Einleitung* (1859), 231–33, 236–37.

matics had to make cautious use of the best philosophical tools available for expressing the tradition in a way that was sensitive to the needs of the Christian community at the present time. In short, Kuhn was convinced that neither theology nor philosophy was essentially dependent upon the other, but rather that both were intimately related. Consequently, Kuhn rejected a common interpretation of the claim that philosophy is the handmaid of theology. He argued that the saying is not to be understood to mean that philosophy only helps theology do more easily what it could do on its own. On the contrary, theology can become what it should be, "the science of faith," only through "application of human rational thought and knowledge, that is, philosophy."[32] Philosophy prepares for theology by demonstrating the possibility of revelation and the reasonableness of Christian faith, and it assists theology in determining the appropriate form in which divine truth ought to be expressed in the present age.

Theology, according to Kuhn, needs therefore to be both perceptive and creative if it is to succeed in formulating Christian faith in a suitable way for contemporary culture. Theology has considerable freedom with regard to how to express the content of faith since the divine communication of truth is "not a communication of real knowledge in ready mental images and concepts, but an enrichment of the source from which real knowledge of God proceeds through the self-activity of the mind."[33] Thus, theology is dependent upon the fact of revelation for its content, but it is not absolutely bound to past expressions of that content. This relatively dependent, relatively independent relationship is evident in the relation of the history of dogmatics to the history of doctrine.

Kuhn held that dogmatics presupposes doctrines (and their development), but he also insisted that dogmatics was not exclusively dependent upon them. Dogmatics has its own principle (the reflection of individuals) and its own goal (critical understanding of the meaning of doctrine). Consequently, there is a constant element or thread of continuity in theological reflection (provided by the doctrine under consideration), but also variables, in terms of the different educational levels of the Christian community and different degrees of success in the

---

32. Ibid., 275; see also 255–58.
33. Ibid., 230.

theological explication of a doctrine's meaning for today.[34] Theology, or what Kuhn called the process of dogmatic knowledge, influences doctrinal development in two ways. First, it presents the meaning of Christian faith in a conception and expression that are suited to the needs of the age. Second, it draws out the meaning of Christian doctrines in such a way that heresy is excluded and the purity of faith is preserved. In these two specific ways, theology directly assists the church's proclamation of the good news.

> The immediate goal of the church's proclamation consists in presenting and exhibiting Christian truth in such a way as the present need of the age requires. The modification of the form of the presentation and the expression—without detriment to the essential content—the bringing forth of now this, now the other side of the same truth... and similar things necessary for the attainment of that goal: all this can be achieved only from the standpoint of knowledge and science [i.e., theology].[35]

Kuhn perceived theologians to exist in a subordinate, yet dialectically creative relationship with the institutional leadership of the church. Since theologians are relatively free in the expression and formulation of the meaning of the church's confessional statements and since they strive for a rigorous, academic comprehension of Christian faith, their formulations of the meaning of faith can be quite different from the church's official instruction.[36] But Kuhn also insisted that orthodoxy and faithful communion with the church are the necessary conditions of one's proper relationship with God and of beatitude.[37] Without communion with the church, Christian faith is not possible. It is in the church that one encounters Christ, and Christ insures the right form of one's encounter with God. Moreover, the content of faith is something revealed, and truths of revelation are neither innate to individual human consciousness nor discoverable through mere thinking. Human

---

34. Ibid., 298.
35. Ibid., 299.
36. Ibid., 283.
37. Kuhn cautioned, however, that the degree of concurrence of one's faith with that of the church is qualitative, not quantitative. That meant that individuals could be in full communion with the church even if they did not consciously affirm all that the church taught. See ibid., 200.

individuals—and this of course includes theologians—are initially dependent on a source outside themselves (God) for certain (not all) truths of revelation, and they are subsequently dependent on a source outside themselves (the church) for the reception and proper understanding of those truths.[38] Thus, theologians do their work in and for the church. And, as Kuhn observed in his later works, since the church culminates in its leadership, theologians never do their work independently of the oversight of the hierarchical magisterium or in basic opposition to it.

At this point, when Kuhn speaks of the church and its teaching office, one begins to perceive that Kuhn held that theology's functions are more properly apologetic and explanatory, not creative and prophetic. That Kuhn held theology's primary task to be explanatory derives from his ecclesiology and from his understanding of revelation. The important truths that theologians have to expound and defend are divinely revealed truths. Divinely revealed truths, by definition, are not truths innate to the human intellect. They cannot be known as true by means of a simple recourse to the individual's rational reflection or experience. Rather, they are known to be true on the basis of the reliable authority by whom and through whom they are communicated.[39] The hierarchical magisterium of the Roman church constitutes, according to Kuhn, the reliable authority that communicates and preserves God's revelation. Its teaching is true and sure because it is the successor of the apostles to whom Jesus entrusted his message and it is assisted by the Holy Spirit.[40] A consequence of this ecclesiology is the minimization of the autonomy of theologians. Such minimization is reflected in Kuhn's conviction that the theological task of demonstrating the reasonableness or credibility of doctrines is more important than the task of demonstrating that the received doctrines are in essential agreement with the teaching of Jesus.[41]

And yet there is a real tension in Kuhn's writings. For in addition to his staunch loyalty to the hierarchy and his failure to see theological expertise as establishing the relative autonomy of the theologian, Kuhn also resisted those who wanted to vest absolute authority in the per-

---

38. Ibid., 200–203. See Dietrich, *Goethezeit,* 183–84. See also Wolfinger, *Der Glaube,* 121–24, 126.

39. Kuhn, *Einleitung* (1859), 201–2.

40. Ibid., 75, 101.

41. Ibid., 205–6.

son of the pope or who wanted the bishops to control thought. Kuhn
maintained that God's revelation was given to all, not only to the hierarchy of the church, and he insisted that no leader in the church
had absolute teaching authority independently of God's word. In the
first edition of his *Dogmatics,* he declared that the consciousness of the
entire community "still remains however the highest court for interpreting and identifying what has flowed from divine revelation." Although
in the second edition he moved toward identifying the church with
the hierarchy, even there he set limits to the hierarchy, which he described as servants of God's word, not lords over it.[42] Moreover, Kuhn
opposed the attempt to establish a private Catholic university in Germany because he feared that it would stifle critical thinking and creative
theology.[43]

In Kuhn's view, theology contributed to the church's life by helping the church, especially its hierarchy, to comprehend and adapt the
meaning of the gospel for the present age. Kuhn argued that if theology merely repeated the words of scripture, the church would fail in its
mission, which is to pass on the living meaning of Christ's message.

> The proclamation of the gospel ... must represent and state the di-
> vine truth in a way corresponding to the changing needs at any
> given time, according to time and place, individuality and spirit-
> ual direction of individuals and peoples, without detriment to the
> truth's completeness and purity. It must do justice to the antithe-
> ses that arise and generally keep even pace with the movement
> of worldly science and culture (which is founded upon experience
> and rational investigation), for its effect upon people, as is rarely
> noticed, depends upon this. The continuous repetition of the same
> truth in the same expressions and turns of phrase, by means of
> the same intuitions and conceptions, would be counterproductive

---

42. Kuhn, *Einleitung* (1846), 67. On account of this text and others, Wolfinger criticizes
Geiselmann for suggesting that "church" always means for Kuhn the authoritative magisterium of the hierarchy. See Wolfinger, *Der Glaube,* 124–25; cf. Geiselmann, *Die lebendige
Überlieferung,* 287–88. Geiselmann believes that Strauss's theory of the *Volksgeist* so horri-
fied Kuhn that he removed all romantic references to the consciousness of the community
or the consensus of the faithful from his later writings.

43. See my article, "Does Theology Belong in the University? The Nineteenth-Century
Case in Ireland and Germany," in *Theology and the University,* ed. John Apczynski (Lanham,
Md.: University Press of America, 1990), 173–76.

since unfruitful. And for this reason it never happened that way. Didn't the apostles proclaim the gospel each in his own way?[44]

Kuhn, then, agreed with Schleiermacher's assertion that dogmatic theology serves the leadership of the church "by showing in how many ways and up to what point the principle of the present period has developed itself on all sides, and how the germs of improved formulations still to come relate to this principle."[45]

Kuhn in Retrospect

Kuhn conceived his specific theological task to consist in formulating and defending an understanding of Christian faith that reconciled the natural and the supernatural, avoided the extremes of rationalism and biblicism, and joined modern philosophy with the inherited theological tradition. In short, Kuhn faced the challenge of writing theology that utilized the best insights of romanticism and idealism without succumbing to either the subjectivism or pantheism he believed to be inherent in their most penetrating representatives.

In carrying out his project, Kuhn drew upon not only Catholic sources, but also Protestant sources—most notably Schleiermacher and Hegel. From both thinkers, he adopted and adapted what he found useful; he criticized and rejected what he found deficient or untrue. Like Schleiermacher, Kuhn recognized and underlined the historical character of theology. Like Schleiermacher, he spoke of doctrines, particularly clearly in his early works, as the objective expression of the Christian consciousness of the age. He believed that doctrinal forms are bound to a particular time, and that there is a relative quality even to the New Testament writings. Like Schleiermacher, he maintained that new expressions are to be worked out in continuity with the prior history of the church's faith.[46] But Kuhn was also critical of Schleiermacher, es-

---

44. Kuhn, *Einleitung* (1859), 48.
45. Schleiermacher, *Brief Outline*, §198, p. 73.
46. Although Kuhn could state that dogmatics "necessarily proceeds from the Christian consciousness of the time and appeals to the most recent ecclesial determinations of the faith for its propositions," he tended to see less mobility in the data of dogmatic reflection than did Schleiermacher (Kuhn, *Einleitung* [1859], 207). Concerning scripture, Kuhn wrote: "Therefore, not only the word of scripture, but also the oral discourse of the apostles and of Christ himself possesses this relative aspect in itself" (ibid., 47). And again: "For although

pecially the "subjectivism" of Schleiermacher's understanding of faith and dogmatics. In some of his criticisms, Kuhn echoed the voice of Hegel. Neither Hegel nor Kuhn was content to abandon attempts designed to demonstrate the truth, necessity, and universal validity of Christianity. Like Hegel, Kuhn affirmed that Christianity as the absolute religion ushered in a new and final stage in religious history.[47] In contrast to Schleiermacher, he, like Hegel, sought to establish the necessity of the doctrine of the Trinity.[48] And Kuhn was convinced, as was Hegel, of the scientific character of theology. Both thinkers agreed that theology was more than a description of subjective states of consciousness; both maintained that theology had an objective quality. Kuhn, however, sharply criticized Hegel for blurring the distinction between the finite and the infinite and for overestimating the power of human reason.[49]

Kuhn took these various insights and concerns and attempted to integrate them into a contemporary, credible, and tenable Roman Catholic theology. Considered within its own Catholic and nineteenth-century context, Kuhn's writing is historically oriented, conceptually detailed, and theologically progressive. Considered from a contemporary perspective, however, the value of his work, though real, is limited. If that

it contains the absolute truth valid for all times, the Bible does not represent it in a manner immediately appropriate to every age, but rather in a manner that was the most appropriate and most effective at the time of the composition of its individual books" (ibid., 48). Cf. Schleiermacher's letter to Jacobi, 30 March 1818: "The Bible is the original interpretation of the Christian feeling, and for this very reason so firmly established that we ought not to attempt more than further to understand and develop it. This right of development, however, I, as a Protestant theologian, will allow no one to defraud me of" (cited by Gerrish, "Continuity and Change: Friedrich Schleiermacher on the Task of Theology," in *Tradition and the Modern World: Reformed Theology in the Nineteenth Century* [Chicago: University of Chicago Press, 1977], 44).

47. G. W. F. Hegel, *Lectures on the Philosophy of Religion,* trans. E. B. Speirs and J. B. Sanderson, 3 vols. (New York: Humanities Press, 1962), 2:327–30. Cf. Schleiermacher, *The Christian Faith,* trans. of 2d German ed., ed. H. R. Macintosh and J. S. Stewart (Philadelphia: Fortress Press, 1976), §11.5, p. 60: "We entirely renounce all attempt to prove the truth or necessity of Christianity; and we presuppose, on the contrary, that every Christian, before he enters at all upon inquiries of this kind, has already the inward certainty that his religion cannot take any other form than this."

48. Just as Hegel's student Philipp Marheineke adopted the trinitarian idea as central to dogmatics and developed its necessity in speculative fashion, so too Kuhn. See Kuhn, *Einleitung* (1859), 289–92; Philipp Marheineke, *Die Grundlehren der christlichen Dogmatik als Wissenschaft,* 2d ed. (1827). See Claude Welch, *Protestant Thought in the Nineteenth Century,* 2 vols. (New Haven, Conn.: Yale University Press, 1972), 1:100–101.

49. See, for example, Kuhn, *Einleitung* (1859), 240 and 292. Also see Wolfinger, *Der Glaube,* 154–57.

is the case, then why should we take a careful look at Kuhn? One answer is that insofar as the present is the outcome of the past, we cannot understand the current situation in theology without comprehension of the theological past. Kuhn is part of that past, albeit a forgotten part in the English-speaking world. But Kuhn did leave a mark upon contemporary Catholic figures, such as J. R. Geiselmann, Karl Adam, and Walter Kasper; more importantly, he and his Catholic Tübingen colleagues sounded many of the themes that were enunciated at the Second Vatican Council. Kuhn specifically contributed to Vatican II's understanding of the relation of scripture and tradition and its conception of a hierarchy of truths.[50]

Another answer is that study of Kuhn, and of other nineteenth-century figures, can keep our present theological endeavors from becoming provincial as well as help them in contributing positively to the further development of the church's life. As H. Richard Niebuhr has argued, the study of history is "never only the effort to understand the past, or even to understand the human present that has grown out of the past." Rather, it is the attempt to understand important issues that are common to both past and present. As such historical inquiry involves "a kind of resurrection of the minds of predecessors in the community of inquiry, and an entering into conversation with them about the common concern."[51] Or as Schubert Ogden has put it, historical theology "should never be content with merely exhibiting the past for its own sake."[52] By engaging in conversation with past theologians, we hear other ways of conceiving our common concern and we gain perhaps a more complete understanding of our faith. Both the strengths and weaknesses in the arguments of our theological predecessors can instruct us in how better to engage in theology today. In this sense, historical theology has a constructive as well as an explanatory function, a forward-looking as well as a retrospective aspect. Schleiermacher was correct in believing that historical knowledge of Christianity constitutes

---

50. Franz Wolfinger, "Glaube und Geschichte bei Johann Evangelist Kuhn," *Theologische Quartalschrift* 168 (1988): 135–36. See also Walter Kasper, "Verständnis der Theologie Damals und Heute," in *Glaube und Geschichte* (Mainz: Matthias Grünewald, 1970), 9–32, esp. 11, 14, 16–20. Also see Kasper's *Jesus the Christ* (New York: Paulist Press, 1976), 9.

51. H. Richard Niebuhr, *The Purpose of the Church and Its Ministry: Reflections on the Aims of Theological Education* (New York: Harper & Brothers, 1956), 122.

52. Schubert M. Ogden, *On Theology* (San Francisco: Harper & Row, 1986), 9.

"the indispensable condition of all intelligent effort toward the further cultivation of Christianity."[53]

What are some of the weaknesses in Kuhn's theological program? What blind alleys in his work should we refuse to follow?

One of Kuhn's weaknesses is insufficient self-criticism. Kuhn seems to have been genuinely unaware of how his dogmatic convictions undercut his ability to engage in a *consistently* critical historical analysis of the church's teaching. Consequently, Kuhn sometimes violated in practice his espousal in theory of truly historical methods in interpreting scripture and tradition. As we saw above, Kuhn did this by taking as his starting point the position that the official teaching of the Roman church was always true and always in fundamental continuity with the message of Jesus and the apostles.

One of the blind alleys in Kuhn's work is his subordination of theology in a quite restrictive way to the hierarchical magisterium. Insofar as theology's primary task was to explain the official teaching of the church, to defend it, and to express it in terms appropriate to the age, any critical or prophetic function of theology became at best secondary. Kuhn's theological silence from 1869 to the end of his life (1887) is one indication of his belief in the subordinate status of theology. Because the hierarchy during this period chose to favor, for example, the theology of Kleutgen and not the theology of Kuhn, Kuhn apparently thought that the appropriate response was to accept in silence the new hegemony of neo-scholasticism. As Kuhn grew older he came to believe more firmly in the role of theologians as ancillaries to the hierarchy. This belief is revealed in his response to the definition of infallibility at Vatican I. Although Kuhn believed that theologians could support the minority bishops who initially opposed the proposed definition of infallibility, once the majority of the bishops at the council had accepted the definition, criticism or rejection of it by theologians was no longer permissible. In fact, after the council Kuhn refused to publish a scholarly article on the Honorius question and he did not allow a French theologian, excommunicated on account of his rejection of infallibility, to visit him. Kuhn justified his position, which was in sharp contrast with that of his contemporary Ignaz von Döllinger, with the assertion that the job of theologians was "not to create dogma, but to expound

---

53. Schleiermacher, *Brief Outline*, §70, p. 41.

it."[54] Moreover, Kuhn's conception of the church in his later works is too narrow. Although he spoke of the church as the whole people of God in the first edition of his *Dogmatics*, in later works he tended to equate the church with the hierarchy. These weaknesses are apparent in Kuhn's reflections upon the nature of Christian doctrine and the theological task.

What then are the strengths of Kuhn's work? How can conversation with his work help the church to develop further? The notion that there can be—even ought to be—real change in the teaching of the church, without deviating from the essence of Christian faith, is an idea under attack from several quarters within the Roman church today. Yet it is an idea that Kuhn advanced, albeit cautiously, in an ecclesiastical context suspicious of change and critical of modern thought. Kuhn reminds Roman Catholic theologians today of the necessity of demonstrating again the truth of this idea. Moreover, Kuhn is a good example of how a theologian can make legitimate use of modern thought, even when ecclesiastically unpopular, in the service of truthfully and faithfully expressing Christian witness. And although his silence in his last years is not necessarily a wholesome example to follow, his silence and the fate of his work offer us an occasion for considering seriously when it is appropriate to dissent publicly and loudly from the official direction of the church and when it is appropriate to continue to teach quietly and within the church what one considers to be a better understanding of the Christian faith. For it must be remembered that, before his final silence, Kuhn resolutely opposed the neo-scholastic and antimodern theological programs that received institutional approbation from the midpoint of the century on. Kuhn thus serves as a reminder of the diversity of the church and an example of the necessity of different voices in the theological conversation. Kuhn engaged in honest, critical dialogue with the outstanding philosophers and theologians of his time in order to comprehend the living spirit of Christ as adequately as possible and in order to express that spirit as effectively as possible to his age. He carried out his work with basic fidelity to the essential Christian truths conveyed in the church's living tradition, but also with a creativity that ruptured more traditional or scholastic modes of thought. His

---

54. See August Hagen, *Gestalten aus dem schwäbischen Katholizismus*, Zweiter Teil (Stuttgart: Schwabenverlag, 1950), 86. See also Heinrich Fries, *Johannes von Kuhn* (Graz: Verlag Styria, 1973), 44–46.

sense of fidelity and creativity, his understanding of church teaching as living and developing, and his sense of theological responsibility to contribute to that development can rightly be retrieved, refined, and applied today.

TWELVE

David W. Lotz

Albrecht Ritschl and
the Heritage of the Reformation

The great tradition of nineteenth-century liberal Protestant theology, from Friedrich Schleiermacher to Ernst Troeltsch, was itself preoccupied with the *problem* of tradition: the exigent issue, namely, of handing on the Christian message in a way that would be at once faithful to the essence of biblical-Reformation Christianity and truthful to the church's new historical situation in the post-Enlightenment world.

One finds important and even irreconcilable differences among the liberal theologians in their respective interpretations of the biblical gospel, the church, the essence of Christianity, the principle of Protestantism, the modern world, as well as in their individual determinations of what constitutes faithfulness and truthfulness. They differed, likewise, in their assessments of the degree of continuity and discontinuity between the Christian past and their present, especially between the Reformation era and the new age following upon the Illumination. Such differing assessments entailed differing perspectives on the need for, and extent of, innovation (doctrinal revision and reconstruction) vis-à-vis the "inheritance." Still, these signal differences were themselves generated by the theologians' confrontation with a common problem: the overarching issue of tradition itself. All were agreed, moreover, that the specific content (the *traditum*) of the historical process of transmission (the *actus tradendi*) was the Christian faith in a recognizably Reformation-Protestant guise.

In this light, then, B. A. Gerrish has justly asserted that "the question of nineteenth-century Protestant thought was precisely that of tradition and the modern world: What is to be done with the Reformation heritage in a world of which Calvin [and Luther] never dreamed?"[1]

No representative of liberal Protestantism devoted more sustained attention to the problem of "traditioning" the Reformation heritage in the modern church and world than did Albrecht Ritschl (1822–89), the most prominent member of the theological faculty at the University of Göttingen from 1864 until his death. Already in 1857, having just completed his seminal study of the development of the old Catholic church (of the second and third centuries), Ritschl—in the words of his son and biographer—"directed his interests to a new field of labor where they were firmly to remain for many years. He began his studies on the doctrine of justification, commencing specifically with his researches into Luther."[2] Such research soon expanded into a comprehensive investigation of the whole of Reformation thought and, indeed, of the main theological developments within post-Reformation Protestantism down to his own time. This penetrating inquiry also moved retrospectively into the Middle Ages, into the pre-Reformation centuries since Augustine: all with a view to tracing the provenance and historical course of what Ritschl called the Reformation's "practical root ideas" (*praktische Grundgedanken*), that is, those foundational religious ideas, centering on the thought of God's unconditional grace, whereby Luther and Zwingli and their associates effected their epoch-making reform of religious life within the late medieval church.

This epochal reform of the Christian *religion,* however, was not—so Ritschl judged—accompanied by the necessary reformulation of Christian *theology,* neither by the reformers themselves (including, not least, Melanchthon and Calvin) nor by their sixteenth-century epigones. Indeed, the whole subsequent history of Protestant thought is a painful record of continuing failure to construct a homogeneous theological system informed throughout by the reformers' religious root ideas, by the original "principle of the Reformation" (*das Princip der Reformation*). Theologically considered, therefore, the Reformation has remained unfinished, with the most deleterious consequences over the centuries for

---

1. B. A. Gerrish, *Tradition and the Modern World: Reformed Theology in the Nineteenth Century* (Chicago, 1978), x.

2. Otto Ritschl, *Albrecht Ritschls Leben,* 2 vols. (Freiburg im Breisgau, 1892, 1986), 1:294. The second edition of Albrecht Ritschl's *Die Entstehung der altkatholischen Kirche,* which marked his dramatic break with F. C. Baur and the Tübingen school, was published in 1857; the first edition had appeared in 1850.

evangelical piety and church life, relegating Protestantism to a state of perpetual immaturity through its dependence on a deformed Reformation heritage. Albrecht Ritschl, accordingly, understood his vocational task as that of at last bringing the Reformation to theological completion, and Protestantism to maturity, through a reconstruction of evangelical dogmatics on the basis of the Reformation principle.

Ritschl's historical findings and his "new" dogmatics, itself based on history and on biblical (New Testament) exegesis, were presented most fully in *The Christian Doctrine of Justification and Reconciliation* (3 vols., 1870–74) and *History of Pietism* (3 vols., 1880–86).[3] These two monumental works secured Ritschl's standing among the century's premier historical theologians, in company with his teacher, Ferdinand Christian Baur, and his disciple, Adolf von Harnack. These same works and their related monographs—*Christian Perfection* (1874), *Instruction in the Christian Religion* (1875), *Theology and Metaphysics* (1881), plus his many essays and addresses—accorded Ritschl an influence as a systematic theologian, during the century's last three decades, comparable to that of Schleiermacher in midcentury.[4]

My intent in this essay is to examine the leading features of Ritschl's Luther and Reformation scholarship: its primary aims and results; its broad textual basis; its foundational role in Ritschl's total theological system; and its influence in its own time. I do not propose to evaluate its relative strengths and weaknesses; nor (apart from some cursory remarks) to relate it to its larger nineteenth-century context; nor to identify and analyze its main theological innovations vis-à-vis the Reformation-Protestant tradition; nor to consider its lines of connection

---

3. Albrecht Ritschl, *Die christliche Lehre von der Rechtfertigung und Versöhnung,* vol. 1: *Die Geschichte der Lehre* (Bonn, 1870), Eng.: *A Critical History of the Christian Doctrine of Justification and Reconciliation,* trans. John S. Black (Edinburgh, 1872) (hereafter cited as *Justification* 1); vol. 2: *Der biblische Stoff der Lehre* (Bonn, 1874); vol. 3: *Die positive Entwicklung der Lehre,* 3d ed. (Bonn, 1888), Eng.: *The Christian Doctrine of Justification and Reconciliation: The Positive Development of the Doctrine,* trans. H. R. Mackintosh and A. B. Macaulay (1900; reprint, Clifton, N.J., 1966) (hereafter cited as *Justification* 3). Idem, *Geschichte des Pietismus,* 3 vols. (Bonn, 1880–86).

4. Albrecht Ritschl, *Die christliche Vollkommenheit: Ein Vortrag* (Göttingen, 1874); idem, *Unterricht in der christlichen Religion,* 3d ed. (Bonn, 1886), Eng.: *Instruction in the Christian Religion,* trans. Philip Hefner, in *Three Essays* (Philadelphia, 1972), 221–91; idem, *Theologie und Metaphysik: Zur Verständigung und Abwehr* (Bonn, 1881), Eng.: *Theology and Metaphysics: Towards Rapprochement and Defense,* trans. Philip Hefner, in *Three Essays,* 151–217. See also Albrecht Ritschl, *Drei akademische Reden* (Bonn, 1887); and Otto Ritschl, ed., *Gesammelte Aufsätze von Albrecht Ritschl,* 2 vols. (Freiburg im Breisgau, 1893, 1896).

with scholarship today. I have attended to the two former topics elsewhere; the latter two call for independent treatment in their own right.[5]
Nevertheless, limited though my discussion must be, it should serve to
clarify what one outstanding leader of liberal Protestantism did with
the Reformation heritage in a world of which the reformers themselves
never dreamed.

I

One must observe, at the outset, that the linkage of Ritschl with Luther
and Reformation research is by no means axiomatic, so far as the historiographical tradition is concerned. Ritschl has often been portrayed as *the*
theologian of Culture Protestantism—hence as the great accommoda-
tor of Protestant Christianity to the Bismarckian zeitgeist. Perspectives
that are less global, less inclined to do history by catchwords, have
represented him as the inaugurator of a new style of dogmatics that
rejected natural theology and banished metaphysics from the theological enterprise—thereby returning to Kant (by way of R. H. Lotze) as
the philosopher of Protestantism. Or he has been depicted as the creator of a novel yet fatally flawed system that equated Christian faith
with the believer's subjective "value judgments" (*Werturtheile*) concerning the existential worth of God and Christ for life in a world where
human spirit is threatened by impersonal society and hostile nature—
thereby undermining faith's cognitive status and succumbing to sheer
theological pragmatism. By far the most pejorative and, until recently,
the prevailing viewpoint has been that of Protestant neoorthodoxy:
Ritschl, according to Karl Barth and his allies, was the betrayer of Reformation Christianity to the rationalistic religion of the Enlightenment
in its chastened Kantian form—thereby surrendering Christian theology to its deadly foes, moralism and anthropocentrism.[6] From about

5. See David W. Lotz, *Ritschl and Luther: A Fresh Perspective on Albrecht Ritschl's Theology in the Light of His Luther Study* (New York/Nashville, 1974); idem, "Albrecht Ritschl and the Unfinished Reformation," *Harvard Theological Review* 73 (July–October 1980): 337–72; and idem, "Albrecht Ritschl," in *The Encyclopedia of Religion*, ed. Mircea Eliade et al. (New York, 1987), 12:403–5.
6. See Karl Barth, "Ritschl," in *Protestant Theology in the Nineteenth Century: Its Background and History* (Valley Forge, Pa., 1973), 644–61.

1925 to 1965 this harsh, unrelenting judgment was accorded well-nigh canonical status.

The so-called Ritschl renaissance of the last quarter-century has repudiated the latter judgment and has corrected or significantly modified the other traditional viewpoints, resulting in a much more nuanced, judicious, and balanced estimate of Ritschl's aims, accomplishments, and limitations.[7] In the process Ritschl the Luther and Reformation scholar has also been given his due.[8] The newer studies have demonstrated that Ritschl's relationship to Luther and Reformation theology was central to his total undertaking—hence it is productive of valuable insights into the core of his thought and indispensable to any fair appraisal of his goals and attainments. This perspective on Ritschl was already much in evidence during the years before the Barthian hegemony. In 1901, for example, Albert Swing maintained that "the relationship which Ritschl sustains to Luther is the most important of all" for understanding the dynamics and substance of his complete system.[9] Most strikingly, in 1938, in the very heyday of neoorthodoxy, Otto Wolff devoted over one hundred pages of his masterly study of modern Luther scholarship to Ritschl's interpretation of Luther, concluding that "Ritschl, for the first time since Schleiermacher, led dogmatic thinking in its multisided totality back to Luther."[10] This "back to Luther," it should be noted, remains a salutary corrective to all those familiar approaches to Ritschl that begin and end with the theme "back to Kant."

Wolff's estimate of Ritschl's study of Luther has been confirmed and elaborated by Walther von Loewenich, whose investigation of "Luther and liberal theology" led him to the weighty conclusion that "Ritschl is the first of the modern systematicians to make Luther's thought the foundation of his own theological system," with the result that "with

---

7. See James Richmond, "The Ritschl Renaissance," in *Ritschl: A Reappraisal* (London, 1978), 13–45, which surveys both older and newer literature. The most recent scholarship is well represented by the essays presented at the Ritschl Colloquium held at the University of Göttingen in 1989, published as *Gottes Reich und menschliche Freiheit*, ed. Joachim Ringleben (Göttingen, 1990).

8. In addition to the works listed in note 5 above, see Walther von Loewenich, *Luther und der Neuprotestantismus* (Witten, 1963); Rolf Schäfer, *Ritschl: Grundlinien eines fast verschollenen dogmatischen Systems* (Tübingen, 1968); Karl Hammer, "Albrecht Ritschls Lutherbild," *Theologische Zeitschrift* 26 (1970): 109–22; Martin Ohst, "Ritschl als Dogmenhistoriker," in Ringleben, *Gottes Reich*, 112–30; Karl H. Neufeld, "Ritschl und Harnack in der Frage nach der christlichen Tradition," in Ringleben, *Gottes Reich*, 131–43.

9. Albert Swing, *The Theology of Albrecht Ritschl* (New York, 1901), 35.

10. Otto Wolff, *Die Haupttypen der neueren Lutherdeutung* (Stuttgart, 1938), 176.

Ritschl, Luther research achieved general theological significance for
the first time in the nineteenth century."[11] Ritschl's deep involvement
with Luther, therefore, appeared as a new thing on the landscape of
nineteenth-century Protestant systematic theology. In Bernhard Lohse's
words: "Luther, before Ritschl, was a church father whose writings were
reverently cited but hardly ever read. After Ritschl, Luther was a theologian who had decisive contributions to make to the situation of the
later nineteenth century—even though this was quite different from the
situation of the sixteenth."[12]

To be sure, one must not approach Ritschl's writings with expectations shaped by the massive scholarly encounter with Luther that gave
rise to the so-called Luther renaissance of the mid–twentieth century.
The latter phenomenon is usually dated from the publication, in 1921,
of Karl Holl's magisterial volume of Luther essays, although Holl's work,
in turn, is inconceivable apart from the impetus to such study supplied a
generation earlier by Ritschl and the "Ritschlians."[13] In any case, Ritschl
was not a Luther and Reformation specialist in our current academic
sense. For that matter, viewed in its own setting, his Reformation historiography could not begin to match in breadth, depth, and influence
Leopold von Ranke's great *History of Germany in the Age of the Reformation* (6 vols., 1839–47). Likewise, Ritschl's Luther study lacked the sheer
bulk and comprehensiveness of the two most noteworthy Luther monographs of the nineteenth century: the multivolumed works by Julius
Köstlin and Theodosius Harnack.[14]

One must immediately add, however, that Ritschl did not purport to
write either a general history of the Reformation era or a full-scale treatment of Luther's theology. His intentions were much more limited and
specific. He sought, first and foremost, "to unfold in a scientific manner"
that one, all-important doctrine that "constitutes the real center of the
theological system," namely the Christian doctrine of justification and

11. Loewenich, *Luther und Neuprotestantismus*, 92, 109.
12. Bernhard Lohse, *Martin Luther: An Introduction to His Life and Work*, trans. Robert C.
Schultz (Philadelphia, 1986), 220.
13. Karl Holl, *Gesammelte Aufsätze zur Kirchengeschichte*, vol. 1: *Luther* (Tübingen, 1921).
Concerning Holl's relationship to Ritschl, see Lotz, *Ritschl and Luther*, 153–61.
14. Julius Köstlin, *Luthers Theologie in ihrer geschichtlichen Entwicklung und ihrem Zusam-
menhange*, 2 vols., 2d ed. (Stuttgart, 1883). Theodosius Harnack, *Luthers Theologie mit
besonderer Beziehung auf seine Versöhnungs–und Erlösungslehre*, 2 vols. (1862, 1886; reprint,
Munich, 1927).

reconciliation.[15] This identification of justification as the principal article of evangelical dogmatics—announced in the very first sentence of the first volume of his magnum opus—already displays Ritschl's profound indebtedness to the Reformation tradition. He approached Luther and the reformers not as subjects for scholarly monographs but as normative sources for, and witnesses to, the right understanding of Christian theology's cardinal tenet, that teaching by which the church stands or falls. Ritschl's Luther and Reformation interpretation, therefore, was consistently doctrinal-theological, rather than a specimen of social-political history (in the manner of Ranke) or of cultural-intellectual history (in the manner of Wilhelm Dilthey and Ernst Troeltsch). Furthermore, in carrying out his historical morphology of a single doctrine, Ritschl cast a remarkably wide net as he ranged through the entire course of Western theology from Anselm and Abelard to Hegel and the Hegelians. (Here Ritschl proved himself superior to both Ranke and Theodosius Harnack, neither of whom related Luther's thought to the Middle Ages or to modern times.) Hence Luther and his fellow reformers, while they certainly occupied stage-center in this endeavor, could not each be accorded the equivalent of a book-length exposition.

As regards Reformation history proper, here too Ritschl had restricted aims: not to trace the rise and spread of the sixteenth-century reform movements *in toto,* but to pursue such historical-theological questions as how it came about that the Lutheran Reformation issued in the dogmatically rigid Lutheran church; how it transpired that the reformers' leading ideas failed to achieve systematic-theological form and so became a "stunted growth"; how to account for and appraise the "scholastic narrowing" of Reformation theology among the reformers themselves as well as their successors; how to interpret and evaluate such phenomena as Anabaptism and Pietism, both of which claimed to have "reforming significance" for Protestantism. Reformation history, in short, was also for Ritschl an adjunct of the history of theology and of Christian thought.

Finally, it must be emphasized that Ritschl the historian was one with Ritschl the systematician: he studied the past for the sake of the present, in order to effect the reconstruction of evangelical theology and the reform of Protestantism by the recovery of the Reformation's prac-

---

15. *Justification* 1:1.

tical root ideas. Historical analysis, therefore, was inseparable from, and must culminate in, theological synthesis. One recalls that Ritschl took for his personal motto the old axiom of the medieval Schoolmen, *qui bene distinguit bene docet*, which he characteristically adapted to his purposes by modifying it to read, *qui bene distinguit et bene comprehendit bene docet*: "one teaches well who divides rightly *and combines correctly*."[16] Ritschl, accordingly, did not regard historical study as an end in itself and so would scarcely be disturbed by the charge that he was not a historian in a "pure" sense. The whole of the Ritschlian system was oriented by design to the *bene comprehendere*, to the requisite "summing up" of the heart of Reformation faith, which, in his judgment, was nothing other than the essence of biblical Christianity and the bearer of the loftiest piety of the Western Catholic church.

II

Ritschl's interpretation of Reformation history and theology, like that of his nineteenth-century predecessors, made use of a number of generalizing formulas: "the principle(s) of Protestantism," "the essence of Protestantism," and, above all, "the principle of the Reformation." Such formulas bespoke German historicism's quest for the animating idea or *Geist* of a historical "whole." What distinguished Ritschl's interpretation, however, was its thoroughness, based as it was on a painstaking study of all the primary theological texts, a mastery of the available documentary sources. Thus, with Ritschl, the historical-particular was not lost in or surrendered to the conceptual-universal (as often happened among the speculative historians and theologians inspired by Hegel's philosophy of history). Ritschl's knowledge of the relevant source materials, according to Loewenich, "exceeded by far" that of Schleiermacher, Baur, and Richard Rothe.[17] In this respect he proved himself an heir of Ranke (and a precursor of twentieth-century Luther research).

Ritschl's primary sources for Luther's theology were chiefly the *Vollständige Reformationsacta und Documenta* edited by Valentin Ernst Löscher

---

16. See O. Ritschl, *Albrecht Ritschls Leben*, 2:167–68.

17. Loewenich, *Luther und Neuprotestantismus*, 92. One should add here that Ritschl, in researching the history of Pietism, examined every literary vestige of Dutch, German, and Swiss Pietism.

(3 vols., 1720ff.) and the so-called Halle or Walch edition of Luther's *Sämtliche Schriften* issued in twenty-four volumes by J. G. Walch (Halle, 1740–53). Löscher's edition, containing Luther's writings from 1515 to 1519, was of particular importance to Ritschl because he found here the reformer's religious ideas presented in their purest form—that is, least influenced by polemics and by the controversies of succeeding decades. He also referred frequently to the available volumes of the newer, much fuller, and far more critically sound Erlangen edition of Luther's collected works (1826ff.), especially the seven volumes of Latin writings illustrative of Luther's career as reformer (the *Opera Latina varii*, 1865–73).[18] At times he also cited the very first collection of Luther's Latin writings—the original Wittenberg edition of 1545ff.—as well as the Latin works published in the succeeding Jena edition (1555ff.). Ritschl thus employed all the major editions of Luther's works that had appeared prior to the launching of the definitive Weimar edition in 1883, in connection with the quadricentennial of Luther's birth. In addition, he frequently quoted from the six volumes of Luther's correspondence edited by W. M. L. de Wette (1825ff.) and, on occasion, cited Luther's table talk in the edition of K. E. Förstemann and H. E. Bindseil (4 vols., 1844–48). Among Luther's writings he evidenced special fondness for the classic "Reformation treatises" of 1520, above all *De libertate christiana*, and the Small Catechism (1529). He quoted, however, from a large number of works ranging from Luther's early sermons (1515–17) to his last lectures on Genesis (1535–45).

For his many references to the works of Melanchthon and Calvin, Ritschl used the great *Corpus Reformatorum* launched in 1834 by K. G. Bretschneider. The first twenty-eight volumes of this series were devoted to Melanchthon's writings, edited by Bretschneider and Bindseil (1834–60). Of these Ritschl made extensive use of volumes 1–10, containing Melanchthon's correspondence, but devoted primary attention to volume 21, containing the texts of the major editions of the *Loci communes* (1521, 1535, 1543–59). Calvin's works occupy the next fifty-nine volumes (29–87), edited by G. Baum, E. Cunitz, and E. Reuss (1863–1900). As one would expect, Ritschl concentrated on the two volumes containing the successive editions of the *Institutes*, namely volume 29 (the 1536

---

18. In the Walch edition, Luther's Latin writings were translated into German. In the Erlangen edition, the German and Latin writings were published in two separate series.

and 1539–54 editions) and volume 30 (the 1559 edition). His quotations from Zwingli's writings were based on the eight volumes of the Zurich reformer's *Werke* edited by M. Schuler and J. Schulthess (1828–42, with a supplementary volume in 1861).[19] Approaching Zwingli not as a "superficial imitator" of Luther, but as a truly independent reformer (and thereby confirming Zwingli's own self-estimate), Ritschl referred mainly to his *Sixty-seven Articles* (1522), *Exposition of the Articles* (1523), *On Divine and Human Righteousness* (1523), *Commentary on True and False Religion* (1525), *On the Providence of God* (1530), and *An Exposition of the Faith* (1531).

Besides mastering the chief works of the leading reformers, Ritschl was thoroughly acquainted with the relevant secondary literature treating their lives and thought. He also exhibited a wide-ranging, detailed knowledge of the works of the lesser figures of the Reformation era and of the succeeding confessional generation. He made insightful use of the early evangelical church orders, and, of course, repeatedly cited the Reformed and Lutheran confessions, above all the Augsburg Confession and its Apology.[20] It is pertinent to add that through his efforts to demonstrate the fundamental agreement between the confessions of the two Protestant churches (something one would expect of a determined advocate of the *Unierte Kirche,* i.e., of the union of Lutheran and Reformed churches mandated in Prussian territories since 1817), Ritschl made substantive contributions to the developing discipline of "comparative symbolics."

In addition to the mainline reformers of the sixteenth century, his dialogue partners included the leading Socinians and Arminians as well as the literary representatives of the main currents of theological thought from Pietism through rationalism, Kant, Hegel, and Schleiermacher, down to the neo-Lutheranism and repristinating confessionalism of his own day. What is perhaps most striking, and surely most foreign, to Ritschl's present-day readers, however, is his massive confrontation with the theologians of Lutheran and Reformed orthodoxy. In both his historical and systematic writings he engaged in a sustained

---

19. Publication of Zwingli's *Sämtliche Werke* in the *Corpus Reformatorum,* vols. 88–101, did not begin until 1905.

20. Ritschl's sourcebook for the church orders was A. L. Richter, ed., *Die evangelischen Kirchenordnungen des 16. Jahrhundert,* 2 vols. (Weimar, 1846). For the Reformed confessions he used H. A. Niemeyer, ed., *Collectio Confessionum in Ecclesiis Reformatis publicatorum* (Leipzig, 1840); for the Lutheran confessions, J. T. Müller, ed., *Die symbolishen Bücher der evangelisch-lutherischen Kirche, deutsch und lateinisch* (Stuttgart, 1848).

critical dialogue with at least a score of seventeenth-century Calvinist and Lutheran divines, of whom but a handful are even remembered today. In volume 3 of *The Christian Doctrine of Justification and Reconciliation*, for example, upon taking up the fundamental question of Christ's divinity, he proceeded to argue on the basis of the old doctrine of the three *munera* or "offices" of the God-man (Prophet, Priest, King) and sought to establish his own position through a dense internal critique of the positions of the Protestant scholastics.[21] In this methodological respect, at least, Ritschl showed himself decidedly old-fashioned for an heir of Schleiermacher, the acknowledged founder of modern theology. Little wonder that, in 1896, Adolf Harnack should have styled his erstwhile mentor "the last Lutheran church father": an epithet clearly expressing admiration for the great man's accomplishments, yet tacitly conceding that by contemporary standards the Ritschlian style of dogmatic theology was not a little passé.[22] So also, in 1907, Wilhelm Herrmann—Ritschl's other preeminent disciple—called him "the last great representative of the orthodox *Dogmatik*," which with Ritschl attained "its maturest form."[23]

III

Ritschl's intensive study of the four primary reformers warranted his conclusion (or, perhaps, confirmed his prejudgment) that they shared the same practical root ideas, which thus composed the principle of the Reformation as a whole.[24] As regards their understanding of the Christian revelation attested in scripture, these reformers displayed

---

21. See *Justification* 3:417–34.
22. Adolf Harnack, "Zur gegenwärtigen Lage des Protestantismus" (1896), in *Reden und Aufsätze* (Giessen, 1906), 2:139. The fuller statement reads: "In Ritschl's theology the old Protestant doctrinaire element comes powerfully to the fore. In this respect he is, for the present, the last Lutheran church father; for his uniqueness consisted in this: that he both strengthened and held in closest connection the two elements of Protestantism—the doctrinaire and the original-religious."
23. Wilhelm Herrmann, "Die Lage und Aufgabe der evangelischen Dogmatik in der Gegenwart" (1907), in *Gesammelte Aufsätze*, ed. F. W. Schmidt (Tübingen, 1923), 118–19. Herrmann judged that Ritschl, "in holding fast to the old task of dogmatics, i.e., the demonstration of 'what must be believed,' makes Holy Scripture into a *Lehrgesetz* [a binding doctrinal norm] in the manner of the old Protestantism" (p. 118).
24. See *Justification* 1:121–95. This pivotal fourth chapter is entitled "The Reformation Principle of Justification by Faith in Christ." Cf. Lotz, *Ritschl and Luther*, 31–51, 57–75.

a basic unity, notwithstanding their manifest differences in age, temperament, training, geographical location, and rhetorical locution, as well as in their formal theological productions. (In his New Testament studies, treating the "apostolic circle of ideas," Ritschl also posited a unity-in-diversity among Paul, James, and Peter.)

The reformers' root ideas were "practical" (what today we would call "experiential" or "existential") because they functioned not as theoretical loci (topics) in a system of church doctrine, but as the religious regulators of believers' understanding of themselves in relationship to God, to the church, and to the world. This multifaceted relationship was, in each instance, determined by the New Testament idea of God's unconditional forgiveness of sins bestowed upon God's covenant people for Christ's sake through faith alone. Luther and Zwingli, however, the two earliest reformers, did not derive this fundamental idea immediately from the Bible, but appropriated it from a venerable tradition of *sola gratia* piety that was operative in the church throughout the Middle Ages, from Augustine through Bernard of Clairvaux to Johann von Staupitz. This tradition received powerful expression in the neo-Augustinianism of the fifteenth century, in opposition both to an ascetic piety of works-righteousness and to the scholastic (nominalist) doctrines of justification based on grace *and* merit. Luther, the earnest Augustinian friar, and the other reformers were grateful heirs of these anti-Pelagian currents of medieval devotion and thought.

By means of their evangelical preaching and teaching, Luther and Zwingli and their colleagues successfully brought their adherents to a new self-, church-, and world-understanding based on the regulative thought of justification by grace alone through faith alone: an understanding, therefore, that was entirely theonomous, that is, determined by the God of love and the love of God. The reformers, in short, transformed the religious consciousness of their contemporaries by effecting a radical break with the late medieval church's heteronomous sacrament of penance and its legalistic control of the anxious conscience; with this church's equally heteronomous polity that made salvation conditional upon obedience to the ecclesiastical hierarchy and to the claims of this hierocratic church to be the sole guarantor of salvation; and, not least, with this church's age-old teaching, embodied in all its institutions, that a monastic-ascetic, world-renouncing piety is the sum of Christian perfection and so is the true Christian ideal of life.

In its original sense, therefore, Reformation meant a practical reform of popular religion, not a comprehensive reform of traditional
theology. Nevertheless, held Ritschl, such theological reconstruction
was imperative if Reformation Christianity in its basal form—if *das
Princip der Reformation*—was to be safeguarded and preserved as the ongoing dynamic of Protestant spirituality, church organization, and life
in the world. The reformers themselves, however, above all Luther and
Melanchthon, were not finally equal to this all-important task. In fact,
"the genuine ideas of the Reformation were more concealed than dis-
closed in the theological works of Luther and Melanchthon": so declared
Ritschl in 1883 in a university address commemorating the quadricentennial of Luther's birth. "Until now," he concluded, "the practical root
idea of Luther's Reformation has not been employed in all clarity and
vigor for the regulation of Protestantism's many tasks, i.e., it has still not
been directed to the ordering of theology and its demarcation from all
useless forms."[25]

IV

Ritschl devoted the bulk of his historical scholarship to analyzing the
causes and consequences of this fateful theological deformation (*Miss-
bildung*) that transpired during the Reformation era and that was never
fully overcome during the post-Reformation centuries, resulting in a
theologically unfinished Reformation.[26] One chief causal factor was
the lack of systematic-constructive ability on the part of the two Wittenberg reformers. Luther, from 1521 onward, was engaged in bitter
controversy with both Romanists and fellow Protestants. His theological works, therefore, were polemically overdetermined, which accounts
for their one-sidedness and episodic (ad hoc) character. Luther the

25. Albrecht Ritschl, "Festival Address on the Four-Hundredth Anniversary of the Birth
of Martin Luther (November 10, 1883)," trans. David W. Lotz (from *Drei akademische Reden*,
5–29) as an appendix (187–202) to Lotz, *Ritschl and Luther*, 195, 200–201.
26. Ritschl's critique of the reformers and their heirs is considered at length in my essay, "Albrecht Ritschl and the Unfinished Reformation," on which the following summary
is based; see also my *Ritschl and Luther*, 57–87. The primary texts are A. Ritschl, *Justification* 1; idem, "Festival Address"; and especially the "Prolegomena" to Ritschl's *History of
Pietism*; the "Prolegomena," trans. Philip Hefner, is in *Three Essays*, 53–147. Most valuable
also is Ritschl's brilliant essay, "Die Entstehung der lutherischen Kirche," *Zeitschrift für
Kirchengeschichte* 1 (1876): 51–110 (reprinted in O. Ritschl, *Gesammelte Aufsätze*, 1:170–217).

theologian also subverted his religious root ideas by reappropriating alien ideas of medieval-scholastic provenance: for example, a nominalist concept of the hidden God of absolute, all-determining power who, in implacable justice, appears wholly other than the loving God revealed in Christ; and Anselm's doctrine of Christ's vicarious satisfaction rendered to God's sin-offended honor (which thus gave God's wrath priority over God's love, the law priority over the gospel). Melanchthon, meanwhile, "was only able to use the loose scheme of the *Loci theologici,* which actually produces the opposite of a theological system."[27] To him also was due the reintroduction into Lutheran dogmatics of a scholastic-Aristotelian method, which gave scope to a natural no less than a revealed knowledge of God. Herewith Melanchthon openly contradicted the consistent Christocentrism that had marked both his and Luther's root ideas.

Ritschl particularly focused on the attendant damage done to the three components of the Reformation principle: the believer's new understanding of the relationship between self and God, self and church, and self and world, an understanding arising from the personal appropriation, within the church, of God's unmerited forgiveness of sins proclaimed in the gospel. The relationship between self and God was distorted by a developing legalism that made the assurance of divine pardon no longer dependent solely on the gospel but, in part at least, on the *prior* experience of terrors of conscience before the divine law that one has failed to keep. This deformation can be traced to the correlation between law and gospel that became the fundament of Lutheran theology during the 1520s. The religious self-understanding was further deformed by a developing intellectualism, attributable largely to Melanchthon: during the 1530s he began to make salvation conditional upon a clear knowledge of the church's formal doctrine of justification and of the ancient trinitarian and christological dogmas, rather than basing it strictly on trust in the gospel itself. The evangelical certainty of salvation was thus undermined by both legalism and doctrinalism, hence by a new heteronomy of Protestant origin.

These baneful developments, in turn, subverted the religious church-understanding. Owing to the dialectic between law and gospel, the church was no longer comprehended simply as the assembly

---

27. A. Ritschl, "Prolegomena," 127.

of the faithful, the community of regenerate persons confident of God's grace, but was now viewed as a mixed body of saints and sinners, the latter still awaiting conversion. Likewise, owing to the intellectualist confusion of faith with knowledge, the church was transformed into a "school": an assembly of right doctrine. Even John Calvin, who was "the one systematic theologian of the later Reformation period" and who otherwise proved to be "the most circumspect" of Luther's heirs, abetted this confusion by insisting that Christian faith had to be "scholastically precise." Hence, by the end of the sixteenth century, a new scholasticism—a "reason-centered Christianity" (*Verstandeschristenthum*)—had come to prevail within Protestantism at large.[28]

All things considered, however, it was the religious world-understanding that was most gravely affected by theological deformation in the Reformation era. In his 1520 treatise *On Christian Liberty*, Luther had given consummate expression to the biblical (Pauline) ideal of the Christian life as one of freedom, in faith, from sin and guilt before God and from the world's crushing weight of ills, which very liberation made possible, in turn, the believer's freedom for loving service to needy humankind and thus for the world's moral reconstruction—that is, for the progressive realization in human history of God's universal dominion (the kingdom of God). Precisely this life of faith active in love, grounded on the believer's justification by God and reconciliation with God, constituted Christian perfection or "wholeness" (not to be confused with sinlessness). And precisely this ideal of spiritual lordship over the world marked the Reformation's epoch-making break with the regnant worldview of the Middle Ages and of Roman Catholicism at large: its life ideal of monastic-ascetic flight from the world.[29]

In their formal theological works, however, Luther and Melanchthon never articulated the practical or *teleological* connection between justification by faith and life in the world, between the forgiveness of sins and the believer's *present* experience of salvation or blessedness through spiritual world dominion. Ritschl found it "frankly shocking" that "there is no mention of the practical aim of justification by faith in the fourth ar-

---

28. A. Ritschl, *Justification* 1:281; idem, "Prolegomena," 130–31, 134, 137.

29. The first edition (1870) of vol. 1 of *Die christliche Lehre* did not yet treat the Christian ideal of life as represented by Luther's 1520 treatise. This cardinal Ritschlian theme first came to the fore in the mid-1870s and was later taken up into the second edition (1882) of vol. 1 of *Die christliche Lehre*. See my "Albrecht Ritschl and the Unfinished Reformation," 344–48.

ticle ['On Justification'] of the Augsburg Confession."[30] One reason for this omission was that the Wittenberg reformers made no systematic use of the most important construct in the teaching of Jesus, namely, the kingdom of God. For them this divine rule was purely internal—the gracious rule of God in the trusting heart—rather than God's outward and continuous reordering of human society through the cooperation of those persons who have become children of God by divine adoption. This grievous deformation of the "secular" component of the Reformation principle was rendered even more severe by Calvin, who "linked the thrust of the world-renouncing, holy church to Luther's principles," thereby reverting to the medieval (Franciscan) ideal of ascetic sanctity that also characterized Anabaptism and was later to give rise to Pietism in Calvinist-Reformed circles.[31] Thus Reformation theology, given its methodological and material failings, lost its hold on its unique life ideal: that religious freedom from and for the world that most clearly distinguishes Protestantism from Catholicism and most directly links the sixteenth-century Reformation with a modern age whose very theme is liberty and liberation.

All these deformations continued apace, and were even compounded, during the post-Reformation centuries. Intellectualism—the transformation of the church into a type of school for doctrinal or moral instruction—prevailed within Socinianism, Lutheran and Reformed orthodoxy, the theology of the German Illumination (rationalism), and the Lutheran neoorthodoxy (confessionalism) of the nineteenth century. It also came to expression in the Kantian moral religion "within the limits of reason alone" and in the Hegelian elevation of religious representations into philosophical concepts. Concurrently, there was a new efflorescence of Anabaptist-like sectarianism: the transformation of the church into a visible assembly of the truly "reborn," distinguished by their arduous penitential struggle, their law-regulated empirical sanctity, their withdrawal from "worldly" entanglements, and often by their physical separation from a "secularized" institutional church. This sectarian spirit—in part a reaction against orthodoxy's and rationalism's arid intellectualism, and traceable to the Lutheran law/gospel distinction and, above all, to the reformers' surrender of their original

---

30. A. Ritschl, "Prolegomena," 128.
31. Ibid., 136.

life ideal—came to the fore in Pietism and its offshoots (such as the Moravian Brotherhood) and gained a new lease on life in the early nineteenth-century Awakening following the German wars of liberation from Napoleonic rule. Attendant upon these developments was the emergence within Protestantism of various modes of mystical piety (Spiritualism): radically sectarian, half-Catholic in conceptuality, and (with its leitmotif of "God and the soul, the soul and its God") even more acosmic and ahistorical than Pietism.

Original Reformation Christianity, in sum, had been left in a theologically unfinished condition by the reformers themselves: it was a "stunted growth" (*Verkümmerung*).[32] This theological atrophy persisted throughout the history of Protestantism, bringing with it many and varied deformations in both faith and life. The Reformation heritage, therefore, if not lost, was no longer discernible in wide circles of the Protestant church and academy. This heritage, to be sure, was patently not a homogeneous phenomenon. Critical-historical scholarship was required to separate the wheat from the chaff, the reformers' religion from its defective theological formulation, the Reformation principle from the countervailing principles of post-Reformation piety and thought. Systematic-theological reconstruction was required for the creation of an evangelical dogmatics centered on the Reformation principle and, like it, grounded on both scripture and biblically warranted tradition. Thereby the unfinished Reformation would be brought to theological completion; the Protestant church would be freed from its servile dependence on alien traditions; and essential Protestantism would be vindicated before its Roman Catholic foes and its cultural critics (all of whom were confusing the withered shell of a deformed Protestantism with the thing-in-itself). For over thirty years Albrecht Ritschl devoted himself to this dual task: the historical recovery and theological re-forming of the authentic heritage of the Reformation.

V

Whatever one's final assessment of Ritschl's Luther and Reformation scholarship—and, for that matter, of his total theological system: histor-

---

32. Ibid., 134; cf. A. Ritschl, "Festival Address," 195.

ical, exegetical, constructive—the preceding considerations should have made plain the remarkable breadth and depth of his engagement with Reformation history and theology, as well as the pivotal role played by this scholarship in his complete system, which itself turns on the idea of the unfinished Reformation.

It remains to emphasize, in conclusion, that this engagement did not end with Ritschl himself or mark merely an episode in the history of modern theology. Quite the contrary. Ritschl's example, his distinctive mode of theologizing out of the Reformation heritage, proved to be magnetic. From the 1870s onward he attracted to himself an extraordinarily talented group of young scholars who at once continued and deepened this enterprise, leading to impressive results in Luther research and Reformation historiography.[33] The valuable contributions of this "Ritschlian school," though all too often overlooked (whether through ignorance or forgetfulness), formed a bridge to the work of Karl Holl and later scholars, and thus to the "Luther renaissance." Indeed, if "owing to Holl, Luther's theology has been removed from the province of purely historical investigation and has become an object of systematic theology," then it must be said that "Holl, in his own way, continue[d] the tradition of Albrecht Ritschl."[34] And if the phrase "Luther renaissance" means, above all, that "on the evangelical side one can no longer conceive of any serious theological undertaking of a comprehensive sort which does not attach itself to Luther and make positive use of his basic religious ideas," then it must also be said that Ritschl clearly prepared the way for *this* phenomenon.[35] (Thus Ritschl, no less than Holl, stands behind what some contemporary historians have called the "theological captivity" that overtook Reformation research in the mid–twentieth century and that has but recently been overcome.)[36] The labors of Ritschl and his school also pointed forward to the so-called neo-Reformation theology of Karl Barth and Emil Brunner, which appropriated the Ritschlian heritage while taking no note of Ritschl the Luther scholar and even pronouncing his theology perverse.

---

33. See Lotz, *Ritschl and Luther,* 55 n. 82, for a representative listing of authors and titles.

34. Loewenich, *Luther und Neuprotestantismus,* 280.

35. Ibid.

36. Cf. Bernd Moeller, "Problems of Reformation Research" (1965), in *Imperial Cities and the Reformation: Three Essays,* ed. and trans. H. C. Erik Midelfort and Mark U. Edwards, Jr. (Philadelphia, 1972), 3–16.

For their part, however, Ritschl's students and younger associates found in his Luther interpretation the distinguishing mark of his theological enterprise.

For example, Martin Rade (cofounder of *Die christliche Welt* and editor from 1886 to 1931) testified that during his own student days at Leipzig "to occupy oneself with Ritschl and to be acquainted with Luther were one and the same thing.... With Ritschl one immediately breathed the spirit of the Reformation."[37] As late as 1937, three years before his death, Rade gratefully recalled the "joy in Luther" of the Ritschlian theology.[38] Julius Kaftan (professor at Berlin from 1883 to 1920) similarly acknowledged that Ritschl had become "a teacher for me and others" precisely because he was "the first to raise the fundamental demand to take up and set about the theological task in the way Luther had originally proposed."[39] And Wilhelm Herrmann (who allied himself with Ritschl in 1875) declared that "Ritschl had the power to rescue Luther's work from that ruin into which it had fallen, even among those who comported themselves as the most loyal of Luther's heirs."[40] Undoubtedly Ritschl's most conspicuous (and poignant) success as a theological mentor occurred in the case of Adolf Harnack (who was, in turn, Holl's teacher). Already in 1874, upon assuming his first academic post as an instructor at Leipzig, this brilliant young scholar turned to Ritschl as his model, breaking decisively with the neo-Lutheranism (and the Luther interpretation!) of his esteemed father, Theodosius Harnack, which led to an irreparable breach between father and son, much to their mutual sorrow. "Ritschl's uniqueness," according to Adolf Harnack, resided specifically in the way he "followed Luther" by approaching "religion, and above all the Christian religion, as a powerful reality in and for itself," thus distinguishing it from all philosophical speculation and natural theology.[41] In view of such recurrent testimony to the impact and appeal of Ritschl's paradigmatic "return to Luther,"

---

37. As quoted in Horst Stephan, *Luther in den Wandlungen seiner Kirche*, 2d ed. (Berlin, 1951), 80.

38. Martin Rade, "Unkonfessionalistisches Luthertum: Errinerung an die Lutherfreude in der Ritschlschen Theologie," *Zeitschrift für Theologie und Kirche* 45, n.s., 18 (1937): 131–51.

39. As quoted in Wolff, *Die Haupttypen*, 139.

40. Wilhelm Herrmann, "Albrecht Ritschl, seine Grösse und seine Schranke," in *Festgabe von Fachgenossen und Freunden A. von Harnack zum siebzigsten Geburtstag dargebracht*, ed. Karl Holl (Tübingen, 1921), 405.

41. Adolf Harnack, "Albrecht Ritschl: Rede zum hundertsten Geburtstag am 30. April 1922 in Bonn gehalten," in *Reden und Aufsätze*, n.s., 4 (Giessen, 1923), 335–36.

Horst Stephan was not exaggerating when he asserted that "it was primarily Ritschl's relationship to Luther that, alongside the power of his
theological thinking, secured his ascendancy over all other theological
leaders of his time."[42]

Over a century has passed since Albrecht Ritschl brought his great
theological system to completion. One can now see—much more clearly,
I think, than was the case fifty years ago—that the uniqueness and
lasting import of his endeavor reside in his creative reappropriation of
the Reformation heritage in the interest of contemporary theological
reconstruction, polemics, and apologetics. It is this masterly elaboration of a unified system out of biblical and tradition-historical materials
that commands our attention and evokes our admiration, rather than
any "assured results" of Ritschl's Luther and Reformation scholarship
(though there are these as well). Ritschl still repays careful study because
one witnesses in his work the subtle interplay between historical analysis and theological synthesis, between the conservation and the criticism
of a heritage, between tradition and innovation. Here one also fathoms
much of the secret of his wide appeal and influence. Unlike Theodosius Harnack, whose estimable Luther book lacked appreciable effect
in its own time, Ritschl established a discipline of Luther-Reformation
study that was truly dialogical, rooted in history yet always directed
to present concerns. Although such an endeavor invites anachronism
on the part of its incautious practitioners, it breaks categorically with
antiquarianism, avoids traditionalism even while respecting and revitalizing the tradition, and so equips a history-based theology to be at
once "responsible" to the past and "responding" to the present.

42. Stephan, *Luther in den Wandlungen seiner Kirche*, 80.

THIRTEEN

Walter E. Wyman, Jr.

The Kingdom of God in Germany: From Ritschl to Troeltsch

Of the many issues being discussed among German Protestant theologians at the turn of the century, the "rediscovery" of the eschatological meaning of the kingdom of God in the preaching of Jesus is perhaps the only one to have achieved the status of a commonplace. The kingdom of God, understood as the highest good to be attained on earth through human action, formed one of the two foci of Albrecht Ritschl's theology. According to the well-known picture, Johannes Weiss showed that Ritschl's understanding of the kingdom of God is not what it meant in the proclamation of Jesus. Jesus' conception is completely eschatological; the kingdom is the apocalyptic transformation of the world to be brought about by the supernatural intervention of God. Along with Albert Schweitzer, who likewise argued for the apocalyptic meaning of the kingdom of God, Johannes Weiss supposedly inflicted a fatal wound on Protestant liberal theology, while inaugurating the modern phase of research into the historical Jesus. Three modern judgments are typical. Leander Keck comments, "Together with Albert Schweitzer, Weiss turned the entire course of Jesus research and undermined the foundations of the prevailing Protestant theology."[1] Richard Hiers and D. Larrimore Holland assert that "the appearance of Johannes Weiss' *Die Predigt Jesu vom Reiche Gottes* in 1892 produced a major crisis in Protes-

---

1. Leander Keck, "Foreword to the Series," in Johannes Weiss, *Jesus' Proclamation of the Kingdom of God,* ed. and trans. R. H. Hiers and D. L. Holland (Philadelphia: Fortress Press, 1971), viii–ix.

tant liberal theology."[2] And James M. Robinson maintains that "when [Albert Schweitzer's] *The Quest of the Historical Jesus* was written, the eschatological orientation of Jesus' and primitive Christianity's message could only bewilder contemporary theology."[3]

But are these judgments historically correct? What, in fact, were the responses of their contemporaries to Weiss and Schweitzer? Were they bewildered by the news of the eschatological meaning of the kingdom of God? Did they sense that a whole era of systematic theology had been thrown into crisis? The purpose of this essay is to test the commonplace judgments on the period by studying a number of theologians who might be loosely termed "liberal Protestants."

I will not in this context attempt an extensive definition of Protestant liberalism, or inquire into the varieties of liberalism at the end of the nineteenth century. Rather, it suffices to single out two characteristics that are relevant for my theme. First, the Protestant liberals fully accept the historical-critical method, with its presuppositions and implications. Second, they do not view either Christianity or Jesus of Nazareth through the lens of orthodox doctrines, such as incarnation and atonement. Rather, they approach Jesus of Nazareth as one would any important historical figure and ask about his religious significance within the framework of the historical consciousness. The significance of these two characteristics should be clear. Insofar as liberal systematic theology rests its estimate of the religious significance of Jesus upon historical claims, and insofar as it accepts the historical-critical method without reservation, it makes religious believing dependent upon historical claims and cannot take refuge in traditional doctrinal beliefs. This means that the liberal theologians are obliged by their principles to take into account the results of historical scholarship and adjust their systematic claims, their statements of belief, accordingly. Thus, given their principles, the liberal theologians were obligated to come to terms with Johannes Weiss's challenge.

My study will concentrate on six figures: three New Testament scholars and three theologians. They are representative figures belonging to the liberal wing of German Protestant theology at the turn of

---

2. R. H. Hiers and D. L. Holland, "Introduction," in Weiss, *Jesus' Proclamation*, 4.

3. James M. Robinson, introduction to Albert Schweitzer, *The Quest of the Historical Jesus: A Critical Study of Its Progress from Reimarus to Wrede* (New York: Macmillan, 1968), xxi.

the century. The New Testament scholars Wilhelm Bousset and Wilhelm Heitmüller employed the history-of-religions method, while Adolf Jülicher did pioneering work on the parables. Wilhelm Herrmann and Adolf Harnack are usually called "Ritschlians," although it is somewhat problematic to consider such original thinkers members of a "school." Ernst Troeltsch has been called the "systematic theologian of the history-of-religions school," although again the "school" designation is problematic. My thesis is that the putative crisis in liberalism inspired by the eschatological school never occurred. Talk of a crisis reflects a later systematic judgment, not a judgment that was made at the time. Moreover, this judgment has been influenced more by Albert Schweitzer's tendentious reading of his contemporaries than by a judicious estimate of these thinkers in their own right. The striking fact about the period is that Protestant liberals were able to respond to the eschatological understanding of the historical Jesus in a number of ways without being thrown into crisis or feeling undermined. To be sure, it was not Ritschl's theology that they defended, but varieties of post-Ritschlian liberalism. And there is no doubt that the kingdom of God tends to disappear from the center of theological interest, but whether this is to be ascribed to the influence of the eschatological school is open to question. In any event, the real shaking of the foundations of German Protestant liberalism did not occur until after the Great War, and for very different reasons.

I

What were the issues at stake between Ritschl and Weiss? Albrecht Ritschl describes the kingdom as "the final end of God in the world" and "the highest good."[4] The goal of human life is "the moral society of nations"; the kingdom of God is a harmonious, peaceful, and just order on earth.[5] "The kingdom of God is the *summum bonum* which God realizes in men; and at the same time it is their common task, for it

---

4. Albrecht Ritschl, *The Christian Doctrine of Justification and Reconciliation: The Positive Development of the Doctrine*, trans. and ed. H. R. Mackintosh and A. B. Macaulay (Clifton, N.J.: Reference Book Publishers, 1966), 326; idem, "Instruction in the Christian Religion," in Albrecht Ritschl, *Three Essays*, trans. Philip Hefner (Philadelphia: Fortress Press, 1972), 222–91; see 222, par. 5.
5. Ritschl, *Justification and Reconciliation*, 10; see also 284–85, 290–91.

is only through the rendering of obedience on man's part that God's sovereignty possesses continuous existence."[6]

Three additional details are important in the subsequent discussion. First, although "the presence of the kingdom is always invisible and a matter of religious faith," still the kingdom really is present where action motivated by love occurs.[7] Yet, the kingdom transcends the world and has not yet fully arrived; "it is in the process of becoming."[8] Second, Jesus as the "founder" of the kingdom both founded the Christian community and entrusted the moral task of the kingdom to his disciples.[9] Third, the kingdom is both a divine gift and a human task. Only through obedient human activity is God's sovereignty actualized on earth; at the same time, the kingdom is "always due to the operation of God," because it "comes to be a reality through the mediation of Christ in his community."[10]

Ritschl's idea of the kingdom of God is an ethically powerful and potentially socially dynamic notion. The "ethical community of humanity" is not a miracle that descends from heaven, but rather the result of human activity and thus a moral obligation. But shortly after his death, Ritschl's theology was challenged by the claim that, however powerful and meaningful his idea of the kingdom might be, it was not what the kingdom of God meant in the proclamation of Jesus of Nazareth.

From the opening pages of *Jesus' Proclamation of the Kingdom of God*, Johannes Weiss makes clear his agenda to test the historical foundations of modern systematic theology's concept of the kingdom of God. He draws attention to the danger of "stripping [biblical] concepts of their original historical character by reinterpreting them or converting them to new purposes in accordance with new viewpoints." This is precisely what has happened with respect to the kingdom of God in Ritschl's theology. In the end Weiss acknowledges both the legitimacy of the procedure and even his agreement with the Ritschlian reinterpretation, but he calls for an explicit acknowledgment "whether and how far we today are removed from the original meaning of the concepts.... One should

---

6. Ibid., 30.
7. Ritschl, "Instruction," pars. 8–9.
8. Ibid., par. 27.
9. Ritschl, *Justification and Reconciliation*, 12; see idem, "Instruction," 271 n. 60.
10. Ritschl, *Justification and Reconciliation*, 290

declare, for the sake of clarity, that he wishes to issue the old coinage at a new rate of exchange."[11]

The main point that Weiss wishes to make against Ritschl is that in Jesus' proclamation the kingdom of God is an apocalyptic concept. The Synoptic summary of Jesus' gospel, "Repent for the kingdom of God is at hand" (Mark 1:15 and parallels), correctly conveys the essence of his message. The kingdom of God is understood as a sudden, destructive, worldwide event brought about by the supernatural intervention of God:

> As Jesus conceived it, the kingdom of God is a radically super-worldly entity which stands in diametric opposition to this world. This is to say that there *can* be no talk of an *innerworldly* development of the kingdom of God in the mind of Jesus! On the basis of this finding, it seems to follow that the dogmatic-religious-ethical application of the idea in more recent theology, an application which has stripped away the original eschatological-apocalyptical meaning of the idea, is unjustified.[12]

Three additional details draw out the opposition of Weiss's view to Ritschl's interpretation. First, the kingdom is in no sense present: it is a future reality. "Either the *basileia* [kingdom] is here, or it is not here. For the disciples and for the early church, it is not yet here."[13] Second, Jesus is not the "founder" of the kingdom of God. Jesus' activity is indistinguishable from that of John the Baptist: they both announce the imminence of the kingdom. Third, human activity has no place in bringing about the kingdom. "Jesus thinks the establishment of the *basileia tou theou* [kingdom of God] will be mediated solely by God's supernatural intervention. Any human activity in connection with it is thus ruled out completely."[14] It follows that Jesus' ethics is an ethics of preparation for the kingdom; his teaching concerning the "ethical goods" (family, state, vocation, etc.) is "heroic": "The things of this world, however high and godly they may be in themselves, have lost all value now that the world is ripe for destruction[.] Now they can only hinder and hold back. Cast

---

11. Weiss, *Jesus' Proclamation*, 59, 60.
12. Ibid., 114.
13. Ibid., 73–74; see also 69, 71.
14. Ibid., 82.

them away, and grasp at what comes from above with both hands."[15]
Thus the kingdom of God cannot be a supreme *ethical* ideal involving human action and initiative in its realization. Rather, the kingdom
is "nothing other than the highest religious good, a good which God
grants."[16]

That Weiss has confronted Ritschl's theology with a challenge to one
of its two foci is incontrovertible. But for all the passionate intensity of
the first edition of his book, Weiss himself thought that one could continue to be a Ritschlian in some sense, only acknowledging that one's
use of the concept of the kingdom differed from what Jesus meant by it.
It was Weiss's younger contemporary, Albert Schweitzer, who picked
up the notion of the eschatological Jesus and forced the systematic
theological issue.

Weiss's eschatological Jesus may be incommensurable with Ritschl's
founder of the kingdom of God, but Schweitzer's tragic apocalyptic
fanatic defies appropriation by modern faith or theology altogether.

> There is silence all around. The Baptist appears, and cries: "Repent,
> for the kingdom of Heaven is at hand." Soon after that comes Jesus,
> and in the knowledge that He is the coming Son of Man lays hold
> of the wheel of the world to set it moving on that last revolution
> which is to bring all ordinary history to a close. It refuses to turn,
> and he throws himself upon it. Then it does turn; and crushes Him.
> Instead of bringing in the eschatological conditions, He has de-
> stroyed them. The wheel rolls onward, and the mangled body of
> the one immeasurably great man, who was strong enough to think
> of Himself as the spiritual ruler of mankind and to bend history to
> His purpose, is hanging upon it still.[17]

Schweitzer forces the issue of the relation of contemporary faith and
theology to the preaching of the historical Jesus. Suppose historical research discloses to us a Jesus whose proclamation is so foreign to our
world that it is utterly irrelevant to our religious convictions and theological systems? What if "the historical knowledge of the personality
and life of Jesus" proves not to "be a help, but perhaps even an offense

---

15. Ibid., 112.
16. Ibid., 132.
17. Schweitzer, *Quest*, 370–71.

to religion"? The historical Jesus, Schweitzer holds, proves to be "to our time a stranger and an enigma"; the quest for the historical Jesus, which believed "that when it had found him it could bring him straight into our time as a Teacher and a Savior," has discovered that "He does not stay; He passes by our time and returns to his own. . . . It could not keep Him in our time, but had to let Him go."[18]

Schweitzer wanted to force the issue because he rejected liberal theology's dependence upon history. Theology should not be based upon historical knowledge alone, but on the present experience of the Spirit. While historical science can clarify the tradition, it cannot mediate between past and present: "The boats with which liberal theology has sailed back and forth between the beginnings of Christianity and our religion are burned; the wooden weapons, with which it wished to fight, are knocked from its hands."[19] Schweitzer's work, in short, is guided by a constructive agenda: a solution to the problem of "faith and history" whereby modern liberal faith is independent of claims about the historical Jesus. His survey of research on the life of Jesus is brilliant, but tendentious. The history of research on the life of Jesus since Weiss is constructed to culminate in an antithesis: either the "consistent skepticism" of Wrede, or the "consistent eschatology" of Schweitzer. There is no third alternative; the reader is led into Schweitzer's camp.

Schweitzer's construction of the story has been very influential. But would his contemporaries have agreed with it? Was liberal, historical theology doomed to collapse in the face of the "eschatological school"?

II

In the same year that Johannes Weiss's work appeared, Wilhelm Bousset published a book that agreed in part with his conclusions, but qualified them. *Jesu Predigt in ihrem Gegensatz zum Judentum* accepts Weiss's premise: Jesus expected "a violent end brought about by God's omnipotent deed, accomplished through the destruction of heaven and earth."[20] But

---

18. Ibid., 401, 399.
19. Albert Schweitzer, *Geschichte der Leben Jesu Forschung,* 9th ed. (Tübingen: J. C. B. Mohr [Paul Siebeck], 1984), 28.
20. Wilhelm Bousset, *Jesu Predigt in ihrem Gegensatz zum Judentum* (Göttingen: Vandenhoeck und Ruprecht, 1892), 65–66.

in the course of arguing his thesis that Jesus' preaching must be understood in opposition to the Judaism of his day, Bousset qualifies Weiss in two important respects. First, Weiss is wrong in understanding the kingdom apocalyptically and as wholly in the future; Jesus has broken through Jewish expectation and holds the kingdom to be paradoxically both present and future. "The Dominion of God is already present, it does not need to be brought into being."[21] Second, the kingdom is not the center of Jesus' proclamation. Rather, the most central and characteristic feature of Jesus' preaching is his faith in God as Father, and this faith cannot be understood eschatologically.[22]

Bousset's essay shows neither bewilderment nor a sense of crisis, but rather a qualified acceptance of Weiss's eschatological Jesus. Bousset does not defend Ritschl, but he sees no gulf between the historical Jesus and ourselves. What was central for Jesus' preaching is also central for us: faith in God's fatherly love. Bousset's qualified eschatology retains the liberal, if not the Ritschlian, image of Jesus.

After the publication of the second edition of Weiss's *Die Predigt Jesu vom Reiche Gottes* in 1900, Bousset modifies his position somewhat. In an essay published in 1902 and in a popular presentation of the life of Jesus from 1904, Bousset completely accepts the thesis of "the exclusively eschatological meaning of the idea of the kingdom of God."[23] Bousset concedes there is a gulf between the historical Jesus and ourselves. We can no longer share Jesus' eschatological worldview. Nevertheless, Bousset is still inclined to see Jesus' preaching as creatively breaking through the nationalistic expectations of Judaism; and if the eschatological form of his preaching is irrelevant, its essence still speaks to us. We do not anticipate the imminent end of the world, but we do anticipate our own deaths and know we must stand before God.[24]

Bousset's Jesus is not, like Schweitzer's, a stranger and an enigma; we may still relate to his "personal" and "spiritual" gospel of God's fatherly love and the paramount importance of "moral personality." But clearly the connection of faith to the historical Jesus has become a prob-

21. Ibid., 102; see also 90–104.
22. Ibid., 41, 67–68, 117.
23. Wilhelm Bousset, "Das Reich Gottes in der Predigt Jesu," *Theologische Rundschau* 5 (1902): 437 n. 1; idem, *Jesus*, trans. J. P. Trevelyan and W. D. Morrison (New York: G. P. Putnam's Sons, 1906), chap. 5.
24. Bousset, "Das Reich Gottes," 446–49; idem, *Jesus*, 96–98.

lem to be reckoned with. A few years later, Bousset acknowledges that Weiss's work has "shaken violently the Ritschlian construction" and that historical work had otherwise complicated the problem of recovering the historical Jesus. Because history cannot offer one an arena free from conflict (*sturmfreies Gebiet*) on which one could base theology or faith, Bousset advocates a rationalistic solution dependent upon the thought of Jakob Friedrich Fries. The content and certainty of faith are not to be grounded upon history at all, but upon reason.[25]

Unlike Bousset, Adolf Jülicher does not adopt the history-of-religions method; his work gives close attention to literary and source-critical concerns in research on the Gospels. Aware of the difficulties of disentangling authentic traditions about the historical Jesus from the creative work of the early tradition and the evangelists, he is wrestling with problems that anticipate later form and redaction criticism.[26] Jülicher's methodological sophistication is crucial for his reaction to Schweitzer. Schweitzer's naive acceptance of the historicity of Mark and Matthew and his ignoring of literary questions are "monstrous"; "with this program Schweitzer has left the ground of historically usable research." Schweitzer's reconstruction of the historical Jesus in chapter 19 of *The Quest of the Historical Jesus* is consequently a "novel." Schweitzer's work is "dogmatic, not historical, criticism," while his claim that current research culminates in a choice between the consistent skepticism of Wrede and the consistent eschatology of Schweitzer is a "legend."[27]

What is Jülicher's picture of Jesus? Jülicher accepts Weiss's contention: he opens his portrayal of the religion of Jesus with the statement, "The germ cell of his Gospel is certainly the sure expectation of the nearness of the kingdom of God."[28] Yet Jülicher mediates the eschatological and noneschatological, finally concluding that Jesus' idea of the kingdom is inconsistent. On the one hand, the kingdom is the future

25. Wilhelm Bousset, "Die Bedeutung der Person Jesu für den Glauben," in *Fünfter Weltkongreß für freies Christentum und religiösen Fortschritt: Protokoll der Verhandlungen,* ed. M. Fischer and F. M. Schiele (Berlin-Schöneberg: Verlag des protestantischen Schriftenvertriebs, 1910), 294–96, 298–305.

26. See, for example, Adolf Jülicher, *Neue Linien in der Kritik der evangelischen Überlieferung* (Gießen: Alfred Töpelmann, 1906), passim; idem, "Die Religion Jesu und die Anfänge des Christentums bis zum Nicaenum," in *Die Kultur der Gegenwart,* ed. Paul Hinneberg, pt. 1, sec. 4, vol. 1: *Die Geschichte der Christlichen Religion,* 2d ed. (Berlin: B. G. Teubner, 1909), 43–47.

27. Jülicher, *Neue Linien,* 3–10.

28. Jülicher, "Die Religion Jesu," 54.

transformation to be brought about by God; on the other hand, the yeast is already at work in a hidden way, and if demons are cast out, the kingdom is already in our midst. Consistent eschatology is qualified by the idea of development. It is not the parables of growth that are crucial for Jülicher, but Jesus' messianic consciousness: he did not see himself as one who just announces the new world, like John the Baptist, but as one who enjoys it already. What is new about Jesus is his personality and his understanding of the right relation of God and humanity: the loving disposition of the individual toward God and other people is the essence.[29]

Thus Jülicher maintains some of the features of the liberal picture of Jesus: Jesus breaks through Pharisaic piety to the religion of loving disposition; the center of his gospel is the love commandment; we are impressed by Jesus' "personality" and "messianic consciousness." At the same time Jülicher acknowledges the eschatological issue; Johannes Weiss could even make fruitful use of his work on the parables in his own second edition—though not agreeing on every point. In sum, then, we see in Jülicher a liberal response to the eschatological Jesus that is not characterized by bewilderment or a sense of crisis, but rather by a qualification of the eschatological thesis (reminiscent of the earlier Bousset) that is based on a sound methodological insight: it is to the parables that one must turn to understand the preaching of Jesus.

Wilhelm Heitmüller, another practitioner of the history-of-religions approach, wrote the major article on Jesus Christ for the first edition of *Die Religion in Geschichte und Gegenwart*. He is familiar with the works of Bousset and Jülicher, and his essay exhibits a response similar to theirs: it accepts the eschatological meaning of Jesus' proclamation concerning the kingdom of God, but qualifies the significance of eschatology in ways that minimize any theological problem.

Heitmüller states in straightforward agreement with Weiss that the kingdom is "the dominion of God in the end time and the state brought about by it—the dominion of God which is realized solely through his action and rule—not an inward community to be brought about by human action."[30] Heitmüller, like Bousset, has no intention of defend-

---

29. Ibid., 54–60, 63, 67, 69–70.
30. Wilhelm Heitmüller, "Jesus Christus," in *Die Religion in Geschichte und Gegenwart*, ed. Herrmann Gunkel, Otto Scheel, and F. M. Schiele, 5 vols. (Tübingen: J. C. B. Mohr [Paul Siebeck], 1909–13), 3:406.

ing Ritschl against Weiss. But he denies the kingdom of God was the center and cardinal point of Jesus' preaching; it was, rather, only the springboard and background for what Jesus had to say.[31] Moreover, Jesus transformed the heritage of Jewish expectation of a future kingdom, for the Gospel accounts contain traces of the view that "the great future is already projected into the present."[32]

If the kingdom was not the center of Jesus' preaching, what was? Heitmüller's answer is: the concept of God and the relation of God and humanity. Jesus proclaimed God's presence, God's immanence in the world, over against Judaism's stress on transcendence. Jesus stressed individualism: the individual, not the chosen people, is the subject of the religious relation, the personal relation of God and the soul. This individualism is also the key to Jesus' ethics: his rigorous and to us foreign demands are due not to the imminence of the kingdom, but to "the exclusivity of life in God, next to which all other goods, family, state, society, culture, disappear."[33] Thus the coming kingdom provides only the context, not the center, of Jesus' ethical demands: he is concerned "only with how the individual, who must give account before God, should comport himself." The characteristic mark of all of Jesus' demands is "unconditional submission to duty, i.e., the will of God."[34]

Thus Heitmüller can both acknowledge Weiss's discovery of eschatology and minimize its theological importance. Heitmüller is like Bousset and Jülicher (with whom he agrees on many details) in that he qualifies the significance of eschatology and so minimizes the gulf between the historical Jesus and the present. In the end, the enduring significance of Jesus turns out—in familiar liberal fashion—to be his personality, with his extraordinary vocational consciousness of being the bearer of a revelation. Jesus' personality is "a sort of religious power station from which new streams and waves" of religious power pour forth into the present.[35]

This all too brief exploration of several liberal New Testament scholars in the period from Ritschl to Troeltsch demonstrates conclusively that the discovery of the eschatological meaning of the kingdom of God

---

31. Ibid., 3:395–96.
32. Ibid., 3:407.
33. Ibid., 3:403.
34. Ibid., 3:401–2.
35. Ibid., 3:409.

did not provoke a crisis. These scholars continue to write lives of Jesus; they take eschatology into account, qualifying it in varying degrees. Weiss has made an impact (but not Schweitzer, whose radical picture of Jesus is not believed). Certainly tensions between faith and history are surfacing, but there is no wholesale break. None of these thinkers defends Ritschl's characteristic understanding of the kingdom of God. But there are no indications of a sense of crisis, or of being undermined, or of a radical turn in Jesus research. To focus on eschatology as provoking a unique crisis is to misread the period.

III

What were the reactions of liberal theologians outside of the community of New Testament scholars?

"The Gospel entered the world as an apocalyptic and eschatological message, apocalyptical and eschatological not only in its form, but also in its contents."[36] This opening sentence of the section on the gospel in the 1893 edition of his *History of Dogma,* as well as the bibliography (which lists Weiss's and Bousset's 1892 works), shows that Adolf Harnack was already informed about the discussion of eschatology. But his very next sentence indicates some massive qualifications of the eschatological thesis: "apocalyptical" means "not merely unveiling the future, but above all the revelation of God as father," while "eschatological" means "the view of Jesus' work as savior." Jesus announces the coming kingdom as the future government of the world by God; but the kingdom is also present, and also means God's government of the soul. In words reminiscent of Bousset, Harnack states that Jesus broke through the "national, political, and sensuous eudemonistic forms" of the eschatological expectation of his day to give them "a new content" and to force them in "a new direction."[37]

Harnack's position remains the same in 1900. In *What Is Christianity?* the kingdom of God is one of the three essential characteristics of Jesus' gospel: "the kingdom of God and its coming, God the Father and the infinite value of the soul, and the higher righteousness and the com-

---

36. Adolf Harnack, *History of Dogma,* trans. Neil Buchanan from the 3d ed. (1893), 7 vols. (New York: Dover Publications, 1961), 1:58.

37. Ibid., 1:58, 61–62; see the bibliography on 1:75–76.

mandment of love."[38] According to Harnack, the kingdom contains two poles: on the one hand, the kingdom is a future event, the external rule of God; on the other hand, the kingdom is already present, and is something inward. The first understanding—the traditional, Jewish expectation—is the husk; the second, involving Jesus' unique break-through, is the kernel. Thus Jesus' characteristic understanding of the kingdom is that "it is the rule of the holy God in the hearts of individuals; it is God himself in his power. From this point of view everything that is dramatic in the external and historical sense of the word has vanished; and gone, too, are all hopes of the future." The kingdom of God is "the power that works inwardly," redeeming the individual.[39]

Thus Harnack has completely neutralized the eschatological meaning of the kingdom of God as far as modern theology is concerned. Instead of eschatology, he makes the chief category of modern individualism, the infinite value of the soul, constitutive for his constructive theology. Yet he does not lose completely the Ritschlian understanding of social ethics; he only gives it a different warrant. "The Gospel is a social message," Harnack argues; it is "profoundly socialistic," for it "aims at founding a community among men as wide as human life itself and as deep as human need." But the warrant for these claims is not the kingdom of God as ethical task, but the principle of love of neighbor.[40]

In his essay on the ethics of Jesus, Wilhelm Herrmann confronted a problem: obedience to the radical ethical demands of the Sermon on the Mount is inconsistent with "giving ourselves over with moral seriousness to the tasks of civilization."[41] Here Johannes Weiss comes to the rescue. In showing us that Jesus saw the end of the world and the last judgment to be at hand, biblical scholarship opens up a gap between us and the historical Jesus. We cannot share Jesus' eschatological mood; we do not confront the end of the world, but an infinity of tasks. Yet this gap is all to the good! For without the work of the biblical scholars, we might attempt that kind of wooden discipleship that consists in trying

---

38. Adolf Harnack, *What Is Christianity?* trans. J. B. Saunders (New York: Harper & Row, 1957), 51.

39. Ibid., 56, 60; see also 52–56.

40. Ibid., 98–101.

41. Wilhelm Herrmann, *Schriften zur Grundlegung der Theologie,* ed. Peter Fischer-Appelt, 2 vols. (Munich: Chr. Kaiser, 1966–67), 1:212.

literally to implement the commands of the Sermon on the Mount. And "this presumed discipleship of Jesus finally ends in insincerity."[42]

It would take more exposition of Herrmann's system than I can offer here to convey the full force of that last line. Suffice it to say that "sincerity" (*Wahrhaftigkeit*) is a crucial technical term in Herrmann's theology and ethics. The essential meaning of the Sermon on the Mount is moral autonomy: the heart of discipleship is that we come to understand and share Jesus' disposition (*Gesinnung*). What counts is not following the literal content of all of Jesus' ethical commandments, but autonomy and sincerity. So Herrmann welcomes the eschatological understanding of Jesus, for it helps us perceive the distance between Jesus' moral demands, conditioned as they were by his eschatological expectation, and our situation, and this is vital to preserving our moral autonomy and sincerity.[43]

Yet despite this positive reception of Weiss, Herrmann could still employ the term "kingdom of God" in a completely noneschatological sense: "by the kingdom of God [Jesus] means God's true lordship over personal life, especially in men's own souls, and in their communion with one another." Jesus thought of the kingdom as "God's sovereignty"; "the longing for the kingdom of God must mean, in Jesus' life, perfect surrender to God, or love to God with all the heart and soul."[44] In such statements, Herrmann echoes Harnack.

Neither Harnack nor Herrmann repristinates Ritschl; both are aware of Weiss's work and do not explicitly register disagreement with him. Herrmann even commends his work and makes use of it as grist for his own mill. But in the end, neither of them takes Weiss very seriously. Needless to say, there is no sign whatsoever that they feel their constructive work is threatened or undermined by the eschatological thesis.

If neither Harnack nor Herrmann took Weiss very seriously, Ernst Troeltsch by contrast was, in the judgment of one scholar, "possibly the first systematic theologian to face" the issue Weiss raised.[45] Although

---

42. Ibid., 1:220.

43. Ibid., 1:217–25.

44. Wilhelm Herrmann, *The Communion of the Christian with God*, trans. R. W. Stewart from the 4th ed. (1903), ed. Robert T. Voelkel (Philadelphia: Fortress Press, 1971), 87, 95.

45. This is Robert Morgan's judgment in *Ernst Troeltsch: Writings on Theology and Religion*, trans. and ed. Robert Morgan and Michael Pye (Atlanta: John Knox Press, 1977), 221.

Troeltsch does not cite Weiss directly in his writings, referring instead to such authorities as Holtzmann, Wernle, Wrede, and Jülicher, it is clear that Troeltsch does accept the eschatological Jesus. Jesus saw the kingdom of God as a "miraculous gift of God," a "miraculous intervention of God in the world."[46]

> [The] fundamental idea of the preaching of Jesus . . . deals with the proclamation of the great final judgment of the coming "kingdom of God," by which is meant that state of life in which God will have supreme control, when his will will be done on earth, as it is now being done in heaven; in the "kingdom," sin, suffering, and pain will have been overcome, and the true spiritual values, combined with single-eyed devotion to the will of God, will shine out in the glory which is their due.[47]

Troeltsch's historical work is thoroughly informed by this eschatological understanding of Jesus. Indeed, *The Social Teaching of the Christian Churches,* a book of several complex agendas, has one major issue set by it: the issue of "compromise." Jesus' ethics is shaped by his eschatology; it is an ethics of preparation for the kingdom. The ethics of the gospel are indifferent to inner-worldly ethical goals. The radicalism of Jesus' demands "and their indifference towards questions of practicability" can be understood only from the fact that "they were formulated in the expectation of the final judgement of the imminent end of the world."[48] Only the coming kingdom of God really matters; the inner-worldly values or goods (i.e., ethical goals or ends [*Zwecke*]—the family, state, economic life, art, and science) are set aside. "The Gospel poses and solves no social problems, for the days of society are numbered, and the days of the kingdom of God are at hand."[49] The problem for subsequent Christian ethics becomes how to develop a positive relation to society, that is, a social ethics, in light of the nonarrival of the kingdom. *The Social Teaching of the Christian Churches* traces the story of the adjustments of the gospel to the world. The gospel ideal "demands a

---

46. Ernst Troeltsch, *Gesammelte Schriften,* 4 vols. (Aalen: Scientia, 1961–66), 2:638. Hereafter cited as *GS.*

47. Ernst Troeltsch, *The Social Teaching of the Christian Churches,* trans. Olive Wyon, 2 vols. (London: Allen & Unwin, 1931), 1:51 (= *GS* 1:34); cf. *GS* 2:634–36.

48. Troeltsch, *Social Teaching,* 55 (= *GS* 1:40).

49. *GS* 2:636; see also 634–35.

new world for its full carrying out, which Jesus correspondingly proclaimed in the kingdom of God. But it is an ideal which cannot be carried
out in an ongoing world without compromise. Thus the history of Christian ethics becomes one of ever-new searches for this compromise and
ever new opposition to the mood of compromise."[50] Troeltsch not only
agrees with the "rediscovery" of eschatology; he integrates it into the
design of his book.

Yet the language Troeltsch uses to set up the issue of the eschatological nature of Jesus' ethic suggests a problem: "Next to the command
to love, nothing dominates the ethics of Jesus as clearly as the message
of the infinite value of the soul, insofar as through surrender to God
it raises itself out of the transient world to the sphere of eternal values."[51] Jesus' demand is for love of God and of neighbor; the result is
"an unlimited, unqualified individualism."[52]

Not only are the "infinite value of the soul" and its concomitant individualism familiar liberal themes that we have already seen in Harnack;
the elevation of the soul from the transient to the transcendent is the
central theme of Troeltsch's own characteristic systematic theology.[53]
Moreover, Troeltsch cashes out the love commandment of Matthew
22:37 in terms of his own ethical categories: to love God is "to act out of
the individual goal of the value of the soul to be gained in love of God
and surrender to God," while to love neighbor is "nothing other than the
demand to act out of the social goal of the setting up of a communion
of all God's children."[54] Although putatively describing the teaching
of the historical Jesus, both the conception of an ultimate religious
goal (Zweck) and the definitions of the "individual goal" and "social
goal" are characteristic of Troeltsch's constructive ethics.[55] Moreover, the
content of the social goal sounds suspiciously like that suggested by
Ritschl.

Troeltsch's language invites the criticism that he, too, has modern-
ized Jesus, that is, interpreted the Jesus of history with the categories

---

50. *GS* 1:973; my trans.
51. *GS* 2:630.
52. *GS* 1:36; my trans.
53. Ernst Troeltsch, *Glaubenslehre nach Heidelberger Vorlesungen aus den Jahren 1911 und 1912* (Aalen: Scientia, 1981), secs. 5.3, 12, 14, 20.
54. *GS* 2:630–31.
55. See *GS* 2:616–25; see also the unpublished Heidelberg lectures on *praktische christ-liche Ethik.*

of modern liberal theology. Certainly, he recognizes the eschatological context and meaning of Jesus' preaching of the kingdom of God; yet he cashes out the fundamental traits of Jesus' preaching in the categories of his own constructive thought. The problem is summed up in a single sentence in the *Glaubenslehre:* the impression of Jesus' personality is "his religious-ethical preaching of the value of the soul and of the kingdom of brotherly love as well as an extraordinary consciousness of mission and anticipation of a world-renewal to be brought about by God."[56] In a single sentence Troeltsch both recognizes the eschatological dimensions of Jesus' preaching "rediscovered" by Johannes Weiss and advocates such modern, noneschatological conceptions as "the infinite value of the soul" and the "kingdom of brotherly love."

Much more could be done in terms of exploring what Troeltsch thought about Jesus and the kingdom of God. But enough has been said to situate Troeltsch among his contemporaries. Troeltsch *does* take the eschatological Jesus more seriously than Herrmann and Harnack. Eschatology does not undermine his "liberalism," or cause him to abandon appeals to the "infinite value of the soul" or to the "power of Jesus' personality." Herrmann, Harnack, and Troeltsch accommodated their thinking in different ways to the news of Jesus' eschatology; but to speak of a "crisis" is a profoundly misleading exaggeration.[57]

IV

The agenda of this essay has been to get a correct fix on the past. One of the tasks of historical theology is intellectual history: seeking to understand correctly the ideas of the past in their own context. A case can be made for considering theological notions (particularly such conceptions as the kingdom of God) in their social setting and significance. Indeed, Troeltsch did so himself. But I have not followed his example of "social history"; rather, for reasons that will soon become apparent,

---

56. Troeltsch, *Glaubenslehre*, sec. 8.3.

57. As an additional piece of evidence for my claim that the discussion of the kingdom of God did not occasion a crisis in liberal systematic theology, consider sec. 8 of Troeltsch's *Glaubenslehre* on "The Significance of Jesus for Faith." It does not even mention the discussion occasioned by the "eschatological school," though it does give attention to the "Christ myth" debate.

my method has been to examine strictly the history of ideas and their scholarly reception.

What I have shown is that some of the generalizations about German Protestant theology at the turn of the century are incorrect. It is an exaggeration to say that the eschatological "school" bewildered or even caused a major crisis in liberal theology. Such generalizations not only fail to capture the actual response of the thinkers involved; they exaggerate the significance of eschatology while overlooking other developments current in New Testament research in the same period (such as the history-of-religions method and the recognition of the difficulties of disentangling the historical Jesus from the theology of the primitive Christian community). It is not even correct to say that the eschatological school "turned the entire course of Jesus research." But I would not go to the opposite extreme of claiming it had little or no impact. The major Protestant thinkers in the period knew of and took into account, in one way or another, the eschatological understanding of Jesus. On the whole, liberal theology after Ritschl shows a perhaps unexpected ability to concede the eschatological meaning of Jesus' preaching of the kingdom of God without surrendering its fundamental orientation.

Yet there is undeniably a difference between the theologies of Ritschl and of Troeltsch, to name just the beginning and end points of this study, and especially so with respect to the meaning and role of the kingdom of God in their systems. In none of the major thinkers studied here does the kingdom of God have the same meaning or play the same role as it did in Ritschl's thought. That fact in itself may be taken as evidence of the impact of the eschatological school. But it would be a mistake to overemphasize its importance in the development of post-Ritschlian liberal theology. Other theological factors, having nothing to do with the kingdom of God, led Ritschl's pupils and his successors to depart from his system. Harnack and Herrmann were already going their own ways before 1892, and Troeltsch, when he states his reasons for dissatisfaction with Ritschl, never mentions the kingdom of God. The most reasonable conclusion is a nuanced one: the work of the eschatological school was not the sole or even the decisive reason for the break with Ritschl, which was already under way for other reasons; but once it had made its case, few thinkers interpreted the kingdom of God in exactly Ritschl's sense. Claude Welch's thesis more accurately catches the spirit of Protestant theology at the turn of the century than generalizations about a "crisis" in liberal theology. What was in harmony with Ritschl (faith, ethics, history) was in tension with Troeltsch.[58]

But the historical theologian is more than an intellectual historian. The term *theology* denotes normative critical reflection: the central theological question is the question of the meaning and truth of religious beliefs.[59] Theology asks: What is it reasonable to believe? This implies that the task of the historical theologian, insofar as it is a *theological* task, is not exhausted by the hermeneutical task of understanding the past, whether that task be conceived as intellectual history or as social history. If the historical theologian is a *theologian,* and not just an intellectual historian whose area of interest happens to be theological ideas, his or her work must finally be guided by the normative theological questions of meaning and truth.

In saying this, I do not intend to collapse the distinction between historical and constructive theology. While historical theologians are guided by an interest in normative questions, it is not their task as historical theologians to propose constructive solutions for the present. Rather, historical theologians reflect critically upon the constructive solutions of the past, not only to understand them in their own (now past) context, but to judge their adequacy.

So why, if we are interested in normative questions—questions of what it is reasonable to believe—should we raid the libraries to free these figures of a century ago from the oblivion of their musty bookshelves? One answer is that we are wrestling with the same issues that they were. First, contemporary Christian theology is confronted with the task of understanding Jesus' proclamation of the kingdom of God. Second, the discussion of the eschatological Jesus raises the perennial issue of the relation of faith to history, specifically the relation of present faith and theology to the preaching of the historical Jesus. Third, the discussion raises the still troublesome methodological question of the relation of historical scholarship to constructive theology.

In terms of the first issue, do Weiss, Schweitzer, Bousset, Jülicher, and

---

58. Claude Welch, *Protestant Thought in the Nineteenth Century,* 2 vols. (New Haven, Conn.: Yale University Press, 1972, 1985), vol. 2, chaps. 1 and 8.

59. For my understanding of the nature of theology I am indebted to the work of Schubert Ogden and David Tracy. See especially Schubert Ogden, "What Is Theology?" in *On Theology* (San Francisco: Harper & Row, 1986), 1–21; and David Tracy, *Blessed Rage for Order* (New York: Seabury Press, 1975).

Heitmüller offer conclusions regarding the historical Jesus and his proclamation of the kingdom that still commend themselves? Or has their
work been superseded by nearly a century of research? Obviously a decision on that issue cannot be argued here; the groundwork must first
be laid through a discussion of contemporary research on the problem.
I would only suggest that, insofar as the question of the eschatological Jesus refuses to stay settled, but has once again been reopened, the
arguments and evidence discussed at the turn of the century remain relevant.[60] We may or may not be persuaded by Weiss's presentation of an
eschatological prophet, by Schweitzer's vision of an apocalyptic fanatic,
or by the qualified portrait of an eschatological Jesus offered by Bousset, Heitmüller, and Jülicher. But insofar as we are still struggling with
the question, we cannot ignore the relevant data of their evidence and
arguments.

Analogously, the thinkers surveyed confront us with a range of
options on the second issue: the question of the significance of the
historical Jesus and his proclamation (however we reconstruct it) for
contemporary faith and theology. With Weiss, we can reissue the old
coinage at a new rate of exchange; with Bousset and Schweitzer, we can
declare the independence of faith from any constitutive relation to the
historical Jesus; with Harnack, Herrmann, and Troeltsch, we can seek
some positive form of relationship. Because this essay has not set about
constructing a case on this issue, I will not attempt to draw a conclusion
on it here. My point is that the issue of faith and history, like the question of the eschatological Jesus, has not gone away; insofar as we are still
struggling with the issue, we give content to our thinking by exploring
other thinkers who have wrestled with the same questions.

The same can be said with respect to the third issue, the question
of the relation of historical scholarship to constructive theology. The
thinkers at the turn of the century present a choice. One can render
historical work more or less irrelevant to the constructive task, either
by opting for some form of rationalism or mysticism (as Schweitzer and
Bousset), or by qualifying historical conclusions or simply refusing to
allow them to have any impact on one's constructive thought (as Harnack and Herrmann). Or one can allow historical conclusions actually

---

60. Marcus Borg, "A Temperate Case for a Non-Eschatological Jesus," *Forum* 2 (1983):
81–102.

to shape the constructive agenda. This last option is exemplified best by Troeltsch, although not always consistently (most successfully in the *Social Teaching,* less so in his constructive thought). The latter choice seems to me to be the more defensible one. Constructive work in a historically conscious theology ought to be dependent upon historical conclusions. By the same token, certain historical questions first become interesting because of the agenda of contemporary constructive theology. Thus a certain interdependence of historical and constructive work is inevitable, and proper.

Thus, there are compelling reasons for revisiting the thinkers of "liberal theology at its height."[61] They sought to reconstruct Christian theology on the basis of the historical consciousness, without assuming the truth of either a supernaturalist metaphysics or the dogmas of the tradition. Troeltsch spoke for many others when he stated the agenda was to solve the systematic task "of thinking through and formulating, now independently, the Christian world of ideas and life-world with unreserved delving into the modern world."[62] Insofar as contemporary theology finds that agenda still persuasive and finds the historical consciousness still to constitute one of the fundamental conditions of theological reflection, a reassessment of Protestant liberal thought at the turn of the century remains in order.

So we raid the libraries because we are troubled by some of the same issues that troubled thinkers of the past, and we are looking for their wisdom. Historical theology is an ongoing conversation with the past on issues that concern us still, undertaken in the conviction that we ought to do our thinking in the best company.[63]

---

61. The subtitle of Martin Rumscheidt's selection of Harnack's writings in the Making of Modern Theology series (London: Collins, 1989).

62. *GS* 1:vii–viii.

63. For the notion of theology as "a determination to make one's theological decisions in the best company," see B. A. Gerrish, "Theology and the Historical Consciousness," below.

Afterword

B. A. Gerrish

Theology and
the Historical Consciousness

You have invited me to speak on "the significance of historical studies for the life and thought of humanity." But the original assignment was accompanied by full permission to define my topic in my own way. In announcing as my theme "Theology and the Historical Consciousness," I do not imagine that I have made it any smaller. (One infinite is as big as another.) All I have done is to hint at the angle of approach. You will not hear from me very much propaganda on behalf of historical studies. At least, it will be subtle, indirect propaganda. It comes in the form of a counterinvitation, since I am asking you to think with me about a theological problem that concerns history, but that is by no means the private domain of historians.

Perhaps I should have picked a safer path, since I am inviting you to reflect with me about a matter on which I have not myself attained clarity or assurance. But at least I shall be talking about history precisely from the standpoint of my own interest in it. The study of history is not now, and never has been, an instinctive passion that I am prepared to defend at all costs. It is rather, for me, an unexpected detour. I should prefer to get on with the business of systematic theology, lecturing from prolegomena to eschatology in two or three semesters, recording the simple truth about God, human beings, and the universe. And I was, at first, diverted into historical studies by my belief that the best systematic

A lecture delivered at McCormick Theological Seminary on March 2, 1967.

theologian lived in the sixteenth century—as did a very good unsystematic one, too. But to read history is to be thrown into a pluralistic world, which plays havoc with our dogmatic certainties. And my powers of resistance, already weakened by some exposure to linguistic philosophy, were further worn away by nineteenth-century historicism.

My topic, then, is *"Theology* and the Historical Consciousness."[1] It is a strictly theological question that I am asking. And I mean "theology" not in a descriptive or interpretative sense—as when we speak of the theology of Paul or of Calvin—but in the strictly constructive sense of a disciplined attempt to state the content of the Christian gospel for our time. The question is: What does the historical consciousness do to us as Christian believers who want to theologize in the present? This is a question that none of us can escape, since the gospel and we ourselves are caught in the web of history. The study of history, for us, is not merely a matter of providing a small-scale map to a territory we may never visit, but rather of trying to chart our way through a territory where we already find ourselves. It is this that I want to suggest by the second expression in my chosen title: "Theology and the *Historical Consciousness.*"

By the "historical consciousness" I do not refer to any extra faculty of the human soul or to any special "sixth sense" that is possessed only by historians. I mean the awareness, which we all have, in greater or lesser degree, that our entire existence is given under the categories of space and time. This, certainly, sounds obvious and innocent enough. And I fully grant that we do not need historians to state the matter in this rather truistic form. Nevertheless, the historical consciousness, so defined, has far-reaching consequences for the discipline of theology, which presumes to make normative judgments and includes within its scope objects (such as God) that cannot be wholly enclosed within the categories of space and time. The study of history should have the effect of heightening the historical consciousness and making us more fully aware of what it implies. But I freely admit that this does not always happen, even though it should. In actual fact, it *may* even be true that the systematic theologian acquires a clearer understanding of the historical consciousness than does the historian. Historiography (the writing

---

1. A number of discerning questions were raised after the lecture was originally given (March 2, 1967), and I wish to thank my critics for their comments. Instead of changing the spoken version, I have added footnotes that convey the gist of my replies.

of history) and historicity (the existence of human beings as historical beings) may be divorced in our actual thinking, and there is no necessary
transition from doing history to becoming aware of history as the form
of our existence. But in a theological school, at any rate, the connection
has to be made explicit.

Obviously, I cannot even begin to cover the full range of questions
that are posed for theology by the historical consciousness. But I think
we can get at the heart of the matter if we take a look at three basic ideas:
relativity, tradition, and transcendence.

The question of history and relativity is whether it is possible to find
in the flux of history any fixed and stable norms that may serve as un-
questionable authorities for the work of the theologian. In short, can we
locate an absolute amid the relativities of history? Since my answer to
this will be no, we shall have to move on to the second question, which
is a kind of chastened reformulation of the first.

The question of history and tradition is whether the Christian heritage can yield at least some relative norms, which may serve as valid
guidelines for the work of theology. My answer to this will be yes, but
only by means of a conscious decision of faith that can never be fully
justified by history itself. The study of history has its value insofar as it informs, perhaps even occasions, this faith. But faith, in its very essence, is
a free choice: it is a decision to let the future be determined by a selective
use of the past. This leads on to the third problem.

The question of history and transcendence is whether there is present in our relative historical judgments an absolute that itself cannot
be fully contained within them. In other words, we have to ask, finally,
about the reference of that talk about "God" that lies at the heart of our
theological language. And what I think about *that* question I shall reveal
when the time is come.

I am sure I do not need to emphasize that these three questions are
only distinguished for the sake of orderliness. They cannot be separated,
but belong together in the constructive theological enterprise. It is, for
example, logically possible to build a theology on the basis of Christian
tradition without raising the question of transcendence. But I suspect
that psychologically it is *not* possible. Unless we come to terms with the
question, To what does our theological language refer? we may take the
drive out of our theological labors, although it does not therefore follow that only one kind of answer will be able to support the theological

enterprise. Indeed, as I shall suggest, though we dare not ignore the question, we may not be in a position to answer it very confidently.

History and Relativity

The attempt has often been made, and still is made, to find a security in history that history itself cannot give. The most obvious examples are credalism and fundamentalism. Each of these phenomena, in its own way, seeks to build its assurance on the apparent solidity of the past; but the past to which they appeal is exempted from the canons of historical criticism. A parallel phenomenon is the appeal to an apostolic succession. At first sight, it appears as though the intention of such an appeal were to rest dogma upon the facts of history. On closer inspection, it is clear that the movement of thought is in the reverse direction, *from* dogma *to* history (or alleged history). Hence it is not considered necessary to demonstrate, by historical evidence, the actual fact of an apostolic succession, since gaps in the evidence are bridged by the belief of the church. The same holds for the authority of apostolic traditions. This, too, looks at first glance as though it were an attempt to rest faith on historical certainties. And in a sense it is; at least the intention is to give an aura of historical definiteness to the concept of tradition. But once again the historicity[2] itself is a dogmatic assertion, not contingent upon the test of historical methods. Hence it may be claimed that the bodily assumption of Mary is part of a tradition that goes back to the first apostles, and yet that the truth of the claim is guaranteed by papal definition of the dogma, not by historical verification.[3]

Now, the fact that such claims do not really rest on history does not prove that they are false. It merely assigns them their correct classification as dogmatic assertions about history and not historical sup-

---

2. I use "historicity" always in the sense of "historical existence," that is, existence under the categories of space and time. But it is obvious that the concept may sometimes suggest the specific sense of "actual," rather than "contingent," existence.

3. See, for example, Semmelroth's statement quoted by Gerhard Ebeling, *The Problem of Historicity* (Philadelphia, 1967), 59–60. I did not receive the English version of Ebeling's penetrating little study until the draft of my lecture was completed, and I had not seen the German original; otherwise I might have made further reference to it. My chief debts on the problems of theology and history have been to Adolf Harnack and Ernst Troeltsch, though I should not wish to be identified with either of them any further than my explicit statements allow.

ports of dogma. Historical criticism could only falsify such assertions if they could be shown contrary to historical evidence. They remain secure as long as the evidence is not contrary, but fragmentary or even nonexistent. But when we turn to the phenomena of credalism and fundamentalism, the problems run deeper. Like the appeals to apostolic succession or apostolic tradition, credalism and fundamentalism have shown a remarkable ability to ride out the storms of historical criticism. The Apostles' Creed, for instance, which once borrowed its authority from the belief that the apostles dictated it, still retains authority long after its apostolic origin has been disproved. And in current efforts towards church reunion we are invited to unite on the basis of what began as a local Roman baptismal confession, produced under transient historical circumstances.[4] Again, one could point to conservative Protestant scholars who defend the inerrancy of the Bible on dogmatic grounds because, for instance, Jesus seems to have believed in the verbal inspiration of the Old Testament. In neither case is historical criticism permitted to become the arbiter of theological questions. And I concede that, to this extent, credalism and fundamentalism are immune from historical criticism, or at least will always be considered so immune by many Christian people. However, I suggest that the problem of historicity cuts more deeply into credalism and fundamentalism than I have so far shown. For behind both of these phenomena there lies the assumption that truth can be formulated in language that is valid for all people, in all places, and at all times.

This assumption has, indeed, been affirmed explicitly in the encyclical *Mysterium Fidei* (1965) of Pope Paul VI. The pope was disturbed by the attempt of certain Roman Catholic theologians to speak about the Eucharist in other terms than the traditional doctrine of transubstantiation. In response, he makes a pronouncement "with apostolic authority" (which means, being interpreted, that he is not speaking *ex cathedra*, but is not giving a private opinion either).

> The norm of speaking which the Church . . . has established and confirmed by the authority of Councils . . . is to be religiously preserved and let no one at his own good pleasure or under pretext

---

4. One need not agree entirely with Arthur Cushman McGiffert's views on the Apostles' Creed (e.g., in his *A History of Christian Thought* [New York, 1932–33], 1:157ff.), but I believe he was right to stress the historical limitations of the creed.

of new science presume to change it. Who indeed would tolerate it that the dogmatic formulae which the ecumenical councils
used concerning the Mysteries of the Most Blessed Trinity and the
Incarnation be declared unsuited to the men of our age and that
other formulae be rashly substituted? In like manner we are not to
tolerate anyone who on his own authority wishes to modify the
formulae in which the Council of Trent sets forth the Mystery of
the Eucharist for our belief.

So far, this could be interpreted to mean simply that the task of stating
the content of the Christian faith belongs not to any individual or individuals, but to the church. However, the reason for not tampering with
old dogmas follows:

For by these formulae as by the rest which the Church uses to express the dogmas of the faith, concepts are expressed which are
not tied to one specific form of human civilization, nor definite period of scientific progress, nor one school of theological thought,
but they present what the human mind by universal and necessary experience grasps of realities and expresses in suitable and
accurate terminology taken either from the language commonly
in use or from polished diction. For this reason, these formulae are
adapted to men of all times and all places.[5]

This, I need hardly add, is the very antithesis of what I understand by
historical thinking. It represents very clearly that credal or dogmatic
Christianity, the essence of which is the belief that theological formulas
can be absolutized—treated as the final truth for all times, freed from
the limitations of historical circumstances. Historical thinking, by contrast, views theological formulas as always relative to a particular time
and a particular place.

It would, of course, require an extended argument to clarify and defend the case of historical relativism against dogmatic Christianity. It
requires, in fact, nothing less than a history of Christian thought. Our
claim is not simply a counterdogma: that theological language *must be*
relative to time and place and therefore not permanently valid. On the

---

5. I quote from the English version published by the National Catholic Welfare
Conference (Washington, D.C., 1965), 6.

contrary, it is a historical judgment, an inductive generalization (so to say). I would have to show that as a matter of historical fact the language of the Christian faith has undergone successive transformations throughout the course of the church's history; further, that even when the language has appeared to remain constant, it has nevertheless been filled with new meaning. Precisely because history never repeats itself, the church can never proclaim the same gospel today that it proclaimed yesterday. The repetition of old formulas by no means guarantees the identity of our proclamation with that of a previous age, for the meaning that the words have will be given by their new environment. Language, then, is a historical phenomenon, subject both to external and to internal change. A good example of the former pattern of change can be seen in the word "Christ," which begins its course in the Jewish world as a title, but becomes a mere proper name in the Greek world that understood nothing of the messianic expectations of the Hebrews. An example of internal linguistic change could be sought in the notion of God's "fatherhood." Of course, it is true that the meaning of the symbol "father" ought to be determined by what revelation says about God's fatherhood. But in the concrete situations of actual life it is obvious that there are some locations in the modern world where the name "father" could only prove a liability to the evangelist.

I have already made the transition, in these remarks, from credalism to fundamentalism. The only difference between them (from the point of view of the historical consciousness) is that each finds its absolutes in a different place: the one in dogma, the other in scripture. And frequently enough the absolutist may be both a credalist and a fundamentalist at the same time. Now, I have already hinted that the problem of fundamentalism does not lie in the doctrine of verbal inerrancy, over which many a futile battle has been fought. The question we have to ask of the Bible is rather: What shall we do with it in the twentieth century, infallible or not? In a characteristically brilliant essay, Benjamin B. Warfield, the great Princeton theologian, undertook to answer the charge that the scriptures are colored by the personality of their authors and cannot therefore be the pure word of God. Warfield inquires:

But what if this personality has itself been formed by God into precisely the personality it is, for the express purpose of communicating to the word given through it just the coloring which it gives

it? What if the colors of the stained glass window have been designed by the architect for the purpose of giving to the light that
floods the cathedral precisely the tone and quality it receives from
them?[6]

That is, I think, a point well made, certainly worth debating. But the
point *I* want to make is of another order. Suppose the fashions of architecture and the style of ornamentation change. Suppose we twentieth-
century persons find ourselves as mere tourists in an ancient Gothic
shrine. What then? Can the architect and the artisan still reproduce in *us*
the impression their workmanship made on medieval men and women
who once prayed there? This, surely, is the question. And it says nothing
about the perfection of the artist's handiwork.

I do not wish to suggest that the Roman Catholic and the Protestant
conservative are simply unaware of the problem of historicity. And my
remarks are certainly not intended to be polemical. The credalist and the
fundamentalist are perfectly aware of the need to interpret their authorities in the present by encyclicals, preaching, and the like. To this extent,
I welcome them as sister and brother historicists. But there is still a difference. To make it concrete: it is the difference between those who insist on
clinging to the Westminster Confession at all costs and those who want
the Presbyterian church to do for itself in the twentieth century what
the Westminster Divines did so well for themselves in the seventeenth.

History and Tradition

The rejection of absolutism requires the abandonment of the pre-
Enlightenment view of external authority. If it is impossible to capture
truth in infallible and irreformable formulas, then it makes little sense to
require theologians to submit their thinking to ancient creeds; and even
new confessions have to be used with a certain reserve and caution. This
confusion, made from the side of historicism, agrees well with the Enlightenment understanding of faith: I may not *say* that anything is true
unless I *see* it to be true. The Reformation was already a decisive step in
the direction of humanity's coming of age. For the reformers rejected

---

6. Benjamin B. Warfield, *The Inspiration and Authority of the Bible* (reprint, London, 1951),
15ff.

the medieval doctrine of implicit faith and insisted that all must do their own believing as surely as they must do their own dying. Nobody else can believe for them, not even Holy Mother Church. But to complete the Reformation, we must add that the assertions of the Bible, too, are not to be accepted as true unless we ourselves see them to be true. Authority, then, if we decide to retain so misleading a term, has to be internalized.[7]

But this by no means requires us to cut ourselves off from the life of the church or the word of scripture. Rather, we view them as the spiritual environment in which we do our thinking, if we want to be Christian theologians. The best description of the theological task, as I understand it, is contained in the rules with which Ignatius Loyola concluded his *Spiritual Exercises*.[8] Theology is *sentire cum ecclesia* (thinking with the church). But I hasten to add that I give the expression a sense that St. Ignatius would not have approved. (Indeed, this particular group of rules was plainly anti-Protestant in intention.)[9] In the first place, *sentire cum ecclesia* meant, for Ignatius, thinking what the church thinks, even against our own insight.

> We must put aside all judgment of our own, and keep the mind ever ready and prompt to obey in all things the true Spouse of Jesus Christ, our Holy Mother.... If we wish to proceed securely in all things, we must hold fast to the following principle: What seems to me white I will believe black if the hierarchical Church so defines.[10]

But is this really to *think* with the church? Or is it to suspend thinking for the sake of the church?

In the second place, when I say "church" I mean not the hierarchical church, but the communion of saints, which extends back in time and provides the link between the incarnation and ourselves. Thinking with the church can never be merely a matter of talking with our contemporaries, since the church is what it is by reason of its history. This,

---

7. "Misleading" precisely because it is a hard concept to internalize. It suggests outside coercion rather than inner conviction.

8. *The Spiritual Exercises of St. Ignatius*, trans. Louis J. Puhl, S.J. (Westminster, Md., 1951), 157ff.

9. See Joseph de Guibert, S.J., *The Jesuits: Their Spiritual Doctrine and Practice*, Eng. trans. (Chicago, 1964), 171.

10. *Spiritual Exercises*, 157, 160.

of course, is true of any human society. But it holds true of the church in a special way, since the communion of saints exists, and has always existed, by its relationship to the incarnation. The heart of its life is an *actus tradendi*, a process of handing on what is received from the past. Tradition, in this sense, is the very stuff of which the church is made, and it cannot be otherwise without loss of identity. But the meaning of the *traditum* (the content of the tradition) cannot be abstracted from the church's historical experience: we have it only in the *traditiones*, the great wealth of traditions that we inherit from the past. Doing theology is not parroting any particular tradition, but participating in the *actus tradendi*, the "traditioning" (so to say). And that means really appropriating the tradition so as to transform it. Tradition is not a static, fixed quantity, but a kind of metamorphosis, and theology is an active agent in effecting it.[11]

All theology, in fact, is historical theology, not as a mere recital or reproduction of the past, but as thinking in the context of an ongoing process. It is a determination to make one's theological decisions in the best company; and it assumes that proven durability is at least as good a criterion of the best company as is current fashion. As the Anglican divine Richard Hooker shrewdly remarked, "There are few things known to be good, till such time as they grow to be ancient."[12] This means that in the work of theology we show our highest respect not for the present best-seller, but for the established classics, which have done most to shape the tradition. The church with which we do our thinking is bound to be something of an abstraction from the communion of saints; this, too, is a consequence of our historicity, which places limitations upon us that we cannot fully transcend. But we are duty-bound to make our church as wide a communion as our limitations allow. John Oman has written that

> man's highest hope of advancing is less in his own most strenuous effort than in keeping himself in the directest line of the loftiest progress.... To be faithful to our own spiritual insight, it must be

---

11. This conception of tradition was perfectly expressed in a statement of Calvin in reply to a Roman Catholic opponent, Pighius: "If Pighius does not know it, I want to make this plain to him: our constant effort, day and night, is also to fashion, in the manner we think will be best, whatever is faithfully handed on by us" (*Calvini Opera* [*Corpus Reformatorum*], 6:250.

12. Richard Hooker, *Ecclesiastical Polity*, 5.7.3, Everyman's Library (London, 1907), 11, 29.

our constant endeavour to be faithful to our spiritual ancestry.... This ancestry and kinship form man's true Church. His debt to it is incalculable, and its authority in some form he must perpetually acknowledge.[13]

But one is bound to add that if our "church" is defined as our spiritual ancestry, then it is partly of our own making, since we have a measure of freedom to choose our spiritual ancestors, unlike our natural ancestors, who are forced upon us. And if our intellectual church is of our own making, we had better see to it that we make it as large as we can. Only then will we be justified in adopting it as the environment of our thinking.

"Tradition," in other words, should not become an honorific name for some fragment of the Christian past that we happen to approve—the patristic age, for example, or the Protestant Reformation. Still, each of us has to begin where she or he is; and this implies, I think, that theology has its natural *starting point* within a *particular* confessional tradition. The eternal appears only under the conditions of history. For this reason, it should not become a theological principle always to move from particularity to generality, as though we hoped, in the end, to capture the whole of the eternal. Of course, not everything peculiar is worth preserving. But it may be the duty of religious communities to defend, rather than surrender, their particularity, to maintain their special identity, to keep intact their distinctive witness. The vitality of the Christian tradition is as much aided as hampered by the coexistence of subtraditions within the larger whole; and the attempt to merge them all indiscriminately could involve a serious loss. I say this not to be antiecumenical, but to define my brand of ecumenism, which rates tensions higher than uniformity.[14]

---

13. John Oman, *Vision and Authority*, 2d ed. (London, 1928), 90.

14. For example, the divergence within Christendom in respect to baptism could be said to have expressed and fostered two equally valid theologies, a theology of prevenient grace and a theology of commitment. Perhaps we may appropriate, at this point, one of the positive gains of romanticism over against eighteenth-century rationalism in religion. It was the influence of romanticism that enabled Schleiermacher to reject artificial attempts to reduce religion to a handful of general truths. His defense of "religious plurality" rested on an awareness that individuality is indispensable to living religion. See his fifth "speech" (*Reden über die Religion* [1799], 5th ed. [Göttingen, 1926]), in which he seeks to treat religions in their historical givenness. We may add that Schleiermacher was among the first to "historicize" theology (i.e., to grasp its fundamentally historical character), as is clearly to be seen in his *Kurze Darstellung des theologischen Studiums* (1811), 3d ed. (Leipzig, 1910).

If, then, we consider theology as a way of thinking with the church, but from the starting point of a particular confession, we have an answer to our second question: whether the Christian heritage can yield at least some relative norms for the work of theology. The answer is yes, insofar as one has identified oneself with a particular historical tradition. But this act of identification, though it may be historically conditioned in all kinds of subtle ways, can never be fully justified from history; it is a venture of faith.

The position for which I am arguing, then, in the light of historical consciousness, is a kind of "relativistic confessionalism." I believe that theology profits from being done in conscious identification with a particular tradition; otherwise it will run the risk of becoming a purely academic pursuit, cut off from religious community and perhaps, for this reason, without much power to influence the life of the church. But I do not believe that we have sufficient reason to absolutize any particular confession or even Christianity itself: there must always be an openness to other confessions and, as far as possible, also to other religions.[15] Neither do I understand confessional loyalty as merely a matter of handing on unopened a doctrinal package received from the past. Beliefs that are to serve our generation as relative norms must have their roots in the past, but they must do their living in the present. If they fail in either respect, they will not have much chance of success.[16]

---

15. Consequently, even our Christology cannot escape the relativities of history. We have to admit, I think, that the figure of the Christ will not make large conquests in cultures that resist "Europeanization." This, certainly, will be embarrassing to any theology that does not take the doctrine of the Trinity seriously—that is, a theology that cannot grant an activity of the divine Logos outside of Jesus or the visible church. The temporal conditions of Jesus' *teaching* were indicated in Harnack's *Das Wesan des Christentums* (Leipzig, 1900), which Troeltsch described as "in some measure the definitive book for the historicizing trend in theology" (*Gesammelte Schriften* [Tübingen, 1913], 2:387). Troeltsch himself dealt more radically with the temporal conditions of Jesus' *person,* especially in *Die Bedeutung der Geschichtlichkeit Jesu für den Glauben* (Tübingen, 1911). See also his final statement on Christianity among the religions of the world, published posthumously in *Christian Thought: Its History and Application* (London, 1923), 1–35. I cannot here evaluate the standpoints and arguments of Harnack and Troeltsch on this complex subject, which raises both dogmatic and historical questions about the historical Jesus.

16. Theology, like history itself (in the sense of historiography), takes place at the meeting of past and present; or, at least, I wish to argue that it should, and that this is a proper way to interpret the idea of a "historical theology." (See my statement in *Criterion* 6, no. 2 [Spring 1967]: 33–35.) The primary datum of theology is therefore neither "the Bible alone" (if that is intended to extrude the exegetical tradition or the claims of modernity) nor "the empirical world" (if it is supposed that the theologian can, or should, come to the empirical world with a blank mind or derive theological propositions from nonreligious

Insofar as this position leaves room for a concept of "authority," it does so for the sake of discipline rather than out of dogmatic pretensions. No community can claim absolute truth for its convictions, but it does have the right to protect the integrity of its distinctive witness. Hence it asks certain "constitutional questions" of those who wish to identify themselves with it.

History and Transcendence

It is, no doubt, already clear that the attempt to historicize theology has its limits. We cannot expect history to do for us what dogma once did, and still does, for others. For the historical consciousness there is a greater flexibility and therefore a greater insecurity. Precisely because history confronts us with rich variety, it cannot give us guaranteed beliefs, but can only challenge us to do our own believing without the support of the old infallibilities. This, of course, does not make faith irrational or arbitrary. Although the beliefs of the theologian cannot be demonstrated by rational argument, any more than they can be guaranteed by infallible authority, they are still subject to rational tests, of which the most important is the existence of a community that shares them.[17]

But could not the whole community of faith be living an illusion? Obviously, we have to admit that this is at least possible. Even within the limits of historical thinking, however, it seems to me unlikely. For if

---

evidences). Of course, if we take both modernity and tradition as sources of theological norms, we invite the question, How much weight do we assign to each? But I do not see how we could fix the percentages in advance; we can only seek to set the context for theological reflection by giving recognition, in principle, to both factors, and must then determine each problem on its own merits.

17. The three elements of conviction (the coercive, the pragmatic, and the reflective) outlined by H. H. Farmer in his *Towards Belief in God* (New York, 1947) furnish tests that, as he suggests, are applicable also to nonreligious beliefs. What is missing in Farmer's treatment is a full recognition of the relationship between belief and community, and here there is something to be learned from the philosophers C. S. Peirce and Josiah Royce. See also Theodore M. Greene, "Christianity and Its Secular Alternatives," in *The Christian Answer*, ed. Henry P. Van Dusen (London, 1946), 104ff.; Greene proposes coerciveness, coherence, and publicity as the criteria of reality. It remains problematic, of course, why there have been, and still are, so many different ways of talking about this alleged "reality." A philosophical analysis of what Willem F. Zuurdeeg taught us to call "convictional language" is a necessary prerequisite for dealing with the problem. See his *An Analytical Philosophy of Religion* (Nashville, 1958).

the evidences of history make it hard to credit the claim of any group to possess absolute truth, they also make it hard to imagine that the whole religious story of humankind is a gigantic illusion. The historical experience of religious groups points constantly to something that lies beyond history, even though it makes its appearance only in time and space. It is this something that the theologian names "God." And here is the dilemma: we want to take seriously the historical character of our existence, and yet our historical experience, as a religious community, itself makes us talk about something that lies outside our history—in short, about something transcendent.[18]

Historians, as far as I can see, can do nothing with this odd fact of religious experience: it passes out of their hands and becomes the proper business of the philosopher of religion. All historians can do is report that an appeal to transcendence is ineradicable from humankind's religious history. If they want to examine the problem further, then they have to change hats and return to the stage as philosophers. This was comparatively easy for the historicists of an earlier generation, whose labors were so rudely interrupted by Karl Barth and neoorthodoxy. They had behind them the heritage of philosophical idealism, by which to interpret the phenomena of religion. Ernst Troeltsch, for example, invoked the idea of the absolute in order to prevent historical relativism from disintegrating into skepticism and confusion. He denied that absolutism and relativism were the only alternatives. In our historical experience the relative and the absolute meet together, since all our historically conditioned values strive after the absolute as their ideal.[19] Hence Troeltsch argued, against William James, that an empiricist philosophy alone cannot provide an adequate foundation for the philosophy of religion: we need also the idealist tradition of Platonism.[20]

---

18. It is, of course, widely claimed nowadays that theology and religion are debilitated precisely by a weakened sense of transcendence. Naturally, the interpretation of religion has to take account of this phenomenon, but it seems to me too early to judge what to make of it. We can only wait and see.

19. This was the position Troeltsch maintained in his great work *Die Absolutheit des Christentums und die Religionsgeschichte* (Tübingen and Leipzig, 1902).

20. Ernst Troeltsch, "Empiricism and Platonism in the Philosophy of Religion," *Harvard Theological Review* 5, no. 4 (October 1912): 401–22. Troeltsch admits, however, that the empirical-psychological approach of James worked with generalizations that gave him "everything that the Platonist and Kantian gets from *a priori* necessities" (p. 410). The difference between them is thereby reduced to the question, What is the ontological status of the categories of religious interpretation?

History has done unkind things to idealism in recent years, and it is much harder today than it was in Troeltsch's day (1865–1923) to call upon the absolute to defend theology. But a modification of his approach may still be a viable option. Certainly, I do not believe it should be ruled out from the *theological* side, whatever has to be said about it from the side of philosophy. We are all familiar with Pascal's famous utterance, "God of Abraham, Isaac, and Jacob ... not of the philosophers." This, in my opinion, was one of Pascal's less happy thoughts. It misses the point—at any rate, if it is used to assert a necessary incompatibility between the biblical and the philosophical God. The question of transcendence, when posed philosophically, cannot be answered from within the framework of biblical language, since it is a question about the language system as a whole, not about any particular items within it.

Let me try to illustrate my meaning. Suppose we are discussing a Greek play in which the hero is driven to destruction by the goddess Aphrodite. The successive acts of the drama portray the events of the hero's downfall, and the figure of Aphrodite appears on the stage, speaks, and does various actions. Now, you may say: Obviously, the Greek poet believed in a literal Aphrodite, a deity in human form, who really controls human affairs. I say: Not at all; he is representing, in mythological language, the destruction brought upon himself by a man who is possessed by an insane passion. Now, the argument between us would be of a quite different order from a disagreement over some particular item within the play. We could settle a difference of opinion over what Aphrodite said and did in the play simply by rereading the text. But the question, What does Aphrodite represent? will probably never be settled, though each of us might point to clues that seem to favor his or her own interpretation.

The question of transcendence, from the philosopher's point of view, is a total question of a kind analogous to the question, What does the drama mean? And no amount of information from biblical theology can settle it. It is a metalinguistic matter that takes us out of the language system itself and makes us look back on it as a whole. And the difficulty is that we have no privileged access to the transcendent, as we might conceivably have to the poet. Even if we exchange religious language for philosophical language, we are still trapped within the limitations of our own historical existence. We move out of one play into another and never meet the author offstage. So, then, another peculiarity of the

historical consciousness is that we cannot step outside of it, and therefore the question of transcendence remains always tantalizingly out of
our reach.

One possible solution to the problem would be to interpret the idea
of transcendence as a delusion, that is, as a misreading of our experience.
It could be argued, for example, that what religious persons apprehend
as a divine imperative is in fact a misinterpretation of the pressures made
upon them by their social groups; or that the divine being to whom they
turn for solace is merely a projection of a father-image stored in their
psyche since childhood. Such attempts to "naturalize the supernatural"
are attractive in principle, since they do not require us to imagine something that transcends the limits of our historical existence. But they are
vulnerable in detail (as others have argued),[21] and leave one with at least
the suspicion that there must be more to it than this. But what?

Perhaps, in the final analysis, one's objection to attempts at eliminat-
ing the transcendent is not that they are too skeptical, but that they claim
to know too much. Certainly, they claim to know more than Christian
theologians have commonly claimed. The classical theologians of the
Christian tradition have denied that they talk about God as God is in
God's self, but only as God is to us (*quoad nos*). They have let the transcendent remain transcendent, and have admitted the indirect character of
theological language.[22] Perhaps the line of theological progress for us, at
the present time, lies in appropriating and transforming this commonplace, but curiously neglected, feature of the Christian tradition. Even
if we stop short of pushing this old distinction to the limits of agnosticism, we should at least learn from it the unlikelihood that we shall ever
identify the reference of God-language in a manner that will satisfy the
craving for clarity and certainty. Talk about transcendence is precisely an
invitation to remain open to possibilities that cannot be comprehended
in our finite understanding. It would therefore be disastrous to proclaim
a moratorium on God-talk until we have succeeded in "explaining" its

---

21. See, for instance, Charles A. Bennett, *The Dilemma of Religious Knowledge* (New
Haven, 1931); John Oman, *The Natural and the Supernatural* (Cambridge, 1931), chap. 3;
Farmer, *Towards Belief.*

22. It is important to note that this admission is characteristic precisely of those whom
we carelessly stereotype as "traditional theists." See the striking and sophisticated remarks
on theological language in the "compend" of Wollebius (1626), the very model of a traditional dogmatician (*Reformed Dogmatics*, ed. John W. Bearsdlee III [New York, 1965], 38ff.
and 47ff.).

point of reference. We have to start at the opposite end and inquire about the way in which talk about transcendence is generated.[23] And that means that we have to begin by thinking with the church.

In conclusion, I am fully aware that I leave you more with a theological agenda than with a set of theological solutions. But at least I have tried to show how, in my opinion, we have to get at theological questions in the modern world. And above all I have tried to show some of the ways in which the historical consciousness will determine the phrasing of our questions and the answers we try to give them.

Postscript to "Theology and the Historical Consciousness"

At first, I resisted the editors' proposal to add to this volume of new essays a lecture I gave a quarter of a century ago. If asked today for a methodological piece on historical theology, I would surely do it differently. I have not only continued to practice historical theology in the intervening years, but have also reflected further—in conversation with other practitioners of the craft, living or dead—on what exactly it is. I was not at all sure that I would wish to have my latest thoughts on the subject represented by something my younger self had said (a little too chattily perhaps) in the 1960s. Even when the editors countered that I

---

23. There is, I think, something to be learned from the procedure (if not the conclusions) of William James, who presented his pragmatic theory of truth as a "genetic theory of what is meant by truth." His point was that a theory of truth should be concerned to find out how, as a matter of fact, we arrive at the position of stating that so-and-so is true. See "What Pragmatism Means," *Selected Papers on Philosophy* (London, 1917), 198–217, esp. 210. Similarly, I would suggest that we need a genetic theory of transcendence—a theory that begins not from the logical puzzles, but from description of how the belief in transcendence arises.

might add a postscript on how my mind had changed, the misgivings were not immediately laid to rest.

On reading through the old lecture, however, I was surprised, even embarrassed, to realize how little my mind has in fact changed, though I would like to think that it has become better informed. The lecture gave my reflections on how theology should be done, and in essentials I stand by them still. Of course, I would put some things differently today; others I would wish to modify, here and there, in substance. But large, complicated retractions do not seem to be called for—not, at least, if I am simply to indicate where I stand today. (It is entirely possible that I was wrong then, and still am.) At the risk of seeming narcissistic, then, I have agreed to add a postscript to the lecture: to review, if not exactly to "revision," a fragment of my own past and to say in general how far I have kept on the course I once charted for myself. A detailed, paragraph-by-paragraph self-appraisal is out of the question; it would very likely be longer than the lecture itself.

My theme in the lecture was not "Historical Theology," but "Theology and the Historical Consciousness." This was by no means accidental. The term "historical theology" has meant different things to different people, which is one reason why its relation to constructive or systematic theology has been variously understood. My own usage, when I do use the term, may be a little esoteric. At any rate, *esoterisch* is how the late Professor Hans-Joachim Birkner characterized the title of my essay "Ernst Troeltsch and the Possibility of a Historical Theology." (As one of our leading Schleiermacher scholars, he knew who the initiated were, who would be sure to understand what I meant.) The majority view probably takes "historical theology" to be synonymous with "the history of theology." But it was the esoteric usage that lay behind my assertion in the 1967 lecture that all theology—that is, the theological enterprise as a whole and in every part—is historical theology. For me, "historical theology" does not name a discipline or subdiscipline but characterizes an entire field of inquiry that is made up of several disciplines. My guiding interest has been to answer the question: What must the theological task look like to someone who has explored the connection of faith and history in all its ramifications, and who is determined to take seriously the fact that Christian belief is inextricably woven into a web of always particular but constantly changing historical conditions?

One might perhaps do better to call this the quest for a "historicist theology" (a *Theologie des Historismus,* to borrow a Troeltschian phrase). But historicism, unfortunately, is at least as ambiguous a concept as historical theology. In any case, I undertook the quest from the first as a theologian, rather than a historian, by calling. This, too, the 1967 lecture made clear. While I have come to appreciate and to love intellectual history as an autonomous discipline, the constructive theological task has continued to motivate all my historical studies. Conversely, in attempting to formulate my own theological positions, I have turned back for guidance and insight to the old classics of dogmatic literature. It is this two-way exchange that has shaped the work I have attempted in both the history of Christian thought and Christian dogmatics. Without merely repeating what I have written elsewhere since 1967, I will venture some brief afterthoughts on each of these two disciplines and the relationship between them as parts of a historical theology. I recognize, of course, that many of the things I say will evoke puzzlement or dissent and need to be argued much more fully than I should or could attempt here.

I

In one respect, the history of Christian doctrine might seem to be a more fitting theological discipline than the history of Christian thought. "Doctrine," like "dogma," is usually taken to mean a pronouncement of a church through its official channels, whereas "thought" suggests the reflections of an individual, and the theologian is bound to give greater weight to the collective expressions of the church's faith than to the personal opinions even of its leaders. But an old doctrine often strikes later generations as strange. They may be puzzled, or bored, or sickened by the conflicts in which the doctrine was hammered out, unless they are willing to dig beneath the words and to find out what made it a matter of life or death. If they wish not only to know what a church said, but also to understand why it said what it said, then they must read a conciliar decree or a confession of faith, say, as a human document. For this reason, doctrines have to be studied in large part through the theologians whose thoughts led to them.

This is by no means to allow too much to individual ideas. Theological ideas have a distinctive sociology. They arise characteristically

out of the theologian's reflection on his or her own existence in the
believing community. The roots a church's official faith has in the collective life naturally appear more clearly in the making of a doctrine
than in the finished product. Hence the origin of doctrines in collective experience becomes most clearly visible precisely in the history of
Christian thought. It is no coincidence that the theologians who have interested me most have been those, such as Calvin and Schleiermacher,
who made it a matter of principle to limit the scope of their discipline
by constant reference to the actual "piety" of the believing community.
But what makes historical study of such theologians as these "historical
theology"?

The history of Christian thought is historical *theology* as an integral moment in the total theological enterprise, which inquires into the
meaning and truth of Christian faith. The primary texts of the history
of Christian thought are the received classics of Christian literature in
which the life of the Christian community has been thematized. The
theological point of examining the classics is not just to file reports about
them, but to engage their authors in conversation. This, to be sure, does
not mean that the history of Christian thought has to operate with special historical methods, which set it apart from what is done in ordinary
history departments. There is no methodological reason why the historians who practice it must consciously take themselves to be contributing
to the theological enterprise at all, even though what they do is in fact
essential to the work they would rather leave to others. The history of
Christian thought is a branch, or a species, of history: it faces common
historical problems, and it tries to resolve them by common historical
methods. A document from the past, if it is to be read historically, cannot be received as though it arrived in this morning's mail, addressed
to me—to be approved or disapproved simply according to the ease
with which I can incorporate its contents into my own fixed thoughts,
convictions, or prejudices. Historical interpretation calls for an initial
willingness to suspend one's own concern long enough to hear someone else's, and to understand the other with all the resources one has.
The ability to listen may well be the best grace that the study of history
can mediate to us.

And yet, having affirmed the strictly historical character of the history of Christian thought, I would immediately wish to add that this
particular kind of historical activity is likely to be carried out best by a

card-carrying historical theologian: that is, someone committed to the work of the theological guild. Interpretation then becomes explicitly a conversation, which is by definition two-way. Certainly, historians of Christian thought need both the general resources of intellectual history and a good sense of what has been peculiar about the history of religious thinking. But it should be an added asset if they have wrestled with the theological situation of their own day, have some understanding of theological problems from the inside, and therefore know how to interrogate a theological text and let it speak. This is by no means to invite or to excuse willful bias. The point rather is exactly parallel to the one made by Bertrand Russell when he remarked that he would rather be reported by his bitterest enemy among philosophers than by a friend innocent of philosophy.

I would go further and venture to assert that the best, or at least the most fascinating and instructive, histories of Christian thought have been written by interpreters of the past who have had a firm theological standpoint in their own present, a standpoint that enabled them to tell us where (in their view) theology ought to go next. My favorite examples include F. C. Baur, Otto Pfleiderer, Adolf von Harnack, and Karl Barth, all of whom wrote—often combatively—out of robust opinions on the theological needs of their own day. Their theological standpoint was shaped in turn by their historical studies. Some of the greatest theologians have in fact pursued the history of Christian thought neither to find confirmation of what they were determined to believe anyway, nor to run through a vexing exercise that one is supposed to complete before real theological reflection begins, but rather to enter into a genuine engagement with the past. Out of this engagement has emerged the invitation to us to see things one way rather than another. They have not been content to establish what this or that individual theologian has said, but have sought to trace lines of development—indeed, of progress or decay—through the decades and through the centuries. One cannot fairly challenge them merely by showing triumphantly that they had a theological standpoint, but only by arguing that the sources do not provide warrants for their standpoint. This too, mutatis mutandis, holds good for other kinds of history, as distinct from mere chronicle.

I must leave it to others to judge whether I have myself managed to become as strongly opinionated as my mentors. At any rate, the focus of my historical work on the relationship between classical and liberal

Protestantism has been motivated by the quest for a viable method in systematic theology. The case I have come to advocate by consequence is on behalf of an experiential model of theology, which I see as rooted in the Reformation, recovered by Schleiermacher, partially misrepresented by Ernst Troeltsch, and rejected for insufficient reasons by Barth and Brunner. Precisely because the model is experiential, it is also inescapably revisionary: faith, unlike dogmas, is a matter of adaptation and change.

The various historical studies I have made are no longer isolated fragments, if they ever were, but moments in a trajectory that I would like to see continued into the present. In a collection of essays, shortly to appear, I have traced some high points of revisionary theology from the sixteenth century to the twentieth. No one who picks it up will fail to notice that I approve and commend the trajectory I trace. But anyone whose acquaintance with me goes back still earlier than 1967 will know that historical study has formed my theological agenda at least as much as my theological agenda has informed my historical writings. The understanding of the theological task I have come to hold is different from the understanding I started with.

II

Some who come to mind as exemplary historical theologians, notably Baur and Harnack, wrote as if the historical study of Christianity made a distinct systematic discipline superfluous. Harnack was convinced that the systematic theology of his day had neither scientific nor practical worth, because its judgments were governed by confessional interests and led into what he ironically called "mysteries." He sought the quickening power of religious faith—and therefore the guidance needed for present belief and practice—in history, more particularly in the lives of great religious personalities, and he held that the study of history is governed by strictly scientific methods.

Now, as will be plain enough from what I have said already, I do not believe that the logical distinction between what faith has been in the past and what it should be, or may properly be, in the present requires historical description and theological prescription to be two totally separate assignments, which cannot (without willful confusion) be carried out at the same time by the same person. Past facts and present norms are clearly interwoven in some of the best samples of the history of Christian thought. It would be an impoverishment of the discipline to hold it strictly to the positivistic historical ideal of just ascertaining the facts. Nevertheless, I do not see how the systematic task can be simply subsumed under the historical. A historical theology, as I understand it (perhaps esoterically), includes both the history of Christian thought and Christian dogmatics as distinct, but mutually dependent, disciplines. Dogmatics seeks to present Christian beliefs in their logical connections, not to trace their chronological development. And the endorsement of any particular historical trajectory is bound to rest, finally, on warrants that history as such cannot authorize, even if they come to the dogmatician by way of historical study and are in turn employed to interpret the past.

My historical "detour," as I called it in the 1967 lecture, has been a long one. I may seem to have suffered a fate like the fate of one of my favorite philosophers, G. E. Moore, who announced that the first and most important problem of philosophy is to give a general description of the whole universe, yet busied himself for the most part with minute logical analysis. For my part, I have spent a great deal of time on detailed *historical* analysis. But for twelve years now (since 1980) I have also taught a year-long course in which the history of Christian thought has begun to attain its theological goal, and I expect to put the results eventually into book form. Despite the disrepute into which the term has fallen in some academic circles, I have called the course "Christian Dogmatics," chiefly because I wish to count apologetics and Christian ethics as distinct divisions of the constructive theological enterprise.

Traditional usage is not uniform, but there is good precedent for taking "systematic theology" as the inclusive term that embraces all three: apologetics, dogmatics, and ethics. The distinctions among them follow the lines of primary concern. Dogmatics is mainly concerned with the understanding of belief; apologetics, with the justification of belief; and Christian ethics, with behavior appropriate to belief. The main reason for preserving the distinctions is to prevent the curtailment of any of the three tasks, which might easily follow from treating them together. But an absolute division of labor seems to me neither desirable nor possible. If, as I hold, what is characteristic of modern, in contrast to the older, dogmatics is its intention to be answerable to critical norms that do not strictly emerge within the believing community, the dogmatic task is already, in a sense, apologetic. The problem is no longer how to correct tradition by scripture, but how to mediate between tradition (including scripture) and present-day knowledge and experience.

Christian dogmatics, so understood, is *historical* theology in a twofold sense, as I tried to show in "Theology and the Historical Consciousness." First, the heart of dogmatic thinking is "traditioning," the transmission of a sacred heritage or trust from the past, to which we have full access only through historical inquiry. Second, however, reflection on historical existence poses an agenda of difficult critical questions. The constructive resources of tradition must be appropriated through criticism. The historically minded dogmatician is bound to be preoccupied, in particular, with questions of transience, pluralism, and historical knowledge, which have recast our entire thinking about the nature of dogma and the significance of the historical Jesus. But the task is still to hand on by re-forming. And as we approach the end of the present century, it seems clear to me that preeminent among the theologians most likely to be remembered in the next century are those who have wrestled critically, not simply with the Christian tradition, but with particular confessional traditions. I think especially of Tillich, Barth, and Rahner, who worked self-consciously out of the Lutheran, Reformed, and Roman Catholic traditions respectively. If it is true, as I have suggested, that some of the most interesting work in the history of Christian thought has been done by theologians, it is no less true that enduring systematic theology is mostly the achievement of theologians who are thoroughly at home in the history of dogma and religious thought.

This is not the place to summarize the directions my own dogmatic work has taken. But there are at least three points at which I would wish to modify what I said in "Theology and the Historical Consciousness." First, the criteria by which the dogmatic theologian performs the twofold task of transmission and reformation have to be carefully specified, and I would now avoid the language of "decision" that I once took over from Troeltsch. That was to confuse the discipline that thematizes faith with faith itself. The task of dogmatics is to test the inherited forms that each dogmatic theme has taken and to make the case for the line of development proposed, strictly according to the specified criteria. Often, perhaps always, an intuitive grasp of the mass of materials furnished by historical study goes before the actual presentation of the constructive case. But the presentation itself is an argument, accessible to the critical appraisal of anyone who accepts the criteria, even if only hypothetically.

Second, I am less open now to the kind of procedural agnosticism that I flirted with in the last section of my lecture. Not that I find it necessary to retract everything I said there. But I no longer think that the most fruitful approach to God-language is to talk about something transcendent—an "absolute"—that lies beyond history. Once again, I can see that I was too much under the influence of Ernst Troeltsch's formulation of the problem. It falls to dogmatic prolegomena, I would now wish to say, not only to specify the criteria for appraising the language of tradition, but also to show its anchorage in common human experience. The introduction to a dogmatics both states the rules of the game and puts the game on the language map, chiefly by showing that the word "God" has an appropriate use in ordinary, not yet Christian discourse. I myself find the required anchor point in the confidence, underlying all disciplined inquiry and human existence itself, that we encounter the world around us as an ordered environment. The referent, or putative referent, of this confidence is what we mean by "God."

Third, a further point at which I would wish to modify the dogmatic program I envisioned in 1967 has to do with the arrangement of the dogmatic materials. At that time, I had little sense of the logical coherence that a Christian dogmatics must aspire to. I thought that, once I had done my historical homework, I would be ready to move seriatim through all the major loci of the dogmatic tradition, "from prolegomena to eschatology." But to think dogmatically is not only to think with the church; it is also to think everything in strictest relation to everything else. The very meaning of the beliefs in which the Christian community gives expression to its faith can be understood only in their mutual relationship and from their location in the whole. In this sense, they constitute a "system." If constructive theology is to be taken seriously as a discipline for both the church and the academy, it must be pursued not only comprehensively, but also systematically—as something more than a mere assemblage of distinct items. And this forces upon the dogmatic theologian the preliminary question of the best way to order the materials.

It would be inappropriate in this short postscript to describe the shape of the dogmatic system I have come to advocate, although it did, as a matter of fact, emerge from historical study of previous models, particularly Calvin's *Institutes* and Schleiermacher's *The Christian Faith.* (This will surprise no one who is familiar with the several attempts I have made in print to compare Calvin and Schleiermacher on dogmatic method.) Suffice it to say, for now, that for me dogmatics remains the crown of historical theology. In a famous methodological essay, Troeltsch remarked that defining the essence of Christianity is at once the coronation (*die Krone*) and the abdication (*die Selbstaufhebung*) of historical theology. He meant, of course, that to offer a normative judgment on what essential Christianity is, or should be, *for us* goes beyond the doing of history as ordinarily understood. I agree, except that I would prefer to say "the history of Christian thought" where Troeltsch says "historical theology." The development of a normative dogmatics is historical theology, part two. No abdication of historical theology is called for.

I believe that over the years I have stayed on course, though it has been a more deliberate and leisurely course than I anticipated. How much has my mind changed? Not as much, I expect, as many will think it should have. Other kinds of history have challenged the one-time dominance of the history of Christian thought, and other kinds of constructive theology have become impatient with the dogmatic tradition. This is all to the good. But I see no reason to expect that the new will simply replace the old, and I have never felt any necessity to convince others, or even myself, that what I like doing happens also to be the one thing needful. There are many ways of posing and answering both historical and theological questions. I remain convinced, however, that a historical theology—in the two-part sense in which I understand it—will, and must, continue to make its contribution to the cooperative enterprise we call "Christian theology." And precisely because I see the theological task the way I do—in essentially revisionary terms—it has to be adaptable, as open in principle to the new as it is grounded in the past.

Contributors

Marcia J. Bunge is Assistant Professor of Religion and Philosophy at Luther College in Decorah, Iowa.

Mary Potter Engel is Affiliated Scholar of United Theological Seminary of the Twin Cities in New Brighton, Minnesota.

Jack Forstman is Charles G. Finney Professor of Theology at the Vanderbilt University Divinity School in Nashville, Tennessee.

B. A. Gerrish is John Nuveen Professor and Professor of Historical Theology at the University of Chicago, The Divinity School.

Michael J. Himes is Associate Professor of Theology at the University of Notre Dame in Notre Dame, Indiana.

David W. Lotz is Washburn Professor of Church History at Union Theological Seminary in New York.

William Madges is Associate Professor of Theology at Xavier University in Cincinnati, Ohio.

Katy O'Brien Weintraub is Lecturer at the University of Chicago.

Schubert M. Ogden is University Distinguished Professor of Theology at Southern Methodist University in Dallas, Texas.

Jill Raitt is Catherine P. Middlebush Professor of the Humanities at the University of Missouri–Columbia.

Jane E. Strohl is Associate Professor of Church History at Luther Northwestern Theological Seminary in St. Paul, Minnesota.

Claude Welch is Professor of Historical Theology and Dean Emeritus at the Graduate Theological Union in Berkeley, California.

307

Walter E. Wyman, Jr., is Associate Professor of Religion at Whitman College in Walla Walla, Washington.

Randall C. Zachman is Assistant Professor of Reformation Studies at the University of Notre Dame.